MW00614580

Learning to Love God

A GUIDE TO UNDERSTANDING THE BIBLE

DAVID WORLEY

Thelese  Publishing

Thelese Publishing
PO Box 1208
Austin, Texas 78767
1-800-THELESE
Email: thelese@aol.com
Web: http://www.thelese.com/media.html

ISBN 978-0-692-80918-1

Preface

The Bible is a small library of sixty-six documents written and collected over a millennium into one book. Christians call this book "Scripture" which means that it is read as a God-breathed book, in which believers learn about God and how to love Him.

In one story from the Bible, in Acts, a financial official is riding in a chariot and reading from the Scripture a prophetic document called Isaiah. A man named Philip joins the official and asks him if he understands what he is reading. The man responds, "How can I unless someone *guides* me?" (8:31)

This present book is a guide to God's library, the Bible. Each of the sixty-six books in this great library is surveyed with a brief guide to reading the book and quotations which exemplify the book's meaning.

These "guides" were first written explicitly for Russians to hear the Scripture read and explained in the mid 90's in the morning on their nationwide RadioRussia network. Today, Russian Christians continue to reach seekers through the Christian Resource Center Russia in St. Petersburg (www.CRCRussia.com).

In its original use, I must thank Tatiana Andreeva who translated these lessons into Russian. In its present form, I must thank Woody Woodrow who encouraged me to publish the guide for an English-speaking audience and who did much editorial work.

May this guide strengthen the desire to prayerfully read the Scripture with fellow believers, so "to walk worthily of the Lord, fully pleasing to him, bearing fruit and increasing in understanding of God" (Col. 1:10).

grace and peace,
david worley

Genesis 1:1-2:4

In the beginning, God created the heavens and the earth.

As the story in Genesis begins, the earth is a formless void. It is wrapped in deep darkness, engulfed in a watery chaos (1:2). God creates by restraining the chaos and filling the emptiness.

Through His creation in space and time God brings about harmony and purpose to the universe. God brings this order to earth in stages, over a six-day period. He begins by confronting the darkness:

> *And God said, "Let there be light," and there was light. And God saw that the light was good. And God separated the light from the darkness. God called the light Day, and the darkness he called Night. And there was evening and there was morning, the first day.*
>
> Genesis 1:3-5

The day commences with the evening's darkness, not the morning's light. In her rhythm of time, God's special people Israel will reckon the day to begin in the evening.

Through the first three days of creation, God restrains chaos through three separations: light from darkness (1:4), waters above from waters below (1:7), and waters below from the dry land (1:9). Such separations preserve order. So Israel as God's people will also learn that separation from things unclean preserves them as a holy, dedicated people to the Lord (cf. Leviticus).

The space God provides on the first three days becomes the dimensions occupied by His subsequent creations on the next three days: the light is contained in sun and moon on day four (1:14); the sky and waters are populated by birds and fish on day five (1:20); and the dry land becomes inhabited by terrestrial creatures on day six (1:24).

To this point, God has created by His word. God has spoken and creation has appeared. On the sixth day, however, God invites others to join His creative work:

> *Then God said, "Let us make man in our image, after our likeness. And let them have dominion over the fish of the sea and*

over the birds of the heavens and over the livestock and over all the earth and over every creeping thing that creeps on the earth."

Genesis 1:26

God is not acting alone. Who are these "others"? Who are "us"?

Already in Genesis the Spirit of God has been mentioned (1:2) brooding and hovering over the watery chaos. Later in the New Testament, we hear of the association of God's Spirit with water in Jesus' baptism and in the believer's baptism (John 3). Not only is the Spirit present at creation; present also is God's only Son.

In the beginning was the Word, and the Word was with God, and the Word was God. ... All things were made through him, and without him was not any thing made that was made. In him was life, and the life was the light of men.

John 1:1, 3-4

God the Father, God the Son, God the Spirit co-create "adam" (*human*) in the image of God.

God sees His creative work as *good*. "And God saw everything that he had made, and behold, it was very good. And there was evening and there was morning, the sixth day" (Gen. 1:31). God's estimate of creation as "very good" stands as a strong reminder that neither the human body nor the material world should be viewed as intrinsically evil.

For everything created by God is good, and nothing is to be rejected if it is received with thanksgiving, for it is made holy by the word of God and prayer.

1 Timothy 4:4-5

After six days of work, God rests on the seventh day (Genesis 2:2-3). Through their own rest on the Sabbath day, the people of Israel would offer their own living testimony to God's creation of time and of the human rhythm of work and rest (Exodus 20:8-11). Christians, however, would later interpret the Sabbath rest as a profound description of the heavenly reality of God's very presence.

So then, there remains a Sabbath rest for the people of God, for whoever has entered God's rest has also rested from his works as God did from his.

Hebrews 4:9-10

In the beginning, God brought order out of chaos. He created time and space as constraints to disorder. In Noah's time, chaos was unloosed for a moment, the waters threatening. Now it only remains for God's voice to disturb earth's order once more, a final time. Then the created things which can be shaken will be completely removed, revealing only God's kingdom (Hebrews 12:25-29). The first creation will yield to the new creation begun already in Jesus' resurrection.

Genesis 1:26-30

On the sixth day of creation God made the terrestrial animals. On this same day, not another day, God made another creature:

> *Then God said, "Let us make man in our image, after our likeness. And let them have dominion over the fish of the sea and over the birds of the heavens and over the livestock and over all the earth and over every creeping thing that creeps on the earth."*
>
> *So God created man in his own image,*
> *in the image of God he created him;*
> *male and female he created them.*
>
> *And God blessed them. And God said to them, "Be fruitful and multiply and fill the earth and subdue it, and have dominion over the fish of the sea and over the birds of the heavens and over every living thing that moves on the earth." And God said, "Behold, I have given you every plant yielding seed that is on the face of all the earth, and every tree with seed in its fruit. You shall have them for food. And to every beast of the earth and to every bird of the heavens and to everything that creeps on the earth, everything that has the breath of life, I have given every green plant for food." And it was so. And God saw everything that he had made, and behold, it was very good. And there was evening and there was morning, the sixth day.*
>
> Genesis 1:26-31

Only in the creation of the human does God call upon others to co-create with Him: "Let *us* make humans." Later Israelites understood Wisdom as co-creating with God (Prov. 8:22). Christians would confess that this Wisdom was none other than the Word made flesh, Jesus the Son of God, present with the Father in creation (Col. 1:15-17).

Humans—and only humans—did God make in His image. No animal, no angel, no other creature in the universe enjoys this distinction. The Bible, however, nowhere explains exactly what it means to be in God's image (cf. Gen. 5:1). Genesis does state explicitly that humans in God's image are given dominion over God's animal and plant kingdom ("subdue the earth," Gen. 1:28-29). Adam, in fact, very soon in the story begins to exercise such authority, caring for the garden in Eden.

Various kingdoms in the ancient Near East could speak of their kings as representatives of their gods, as bearing the image of their gods. In Genesis, strikingly, it is not one elevated individual, but rather all humans who are created in God's image. God the King extends His rule of the earth to all human creatures, giving man authority over every living thing:

> *You have made him a little lower than the heavenly beings*
> *and crowned him with glory and honor.*
> *You have given him dominion over the works of your hands;*
> *you have put all things under his feet,*
> *all sheep and oxen,*
> *and also the beasts of the field,*
> *the birds of the heavens, and the fish of the sea,*
> *whatever passes along the paths of the seas.*
>
> Psalm 8:5-8

God appoints humans His vice-regents over creation. He empowers them to procreate and populate the earth.

That humans are declared to be made in "our" image—not made only in God the Father's image, but made in the co-creators' image—invites reflection. It may not be too speculative to suggest that we bear the image of God in those capacities which reflect God's mutuality within Himself, which mirror God's intra communication and inner relationship. Certainly, only humans made in God's image—and not animals—can experience relationship with the Creator, can understand the Creator's voice, can communicate with the Creator.

Even after the disobedience of Adam and Eve in the garden, humans continue to bear the image and likeness of God. Murder can still be prohibited because humans remain divine image bearers (Gen. 9:6). No human may slaughter the image of God!

With Jesus' coming and His confession as the "reflection of God's glory, the exact imprint of God's being" (Heb. 1:3), "the image of the invisible God" (Col. 1:15; 2 Cor. 4:4), Christians now have an image of God to imitate.

> *And we know that for those who love God all things work together for good, for those who are called according to his purpose. For those whom he foreknew he also predestined to be conformed to the image of his Son, in order that he might be the firstborn among many brothers.*
>
> Romans 8:28-29

> *Do not lie to one another, seeing that you have put off the old self with its practices and have put on the new self, which is being renewed in knowledge after the image of its creator.*
>
> Colossians 3:9-10

As humans we all share with the first Adam creation in the likeness of God. Through faith, Christians also live according to another image of God—the image of the second Adam, Jesus Christ—and await sharing in His resurrection.

> *The first man was from the earth, a man of dust; the second man is from heaven. As was the man of dust, so also are those who are of the dust, and as is the man of heaven, so also are those who are of heaven. Just as we have borne the image of the man of dust, we shall also bear the image of the man of heaven.*
>
> 1 Cor. 15:47-49

Genesis 2:7-3:24

Male and female as human being are both created in the image of God on the sixth day. The distinctive aspects of man and woman, however, are not described until the story of day six is retold in Genesis 2. Like a master potter, God forms a figure from clay and breathes into it His breath. But alive is no boy; God has molded and enlivened a grown man. God makes an earthling from the earth. God places this earthling in a garden He planted for him to tend. Of the various trees God gives for food and enjoyment in the garden, only one is forbidden.

> *The LORD God took the man and put him in the garden of Eden to work it and keep it. And the LORD God commanded the man,*

saying, "You may surely eat of every tree of the garden, but of the tree of the knowledge of good and evil you shall not eat, for in the day that you eat of it you shall surely die."

Genesis 2:15-17

God had previously evaluated His creation as "good." But not now. Something is not right; man's loneliness is *not* good (2:18). Neither God nor any animal man names can provide the companionship necessary to overcome this loneliness. God's reaction is not to make another creature from the ground, but to cause a deep sleep to fall upon the man. For the first and only time, God forms a woman out of man's rib.

Then the man said,
"This at last is bone of my bones
and flesh of my flesh;
she shall be called Woman,
because she was taken out of Man."
Therefore a man shall leave his father and his mother and hold fast to his wife, and they shall become one flesh.

Genesis 2:23-24

The first speech about God in the Bible comes, surprisingly, from a serpent—a creature whom the man and woman were supposed to rule! With deceitful cleverness, the serpent leads the woman to question God's command and motives. He asserts, "You will not surely die. For God knows that when you eat of it your eyes will be opened, and you will be like God, knowing good and evil" (3:4b-5).

Do I trust what God commands for my good or do I try to become God? Should what God knows limit what I do?

The desire of the eyes, the desire of the flesh, the pride of life are strong impulses in the woman:

When the woman saw that the tree was good for food, and that it was a delight to the eyes, and that the tree was to be desired to make one wise, she took of its fruit and ate, and she also gave some to her husband who was with her, and he ate.

Genesis 3:6

The woman yields to these desires rather than trusting and honoring God's gracious limits. The infectious social consequences of disobedience are quickly realized as the woman gives the fruit to her husband. They do not die physically. Indeed, their eyes are opened; the serpent appears right. However now, in their extra-ordinary knowledge they become extraordinarily self-conscious. They learn the shame of guilt before God; their nakedness is a reproach. They must make clothes; they seek to blame each other.

The trees God had given for enjoyment and food now become a hiding place from God. But the Gracious One who had given all to be enjoyed will not let the man stay hidden:

> *But the LORD God called to the man and said to him, "Where are you?" And he said, "I heard the sound of you in the garden, and I was afraid, because I was naked, and I hid myself."*
>
> *He said, "Who told you that you were naked? Have you eaten of the tree of which I commanded you not to eat?" The man said, "The woman whom you gave to be with me, she gave me fruit of the tree, and I ate."*
>
> *Then the LORD God said to the woman, "What is this that you have done?" The woman said, "The serpent deceived me, and I ate."*
>
> Genesis 3:9-13

What will God do?

God makes more durable clothes to replace the garments of vegetation (3:21). And in another act of care and love, God takes the man from the garden. He positions cherubim and a flaming sword to prevent man from reaching the tree of life, lest he eat and live forever in selfishness and conflict with God (3:22-24).

God establishes within creation reminders of Adam and Eve's mistrust and rebellion. Whenever the pains of childbirth are great for the woman in labor, the daughter of Eve is to remember the first mother and the consequences of disobedience. Whenever a man meets resistance in field or work, the son of Adam is to remember the first man and the consequences of disobedience.

Despite the defiance of the first woman and man, God's grand plan is not thwarted. God had decided and arranged before creating male and female that the separations and brokenness within the universe would one day be made right in a new man, in a second Adam, "in the Christ."

Genesis 4-11

In Genesis, God blesses Adam and Eve with the sharing of His creative power through procreation. Outside the garden, Eve indeed is fruitful. "Now Adam knew Eve his wife, and she conceived and bore Cain, saying, 'I have gotten a man with the help of the LORD'" (4:1).

Another son, Abel, soon follows. And so begins the multiplication of humanity which God had commanded. Tragically, as quickly as the populating of the earth begins, depopulation threatens. Cain becomes indignant when God has no regard for his offering while accepting his brother's (cf. Luke 15:28). The story does not say why.

Cain fails to control his anger; sin masters him (Gen. 4:6-7). Cain, callous to God's injunction to multiply and fill the earth, murders his brother. Violence is unleashed on the earth.

The ground, cursed because of Adam's disobedience, now experiences the bitter taste of Abel's blood. The Living One hears the cry of the dead man's blood. Cain, though a farmer, is cursed from the ground. Only God's mercy protects Cain, in his vagabond wanderings, from the violence of others (Gen. 4:15).

Cain and his third brother Seth have wives and children who begin to fill the earth. But the violence continues. The division between heaven and earth is violated when the sons of God come down from heaven and take the daughters on earth for wives (6:1-4). God is grieved at the wickedness which results in His world, especially the violent affront to fertility.

> *And the LORD regretted that he had made man on the earth, and it grieved him to his heart. So the LORD said, "I will blot out man whom I have created from the face of the land, man and animals and creeping things and birds of the heavens, for I am sorry that I have made them."*
>
> Genesis 6:6-7

God decides to flood the earth, destroying all that had His breath, undoing His division of the waters, letting them return to chaos (7:21-23).

Only one man and his family are saved – Noah, a righteous and blameless man (Gen. 6:9). Noah never speaks in the story. He listens to God and obeys His command to build an ark which protects his family and selected animals. The first Christians understood their own rescue through water as prefigured in Noah's salvation through water (1 Peter 3:20-21).

God promises never again to destroy the world by flood. God sets the rainbow in the clouds as a personal reminder of His covenant with every living creature never again to destroy all flesh by such waters (Gen. 9:8-17). The apostle Peter later confirms that indeed the earth and its works will be dissolved—not by water, but by fire—making way for new heavens and a new earth (2 Peter 3:5-13).

The ground, cursed because of Adam's disobedience (Gen. 3:17-18), yields more pleasant fruit to the hands of Noah. Noah has vineyards and makes wine which provides relief from man's work (5:29). As divine image bearer Noah exercises dominion over the animals (9:2-3). In one sense, God starts afresh with Noah's sons, commanding them to be fruitful and multiply and fill the earth. The genealogies in Genesis 10 reveal the way Noah's sons and descendants spread throughout the earth.

But another major disturbance occurs. In disregard of God's command to "fill the earth," humans decide to stay together in one city. Worse, they determine to live by their own resources, to make a name for themselves by building a monumental tower to touch the heavens (Gen. 11:1-9).

God, however, frustrates their plans by confusing their languages so that they cannot understand each other's speech. As a result, they abandon the city and the tower, renamed Babel. They scatter abroad to fill the earth. Only at Jerusalem on Pentecost—when the church begins and everyone hears the gospel in their own language—is there a reversal of Babel (Acts 2).

In the primary stories of Genesis 3-11, then, violence increases on the earth. Sin dwells in the human heart. Misusing their freedom, God's creatures transgress the limitations of creation. Eve wants to be like God. Cain murders his brother made in the image of God. Sons of God cohabit with human women. The builders of Babel desire to make a name for themselves.

Yet God displays steady compassion and love. He protects Cain from being murdered. He preserves humanity through the rescue of Noah. He allows the Babel inhabitants to scatter across the earth. God's blessings of fruitfulness find their way.

God's blessings, however, will only find their true and full meaning in the Messiah, through whom freedom from master Sin is announced. No longer will Sin's lurking at the door mean inevitable captivity. The Spirit will dwell within and the master will be Christ, not Sin.

Genesis 12-23

At the heart of Genesis is the story of God's promises to Abram. As God's Word in the beginning created, so God's word to Abram also creates—this time not a universe, but a people. Since a great people need land, God promises a great land (Gen. 13:14-17).

> *Now the LORD said to Abram,*
> *"Go from your country and your kindred*
> *and your father's house to the land that I will show you.*
> *And I will make of you a great nation,*
> *and I will bless you and make your name great,*
> *so that you will be a blessing.*
> *I will bless those who bless you,*
> *and him who dishonors you I will curse,*
> *and in you all the families of the earth shall be blessed."*
>
> Genesis 12:1-3

God's decision to choose one person for such extravagant promises seems on the surface unfair to the rest of humanity. As it evolves, however, Abram's family is to be itself the very channel through which God will bless all families of the earth. The way this happens is the core story of the Bible, climaxing in Jesus' coming as the true seed of Abram—or Abraham—who indeed blesses the world (Galatians 3:16).

The story in Genesis 12-23 describes Abram's responses to the promises of God. In the process it defines for us what true faith in God really means.

In the first place, Abram's faith meant obedience. The promises would not have been available to Abram if he had not been willing to leave the familiarity of his homeland and go to the place God would show him. Abraham obeyed, not knowing where he was to go (Hebrews 11:8).

Abram's faith, however, was not always unwavering trust in God. On two different occasions Abram had his wife Sarai say to different officials that she was only his sister (Gen. 12:10-20; 20:1-18). As a result, Abram put two royal families in mortal danger. Abram did not fully trust God to find a way to keep His promises.

Frequently Abram's faith needed reassurance. For example, Abram did not think that God would give him a son by his barren wife Sarai (or Sarah). In fact, both Abraham and Sarah laughed at the idea of her having a baby at 90 years of age. Sarai proposed to Abram that he have a child through a slave girl named Hagar. Abram did and a son was born named Ishmael.

But God's grace and patience abounded with Abram. God went so far to assure Abram that He passed between halved animals in a solemn ritual of covenant making (Gen. 15). On another occasion, God sought to reassure Abraham by appearing to him in the form of three men who came to his tent (Gen. 18; Heb. 13:3).

Through all of this, however, Abram's faith was growing. On no occasion did Abram go into battle to take another's land. Abram waited for God to provide (Genesis 13-14). But strangely, God did not. Abraham had to buy a burial plot for Sarah; he himself died homeless (Genesis 23). Early Christians reckoned that Abraham had actually come to expect not land, but rather a heavenly city in which God dwelled (Hebrews 11:13-16).

In the Genesis account, Abraham's faith grew as he acted as a priest—interceding and pleading for the welfare of others before God—becoming a blessing to many, as with the righteous who lived in Sodom (Genesis 18:16-33).

Abraham's greatest test was his response to God's demand to sacrifice Isaac, the beloved son of promise. Would Abraham try somehow to make God keep His promise of "descendants as many as the stars" by withholding Isaac? Or would Abraham leave God alone to keep His promise, even if meant killing his only son?

As Abram had chosen to give up his past when he left Mesopotamia in Genesis 12, so Abraham in Genesis 22 chooses to give up his future posterity through the death of his son. But God intervenes and spares Abraham's son. By contrast, God refuses to spare His only Son, Jesus, permitting Him to die for the sins of the world.

The apostle Paul recognized that Christians share something fundamental with Abraham—a faith that God brings the dead to life (Romans 4). It is indeed the only explanation for Abraham's willingness to sacrifice Isaac—his belief that God could bring Isaac back to life (cf. Hebrews 11:19).

God's promises to Abraham set in motion on the world's stage a dramatic plan: the blessing of all nations through the seed of Abraham.

The offspring of the patriarch are not mere puppets whose strings are pulled by God. Their choices, faith, and obedience make a real difference in how, where, and when God interacts with His creation. Their failures, however, do not thwart God's determination to keep His promises for reconciling creation to Himself—as He does in the life, death, resurrection, and exaltation of His only Son, Jesus Christ.

Genesis 24-50

The chronicles of family life in Genesis 24-50 have all the drama and flavor of a soap opera: a parent's favoritism, sibling rivalry, a wedding disaster, a brother's revenge, incest, a plotted fratricide. What makes this soap opera unique, however, is the movement of God's promises through the desires, decisions, and reactions of a family which had been blessed with His promises of land, nation, and name.

The main characters in this story are two men—Jacob and Joseph—a father and his beloved son. The two men provide profiles in character. (Isaac, the father of Jacob, merits only passing mention.)

Jacob is the clever, opportunistic man heavily influenced by a doting mother. His son Joseph (by Rachel) parades his father's partiality toward him among his brothers. The character flaws of each—Jacob's deceit and Joseph's arrogance—will lead to special misery in the family. Each, however, experiences a kind of transformation through the weaving of God's promises in the fabric of their lives.

Jacob's story is punctuated by intense sibling rivalry, the long struggle with his twin brother Esau, beginning in the womb (25:22). Through deception Jacob extracts from their father the blessing which should have gone to the firstborn (27:1-29). Because of this, Esau, a rugged outdoorsman, hates his more cerebral brother, and decides to track Jacob down and kill him (27:30-48).

In the meantime Jacob experiences other consequences of his deceptive ways. Jacob the deceiver becomes Jacob the deceived. His father-in-law Laban tricks Jacob, giving him the wrong wife (Gen. 29). Later his own sons will fool him into believing his favorite son, Joseph, has been killed by a wild beast (Gen. 37). And finally, Joseph will trick his father into potentially sacrificing the youngest son Benjamin (Gen. 43-44).

God, however, does not trick Jacob; He struggles with him. In Genesis 32, Jacob is about to confront Esau coming his way with 400 men. Jacob sends his wives and children across the Jabbock, but he remains behind.

> *And Jacob was left alone. And a man wrestled with him until the breaking of the day. When the man saw that he did not prevail against Jacob, he touched his hip socket, and Jacob's hip was put out of joint as he wrestled with him. Then he said, "Let me go, for the day has broken." But Jacob said, "I will not let you go unless you bless me." And he said to him, "What is your name?" And he said, "Jacob." Then he said, "Your name shall no longer be called Jacob, but Israel, for you have striven with God and with men, and have prevailed." Then Jacob asked him, "Please tell me your name." But he said, "Why is it that you ask my name?" And there he blessed him. So Jacob called the name of the place Peniel ["the face of God"], saying, "For I have seen God face to face, and yet my life has been delivered."*
>
> Genesis 32:24-30

Because of this struggle, Jacob is renamed "Israel" which means "struggle with God." Through this encounter, God prepares Jacob to encounter the estranged Esau. When he finally meets the brother whom he had deprived of the blessing, Jacob is able to see in his brother's face the face of God! (Gen. 33:10)

Like his father, Jacob had a favorite son, Joseph, who was hated by his brothers—in part because of his arrogant attitude toward them. Unlike Cain's treatment of Abel, Joseph's brothers do not slay him; they sell him into slavery.

Through a series of incidents—incidents bearing the signature of God—Joseph rises to the position of second-in-command under Pharaoh. He is even given an Egyptian name. Joseph grows before God, even in the face of critical situations, no less than charges of rape and imprisonment. But he is vindicated.

But then the strangest thing happens. Joseph's family faces a severe famine in Canaan. His brothers are forced to journey south to Egypt to buy grain. As it turns out, Egypt is able to escape agricultural disaster largely through the prudent, administrative skill of the son of Israel named Joseph.

In Egypt, Jacob's sons meet their brother, but they do not recognize him. The men who had abandoned Joseph to slavery now find themselves begging at his door for bread. Joseph displays great character in not taking vengeance. He does put his brothers through considerable anxiety, but finally reveals himself and in the process, his great wisdom.

> *So Joseph said to his brothers, "Come near to me, please." And they came near. And he said, "I am your brother, Joseph, whom you sold into Egypt. And now do not be distressed or angry with yourselves because you sold me here, for God sent me before you to preserve life. For the famine has been in the land these two years, and there are yet five years in which there will be neither plowing nor harvest. And God sent me before you to preserve for you a remnant on earth, and to keep alive for you many survivors. So it was not you who sent me here, but God. He has made me a father to Pharaoh, and lord of all his house and ruler over all the land of Egypt."*
>
> Genesis 45:4-8

God was fulfilling His promises.

But God is not finished with surprises in keeping His word. When God begins His grand promise keeping through His only Son, Jesus is not born into a family from the lineage of the great man Joseph. Jesus is born instead through another son of Israel named Judah. Judah was the very brother who had suggested selling Joseph into slavery (37:26-28). Judah was the brother who had abhorrently, unknowingly gone into his own daughter-in-law, thinking her a prostitute (Genesis 38).

God's promises set in motion a whole series of events in the lives of Jacob and Joseph. How they reacted to God's promises was not predetermined. Yet God used the decisions and reactions of these men to accomplish His purposes in the most surprising ways. In the process, Jacob and Joseph were blessed, even as they in turn became blessings to others.

Exodus 1-4

The second book of the Bible, Exodus, begins with the descendants of Jacob, the Israelites, living prosperously in Egypt. Earlier, Jacob's favorite son Joseph had come to Egypt as a slave—sold to a band of traveling merchants by his jealous brothers. But God had been with Joseph, giving him success in everything he did. Eventually he had risen to the position of second-in-command to the king himself. Joseph's family was able to follow, not as slaves but as honored immigrants, invited by the king and given the best land in Egypt.

But times had changed, as they always do. The Israelites now faced increasing hatred, slavery, and the prospect of genocide:

> *Now there arose a new king over Egypt, who did not know Joseph. And he said to his people, "Behold, the people of Israel are too many and too mighty for us. Come, let us deal shrewdly with them, lest they multiply, and, if war breaks out, they join our enemies and fight against us and escape from the land." Therefore they set taskmasters over them to afflict them with heavy burdens. They built for Pharaoh store cities, Pithom and Raamses. But the more they were oppressed, the more they multiplied and the more they spread abroad. And the Egyptians were in dread of the people of Israel. So they ruthlessly made the people of Israel work as slaves.*
>
> Exodus 1:8-13

Despite the oppression, the people continued to multiply and thrive. Pharaoh ordered the Hebrew midwives to kill all the male Israelite babies.

> *But the midwives feared God and did not do as the king of Egypt commanded them, but let the male children live. So the king of Egypt called the midwives and said to them, "Why have you done this, and let the male children live?" The midwives said to Pharaoh, "Because the Hebrew women are not like the Egyptian women, for they are vigorous and give birth before the midwife comes to them."*
>
> Exodus 1:17-19

Pharaoh then ordered every male baby to be thrown into the Nile (1:22). Christians remembered this horrific scene when they spoke of the circumstances which surrounded Jesus' own infancy, when King Herod ordered the murder of all the male infants of Bethlehem (Matt. 1:16).

Under Pharaoh, the Israelites—descendants of Abraham to whom God had said, “I will make you a great nation”—faced extinction. What were they to do? What was God to do?

The answer: God will deliver Israel from Egyptian oppression.

Remarkable: the one God chooses to lead His people.

> *Now a man from the house of Levi went and took as his wife a Levite woman. The woman conceived and bore a son, and when she saw that he was a fine child, she hid him three months. When she could hide him no longer, she took for him a basket made of bulrushes and daubed it with bitumen and pitch. She put the child in it and placed it among the reeds by the river bank. And his sister stood at a distance to know what would be done to him.*
>
> *Now the daughter of Pharaoh came down to bathe at the river, while her young women walked beside the river. She saw the basket among the reeds and sent her servant woman, and she took it. When she opened it, she saw the child, and behold, the baby was crying. She took pity on him and said, “This is one of the Hebrews' children.”*
>
> *Then his sister said to Pharaoh's daughter, “Shall I go and call you a nurse from the Hebrew women to nurse the child for you?”*
>
> *And Pharaoh's daughter said to her, “Go.” So the girl went and called the child's mother. And Pharaoh's daughter said to her, “Take this child away and nurse him for me, and I will give you your wages.” So the woman took the child and nursed him.*
>
> *When the child grew older, she brought him to Pharaoh's daughter, and he became her son. She named him Moses, “Because,” she said, “I drew him out of the water.”*
>
> Exodus 2:1-10

When Moses became an adult, he saw the bitter plight of his people. He tried to take their side, but resorted to violence to settle injustices (2:11-14). As a result, instead of saving his people, Moses himself became a fugitive from justice. He found himself in a foreign land, Midian, in time becoming a shepherd for his father-in-law (2:15-22).

Here Moses was an expatriate, a failed deliverer. But God chose him anyway.

> *Now Moses was keeping the flock of his father-in-law, Jethro, the priest of Midian, and he led his flock to the west side of the wilderness and came to Horeb, the mountain of God. And the angel of the* LORD *appeared to him in a flame of fire out of the midst of a bush. He looked, and behold, the bush was burning, yet it was not consumed. And Moses said, "I will turn aside to see this great sight, why the bush is not burned."*
>
> *When the* LORD *saw that he turned aside to see, God called to him out of the bush, "Moses, Moses!" And he said, "Here I am." Then he said, "Do not come near; take your sandals off your feet, for the place on which you are standing is holy ground." And he said, "I am the God of your father, the God of Abraham, the God of Isaac, and the God of Jacob." And Moses hid his face, for he was afraid to look at God.*
>
> *Then the* LORD *said, "I have surely seen the affliction of my people who are in Egypt and have heard their cry because of their taskmasters. I know their sufferings, and I have come down to deliver them out of the hand of the Egyptians and to bring them up out of that land to a good and broad land, a land flowing with milk and honey, to the place of the Canaanites, the Hittites, the Amorites, the Perizzites, the Hivites, and the Jebusites. And now, behold, the cry of the people of Israel has come to me, and I have also seen the oppression with which the Egyptians oppress them. Come, I will send you to Pharaoh that you may bring my people, the children of Israel, out of Egypt."*
>
> Exodus 3:1-10

Surprisingly, Moses resists God's call. "Who am I?" Moses asks. "It doesn't matter," God answers. "I will be with you" (3:11-12).

Moses asks God, "Who are you?" God replies, "I AM WHO I AM. I am the God of your forefathers. I am the LORD" (3:13-15).

Moses asks, "What if the people don't believe me?" God enables Moses to perform wondrous signs to demonstrate His power and presence (4:1-9).

Moses objects finally, "I am not eloquent; please send someone else" (4:10-13). God refuses to accept these excuses. He appoints Moses' brother Aaron to serve as spokesman. But Moses will be the leader.

Why was God so determined to use this failed, frightened man as His agent of deliverance? The clearest answer comes much later from the apostle Paul, who explains why God would entrust the message of the gospel to imperfect human beings: “But we have this treasure in jars of clay, to show that the surpassing power belongs to God and not to us” (2 Corinthians 4:7).

God called a shepherd boy named David to defeat the mighty Philistines. God used an uneducated fisherman named Peter to be His special spokesman. God took a leather worker named Paul—a violent enemy of Christians—and transformed him into the gospel’s greatest ambassador.

God consistently works through frail human agents to accomplish His purposes. Limited and imperfect though we are, God invests us with His power in order to accomplish His will. He makes the minister competent; the minister does not (2 Cor. 3:5).

God made Moses competent to lead His people. Moses responded to God’s confidence in faith.

> *By faith Moses, when he was born, was hidden for three months by his parents, because they saw that the child was beautiful, and they were not afraid of the king's edict. By faith Moses, when he was grown up, refused to be called the son of Pharaoh's daughter, choosing rather to be mistreated with the people of God than to enjoy the fleeting pleasures of sin. He considered the reproach of Christ greater wealth than the treasures of Egypt, for he was looking to the reward.*
>
> Hebrews 11:23-26

Exodus 5-18

The story of the exodus is the story of a great power struggle: the king of Egypt, Pharaoh, versus the God of the Israelite slaves.

Thinking he is in control, Pharaoh determines to decrease the size of the Israelites and increase the burdens of their bondage (Exod. 5:19-23). God, remembering His promises to increase His people and to make them a great nation, asserts through His servant Moses that Israel is *His* possession and that Pharaoh *must* let His people go.

The line is drawn in the sand. As it happens, Pharaoh will blink.

Time and again Moses and his brother Aaron ask Pharaoh to let the Israelites go into the desert to offer sacrifices to the LORD God (5:3). Pharaoh's heart is hardened and he will not let them go. His obstinacy, however, becomes the opportunity for God's power to be demonstrated and God's name to be proclaimed in all the earth (9:16). As if in response to Pharaoh's threatened genocide of God's people, and his attempted violation of the blessing of creation, the creation turns chaotic. With each of Pharaoh's refusals, God inflicts calamity upon the Egyptians.

A plague turns the Nile River into blood—the great Nile, the lifeline of the Egyptians, from which their fields were irrigated, in which they fished, on which they traveled. The plagues continue: frogs, gnats, and flies everywhere; afflictions to the cattle; boils infecting the people. Hail. Locusts. Darkness.

Through them all Pharaoh begins to relent, but ultimately refuses. That is, until the tenth plague: the death of every Egyptian first-born male—including Pharaoh's own son!

"Enough!" Pharaoh cries to Moses and Aaron. "Leave, and take all your possessions with you!" (Exodus 12:31-32). Israel does leave, free, clothed in Egyptian finery.

But before their departure, they celebrate a special meal—the feast of the Passover—each family sacrificing a lamb, putting its blood on the doorposts, roasting its flesh to eat. The lambs would take the place of Israelite first-born sons whom God spared in the tenth plague. The families would eat bitter herbs to remember their slavery and unleavened bread to recall the haste of their departure (Exodus 12:14).

Centuries later a young Jew named Jesus from the tribe of Judah would eat a last Passover meal with His followers and forever transform the meal's meaning by his own sacrificial death (cf. 1 Corinthians 5:7; 10:17).

The Israelites did leave Egypt. But Pharaoh changed his mind—again. He pursued Israel with his armies and pinned them against the Sea on the eastern boundary of Egypt. Great fear came upon the people of God. They blamed Moses for having led them out only to die.

> *And Moses said to the people, "Fear not, stand firm, and see the salvation of the LORD, which he will work for you today. For the Egyptians whom you see today, you shall never see again. The LORD will fight for you, and you have only to be silent."*
>
> Exodus 14:13-14

As in the beginning when He separated the waters from dry land, so God divided the water of the sea, allowing the Israelites to go forward on dry ground. The pursuing Egyptians were swallowed up by the walls of water that flowed back and covered them. Yahweh, the God of Israel, gained glory through Pharaoh and his army (14:4, 17-18). In the earliest hymn recorded in the Bible, the Israelites sang praises to God:

> *"Who is like you, O LORD, among the gods?*
> *Who is like you, majestic in holiness,*
> *awesome in glorious deeds, doing wonders?*
> *You stretched out your right hand;*
> *the earth swallowed them.*
> *"You have led in your steadfast love the people whom you have redeemed;*
> *you have guided them by your strength to your holy abode."*
>
> *"The LORD will reign forever and ever."*
>
> Exodus 15:11-13, 18

But the gratitude and thankfulness were short-lived. Again in the wilderness, the Israelites became nostalgic about the "better" days:

> *And the people of Israel said to them, "Would that we had died by the hand of the LORD in the land of Egypt, when we sat by the meat pots and ate bread to the full, for you have brought us out into this wilderness to kill this whole assembly with hunger."*
>
> *Then the LORD said to Moses, "Behold, I am about to rain bread from heaven for you, and the people shall go out and gather a day's portion every day, that I may test them, whether they will walk in my law or not."*
>
> *But the people thirsted there for water, and the people grumbled against Moses and said, "Why did you bring us up out of Egypt, to kill us and our children and our livestock with thirst?"*
>
> Exodus 16:3-4; 17:3

Nevertheless, God was merciful to them. He provided bread from heaven in the morning, quail in the evening, and water to drink in the desert. God tested them to ensure their faithfulness and prepare them for an even more dramatic moment around Mt. Sinai.

Exodus 19-40

In Egypt, God's chosen people had become slaves. Through the exodus God carried them on eagle's wings to liberation. They were free! But free to do what? Free to be what?

Through ten "words" God provided structure to their freedom, order to their community. Their position as God's chosen people was not to be enjoyed as elite privilege. They were given a unique vocation among all the nations of the earth:

> *"'Now therefore, if you will indeed obey my voice and keep my covenant, you shall be my treasured possession among all peoples, for all the earth is mine; and you shall be to me a kingdom of priests and a holy nation.' These are the words that you shall speak to the people of Israel."*
>
> Exodus 19:5-6

God had set apart Israel for a holy purpose—to be priests to the nations, mediating between God and other peoples.

God demonstrated His love for Israel by freely choosing to release them from Egyptian bondage. Now God was prepared to make this relationship permanent—if Israel chose to obey Him, leading the free and ordered life of love in return.

God led Israel through the wilderness to a mountain—Mount Sinai—the place where He had first called Moses from a burning bush. Once Israel had reached the mountain, God's presence was overwhelming:

> *On the morning of the third day there were thunders and lightnings and a thick cloud on the mountain and a very loud trumpet blast, so that all the people in the camp trembled.*
>
> *Now Mount Sinai was wrapped in smoke because the LORD had descended on it in fire. The smoke of it went up like the smoke of a kiln, and the whole mountain trembled greatly.*
>
> *Moses said to the people, "Do not fear, for God has come to test you, that the fear of him may be before you, that you may not sin."*
>
> Exodus 19:16, 18; 20:20

In the Ten Commandments God graciously gave Israel a social structure for her freedom and a community behavior for her unique mission (20:1-17). The first four words call the people to exclusive loyalty: "You shall have no other gods before me." They must show Him the honor He is due—refusing to reduce His being to any visual representation or to use His name with disdain. They must "remember" the Sabbath by refraining from work, for "in six days God made heaven and earth" and "rested on the seventh day."

The remaining six commandments defined the people's relationships with one another. Parents were to be honored. Murder, adultery, theft, false witness, and covetousness were to be rejected. Each person's life, marriage, property, and reputation would be respected and protected. Living together in this way, Israel would indeed be a "holy" people, taking on the very character of God. A "kingdom of priests," mediating His blessings to all other peoples of the world.

God also promised to come down from the mountain to dwell among His people in a moveable sanctuary. Moses was given detailed instructions for the building of such a tent-sanctuary and its apparatus (chs. 25-31, 35-40). While he was still on the mountain, however, the children of God violated the command not to make and worship an idol (32:1-8; 20:4-6). They built a calf of gold. God's response is ominous:

> *And the LORD said to Moses, "I have seen this people, and behold, it is a stiff-necked people. Now therefore let me alone, that my wrath may burn hot against them and I may consume them, in order that I may make a great nation of you."*
>
> Exodus 32:9-10

Moses pleads with God to remember His promises. And God does remember. He relents and does not destroy Israel. But Moses, seeing the people dancing around the idol, cannot contain his own anger.

> *And as soon as he came near the camp and saw the calf and the dancing, Moses' anger burned hot, and he threw the tablets out of his hands and broke them at the foot of the mountain. He took the calf that they had made and burned it with fire and ground it to powder and scattered it on the water and made the people of Israel drink it.*
>
> Exodus 32:19-20

The next day Moses addressed the people: “You have committed a great sin. But now I will go up to the LORD; perhaps I can make atonement for your sin” (32:30).

> *So Moses returned to the LORD and said, “Alas, this people has sinned a great sin. They have made for themselves gods of gold. But now, if you will forgive their sin—but if not, please blot me out of your book that you have written.”*
>
> Exodus 32:31

At first God announces He will not go with Israel to the Promised Land, lest He destroy them on the way (33:1-5). Moses pleads with the LORD to guide His people. God listens, agrees, and once again meets Moses on the mountain to inscribe the commandments on stone.

> *The LORD descended in the cloud and stood with him there, and proclaimed the name of the LORD. The LORD passed before him and proclaimed, “The LORD, the LORD, a God merciful and gracious, slow to anger, and abounding in steadfast love and faithfulness, keeping steadfast love for thousands, forgiving iniquity and transgression and sin, but who will by no means clear the guilty, visiting the iniquity of the fathers on the children and the children's children, to the third and the fourth generation.”*
>
> *And Moses quickly bowed his head toward the earth and worshiped. And he said, “If now I have found favor in your sight, O LORD, please let the LORD go in the midst of us, for it is a stiff-necked people, and pardon our iniquity and our sin, and take us for your inheritance.”*
>
> *And he said, “Behold, I am making a covenant. Before all your people I will do marvels, such as have not been created in all the earth or in any nation. And all the people among whom you are shall see the work of the LORD, for it is an awesome thing that I will do with you.”*
>
> Exodus 34: 5-10

When Moses returned, his face glowed from his conversation with God (34:29-35). Centuries later, in the face of criticism and hardship, the apostle Paul would recall the experiences of Moses for insight into the nature of the Christian life and ministry.

Now if the ministry of death, carved in letters on stone, came with such glory that the Israelites could not gaze at Moses' face because of its glory, which was being brought to an end, will not the ministry of the Spirit have even more glory? For if there was glory in the ministry of condemnation, the ministry of righteousness must far exceed it in glory. Indeed, in this case, what once had glory has come to have no glory at all, because of the glory that surpasses it. For if what was being brought to an end came with glory, much more will what is permanent have glory.

Since we have such a hope, we are very bold, not like Moses, who would put a veil over his face so that the Israelites might not gaze at the outcome of what was being brought to an end. But their minds were hardened. For to this day, when they read the old covenant, that same veil remains unlifted, because only through Christ is it taken away. Yes, to this day whenever Moses is read a veil lies over their hearts. But when one turns to the Lord, the veil is removed. Now the Lord is the Spirit, and where the Spirit of the Lord is, there is freedom. And we all, with unveiled face, beholding the glory of the Lord, are being transformed into the same image from one degree of glory to another. For this comes from the Lord who is the Spirit.

2 Corinthians 3:7-18

Leviticus

As the book of Exodus closes (40:34ff), God encamps with the Israelites. As God is wholly other, holy, majestic, a cloud covers God's tent and His glory fills it.

How can a holy God live among defiled humans? How can humans dare approach this holy God? Leviticus offers the answer. Through a series of divine speeches God says to Israel, "You must be holy, for I the LORD am holy" (11:45; 19:2). Being holy will lead to a love for neighbor:

"You shall not go around as a slanderer among your people, and you shall not stand up against the life of your neighbor: I am the LORD.

"You shall not hate your brother in your heart, but you shall reason frankly with your neighbor, lest you incur sin because of

him. You shall not take vengeance or bear a grudge against the sons of your own people, but you shall love your neighbor as yourself: I am the LORD."

Leviticus 19:16-18

Remarkably, the LORD insists that man become like God!

Earlier in the Bible, tragic consequences ensued in man's attempt—on his own—to become like God. Eve had eaten of the fruit of knowledge in order to be like God. For this she and her husband were expelled from the Garden. At the tower of Babel, humans once again tried to become like God. The LORD confused their languages, retarding their arrogant intentions.

But in Leviticus God invites man to become like God, to become holy as He is holy. On the surface, the challenge to become holy like God appears unattainable. God is God and man is man. How can there be intersection? Man is not merely sinful; man is defiled. The book of Leviticus takes such defilement seriously.

Leviticus understands defilement—uncleanness—not merely as an evil act or a bad thought. Defilement is sinister, penetrating like microscopic radiation. It is a contagion, often spreading invisibly. When such defilement encroaches on the sacred, the results can be lethal:

Now Nadab and Abihu, the sons of Aaron, each took his censer and put fire in it and laid incense on it and offered unauthorized fire before the LORD, which he had not commanded them. And fire came out from before the LORD and consumed them, and they died before the LORD. Then Moses said to Aaron, "This is what the LORD has said: 'Among those who are near me I will be sanctified, and before all the people I will be glorified.'" And Aaron held his peace.

Leviticus 10:1-3

Leviticus describes various things as being unclean: certain animals, skin diseases, sexual situations, and biological functions. The prohibitions against contacting unclean things is apparently not for the sake of better hygiene. Nor is it because unclean things are sinful per se.

The book of Leviticus simply does not explain why certain things are unclean. Rather, the designation of uncleanness appears to distinguish the abnormal from the normal, the deviate from the natural, in God's ordering of creation. The strong sense of defilement functions to impart a keen awareness of the caution necessary in approaching the Holy, Holy, Holy God.

To magnify this caution, Leviticus outlines detailed procedures for priest and Israelite to follow—in ritual, sacrifice, and behavior; in the pursuit of holiness—so there may be purity in the community, which will protect from God's holy wrath.

Leviticus also presents the origin of the Day of Atonement, that great annual day in Israel's calendar when the sanctuary and altar are cleansed from the defilement of the people:

> *For on this day shall atonement be made for you to cleanse you. You shall be clean before the* LORD *from all your sins. It is a Sabbath of solemn rest to you, and you shall afflict yourselves; it is a statute forever. And the priest who is anointed and consecrated as priest in his father's place shall make atonement, wearing the holy linen garments. He shall make atonement for the holy sanctuary, and he shall make atonement for the tent of meeting and for the altar, and he shall make atonement for the priests and for all the people of the assembly.*
>
> Leviticus 16:30-33

What happens, then, when the holy God dwells among humans, not in a tent, but in the form of a man—Jesus of Nazareth? Can humans approach such a holy person?

Surprisingly, Jesus takes the initiative to reach out and touch the unclean, the leper, the bleeding woman. In the Gospels, uncleanness becomes personal and speaks through the voices of unclean spirits. In the presence of Jesus, unholy and impure spirits are overwhelmed and feel compelled to acknowledge Him as the Holy One of God.

Such active power of holiness is extended by Jesus after his death to every believer (1 Cor. 7:14; Acts 2:38ff). No longer are frequent bathings and washings required to remove impurity (Heb. 6:2; 1 Peter 3:21). Now the believer needs be immersed in water only once for cleansing, and with such washing receive the Holy Spirit.

Amazingly, God's holy presence now encamps in the human heart (1 Cor. 6:19). Such is possible only because of Jesus' blood and His work as great High Priest.

According to the letter of Hebrews, Jesus' death has made the Day of Atonement a thing of the past—obsolete (Hebrews 9-10). By Jesus' self-sacrifice sins both unintended and premeditated may be forgiven. The blood of Jesus, unlike the blood of bulls and goats, penetrates to the inmost memory of sin, cleansing the heart, freeing the believer from dead works and habits, assuring the Christian of access to the very throne of God.

By the Holy Spirit the believer is enabled to live a life of holiness. Through suffering and discipline, the believer shares in God's holiness (Heb. 12:10).

Numbers

As Numbers begins, it is one year after Israel's escape from King Pharaoh in Egypt. The children of Israel have indeed increased in "numbers" at Sinai. Males, twenty years and older who are able to go to war, now "number" 603,550 (Num. 1:46).

Israel appears to have conscripted a suitable army able to enter and take possession of the land God had first promised to Abraham. Israel is directed to encamp, its twelve tribes in specific areas around the tent of God's glory, and be ready to march on orders into battle.

Surely as God had blessed Abraham with descendants in abundance, surely as He had brought them out of Egypt, surely as He had given them a legal constitution, surely God would now lead His children into the Promised Land. But people's memories are short; expectations outrun patience; nostalgia deceives.

> *Now the rabble that was among them had a strong craving. And the people of Israel also wept again and said, "Oh that we had meat to eat! We remember the fish we ate in Egypt that cost nothing, the cucumbers, the melons, the leeks, the onions, and the garlic. But now our strength is dried up, and there is nothing at all but this manna to look at."*
>
> Numbers 11:4-6

For a nation which has been rescued from destruction expectations run high! After the exodus and the terror of Sinai, Israel expected freedom to offer exhilaration. Israel's desires became more important than her needs.

Still God listened to her cries for meat and answered her prayers of craving, satiating her with quail.

> *"And say to the people, 'Consecrate yourselves for tomorrow, and you shall eat meat, for you have wept in the hearing of the LORD, saying, "Who will give us meat to eat? For it was better for us in Egypt." Therefore the LORD will give you meat, and you shall eat. You shall not eat just one day, or two days, or five days, or ten days, or twenty days, but a whole month, until it comes out at your nostrils and becomes loathsome to you, because you have rejected the LORD who is among you and have wept before him, saying, "Why did we come out of Egypt?"'"*
>
> Numbers 11:18-20

In spite of the complaints, God had Moses send spies into the land promised. They discovered how rich indeed it was—in produce, in grapes, in cattle, in honey—but also how formidable its inhabitants! (Numbers 13:23-33)

Israel failed to trust God as her leader. His people failed to remember how He had defeated Egypt. The children of Israel could only see the strength and size of the land's inhabitants. God's power was invisible to their eyes.

And so, unbelievably so, Israel yearned to return to Egypt: 'Better to be slaves and be told what to do by King Pharaoh than to have the risky freedom of following God as King.'

> *And all the people of Israel grumbled against Moses and Aaron. The whole congregation said to them, "Would that we had died in the land of Egypt! Or would that we had died in this wilderness! Why is the LORD bringing us into this land, to fall by the sword? Our wives and our little ones will become a prey. Would it not be better for us to go back to Egypt?" And they said to one another, "Let us choose a leader and go back to Egypt."*
>
> Numbers 14:2-4

God wants to disinherit Israel on the spot. Moses pleads with God to forgive, just as he had pleaded for the nation before. God forgives the people according to His steadfast love, but with one significant qualification: no one above twenty years of age—except the two spies who trusted God as warrior—would be able to enter the Promised Land. And over the next forty years, the dead bodies of an entire generation would be strewn across a sun-drenched wilderness (Num. 14:20-35). But the children would survive to inherit the Promised Land, testifying to Israel's real dependence on God.

As the story in Numbers continues, the first generation dies. They die in their foolish attempt to conquer the land without the leadership of God (Num. 14:26-45). They die in their foolish rebellion against the leadership of Moses (Num. 15).

In all of this Moses is very lowly and very great. He is humble before the LORD. In fact God calls him "my servant" and entrusts His people to Moses' care (Num. 12:3-8). God listens when Moses intercedes for the people.

Yet Moses is very human. On one occasion, in a moment of frustration with the people's rebellious heart, Moses himself disobeys God. Instead of commanding a rock to yield water, Moses strikes the rock—twice. Water comes out, but Moses failed to honor God's holiness.

> *And the LORD said to Moses and Aaron, "Because you did not believe in me, to uphold me as holy in the eyes of the people of Israel, therefore you shall not bring this assembly into the land that I have given them." These are the waters of Meribah ["quarreling"], where the people of Israel quarreled with the LORD, and through them he showed himself holy.*
>
> Numbers 20:12-13

Joshua, not Moses, will one day bring the second generation into the land "flowing with milk and honey."

Much later, another Israelite, not of the tribe of Levi but of Judah, will appear on the earth. This Jew, the Son of God, will also be thrust into the wilderness. But unlike the first children of God in the desert, this Son will be obedient to the Father, resisting the test to turn stone into bread in His period of dedication to God's care.

As great as was Moses, this Jew will be far greater. As faithful as was Moses in all God's house as a servant, Jesus will be faithful over God's house as a Son (Hebrews 3:1-6).

Christians who read the story of Israel in the wilderness see it as a tale of warning (1 Cor. 10:1-5). Israel was baptized in a cloud; they received God's food and water in the desert. Yet the LORD was not pleased with them because they failed to trust Him—even after great signs and assurances. Christians rightfully sense protection through baptism and security in the Lord's meal, yet they must continue to trust His care.

It is easy to forget past joys. It is easy to expect too much, too soon. The wilderness generation is a reminder for Christians not to be surprised when God leads His people to Rest through difficult times of testing. But He also provides precious, very great promises of an inheritance, undefiled and unfading, kept in heaven for those who continue to trust His care and faithfulness.

Deuteronomy 1-8

The name for the fifth book of the Bible, Deuteronomy, is taken from a word in the Greek translation of Deut. 17:18 which means "second law." Indeed, in Deuteronomy Moses is proclaiming the law of God a second time to Israel—to a new generation—since the first generation (who had heard the law at Sinai) has died in the wilderness.

The setting for Deuteronomy is poignant. Moses is 120 years old. The great leader, the prophet, the servant of God, stands overlooking the Promised Land beyond the Jordan River. He so desires to cross over and enter the good land, but the LORD God has told him he cannot because he had compromised God's holiness (Deut. 3:23ff; 32:48ff).

It is left to Moses, a father to the nation, to tell the story of Sinai and the wilderness to the children and fully engage them in Israel's covenant with God. Deuteronomy functions as Moses' *last will and testament*. It is a series of moving, passionate speeches delivered shortly before Moses dies and is buried outside the Promised Land (cf. Deut. 34).

In these exhortations and warnings, Moses attempts to prepare the people for entering and living in the Promised Land. No longer will they have Moses to lead them. No longer will they have God's guidance by cloud and fire. They will now have the words of God in their memory to guide them—words to obey that they might live long in the land.

For this reason, Moses reminds them that at Mt. Sinai they (through their fathers) did not see God's form. They experienced God through their ears, not their eyes, hearing the sound of words from the fire. So now words inscribed within must instruct them.

Moses warns them they should never fashion an idol (Deut. 4). In the Promised Land, Israel would indeed be tempted to worship other gods and to mold images like the golden calf in the wilderness. Israel was to remember that words, not carved images, convey God's presence and mediate God's will.

Moses composes a song for the children to sing whose lyrics remind them of God's presence and will (Deut. 32). Christians today confess that they too experience the presence of God's Son through the remembrance of His words and the gift of His Spirit.

> *"If you love me, you will keep my commandments. And I will ask the Father, and he will give you another Helper, to be with you forever, even the Spirit of truth, whom the world cannot receive, because it neither sees him nor knows him. You know him, for he dwells with you and will be in you."*
>
> John 14:15-17

In Deuteronomy 5-6, Moses commands the children to hear certain specific words, to learn and obey them diligently. Moses goes so far as to describe their obedience as faithfulness to a covenant. In obeying the Ten Commandments, the children are being faithful to a solemn agreement with God.

> *And Moses summoned all Israel and said to them, "Hear, O Israel, the statutes and the rules that I speak in your hearing today, and you shall learn them and be careful to do them. The LORD our God made a covenant with us in Horeb. Not with our fathers did the LORD make this covenant, but with us, who are all of us here alive today. The LORD spoke with you face to face at the mountain, out of the midst of the fire, while I stood between the LORD and you at that time, to declare to you the word of the LORD. For you were afraid because of the fire, and you did not go up into the mountain. He said:*
>
> *"'I am the LORD your God, who brought you out of the land of Egypt, out of the house of slavery.*
>
> *"'You shall have no other gods before me.'"*
>
> Deuteronomy 5:1-6

In chapters 12-26, Moses elaborates the significance of God's commandments for life in the land. But when Moses anticipates the question of later generations, "What do these commandments mean?" he does not immediately answer with explanations of their application to various situations. Nor does Moses reply with a re-presentation of God's terrifying, awe-inspiring presence at Sinai. No. Instead, Moses emphasizes the loving concern and care the LORD God had shown for Israel in the exodus.

> *"When your son asks you in time to come, 'What is the meaning of the testimonies and the statutes and the rules that the LORD our God has commanded you?' then you shall say to your son, 'We were Pharaoh's slaves in Egypt. And the LORD brought us out of Egypt with a mighty hand. And the LORD showed signs and wonders, great and grievous, against Egypt and against Pharaoh and all his household, before our eyes. And he brought us out from there, that he might bring us in and give us the land that he swore to give to our fathers. And the LORD commanded us to do all these statutes, to fear the LORD our God, for our good always, that he might preserve us alive, as we are this day. And it will be righteousness for us, if we are careful to do all this commandment before the LORD our God, as he has commanded us.'"*
>
> Deuteronomy 6:20-25

Moses' moving speeches are meant to lead the children to long for, to seek, to embrace the care of such a God—to lead them without reservation to confess the words of Deuteronomy 6:4: "The LORD is *our* God, the LORD alone."

Truly the God named Yahweh had fought for Israel and delivered her. In response, Moses commands the children to also love:

> *Love the LORD your God with all your heart, and with all your soul, and with all your strength.*
>
> Deuteronomy 6:5

Love here is not merely the heart's best impulses or the mind's truest allegiance. It is love willing to give up life itself in faithfulness to God. It is love willing to marshal all of life's possessions in adoration to the God who has showered blessings of good.

Love in Deuteronomy is loyalty to God.

Christians confess that only one Israelite ever loved God this completely and faithfully; that this man alone, of all men who have ever lived, truly exemplified the love of God with all heart, all life, and all strength—the man named Jesus.

Deuteronomy 9-34

A parent wants his child to grow up to be healthy and to prosper. At the same time, every parent, knowing life's dangers, seeks to warn the child of the world's evil.

In the fifth book of the Bible, Deuteronomy, Moses tells the children of Israel how to be healthy and thrive in the new land God would give to them. He also warns them about false ideologies and propaganda which could lead them astray.

In entering the Promised Land, Israel was about to confront a native population both prosperous and powerful. Israel's spies reported strong walled cities with impressive buildings. The people as well were imposing—large and strong. The natives appeared fruitful in business, farming, and trading.

> *"Hear, O Israel: you are to cross over the Jordan today, to go in to dispossess nations greater and mightier than you, cities great and fortified up to heaven, a people great and tall, the sons of the Anakim, whom you know, and of whom you have heard it said, 'Who can stand before the sons of Anak?' Know therefore today that he who goes over before you as a consuming fire is the LORD your God. He will destroy them and subdue them before you. So you shall drive them out and make them perish quickly, as the LORD has promised you."*
>
> Deuteronomy 9:1-4

Moses understood that the poor Israelites, having accomplished none of these things, would wonder why the Canaanites were so prosperous. The Canaanites could tell them: "We know how to please the gods of our land." The Israelites might envy their success.

The Canaanites believed that they had to please their gods, Baal and Asherah, who controlled the storms, rainfall, and fertility. Otherwise their crops would fail, their flocks starve, and their children die. They believed that sexual activity could somehow encourage the gods to bring fertility to the soil and flock.

By contrast, Moses reminded the people that their God, the LORD of Israel, did not grant blessings based on such practices. God had chosen Israel, not the reverse. God's directives did not demand rites of fertility, but rather lives of loyalty to the only true God; lives of justice to the neighbor; and lives of care for the disadvantaged, the widow, the orphan, the resident alien.

> *"And because you listen to these rules and keep and do them, the LORD your God will keep with you the covenant and the steadfast love that he swore to your fathers. He will love you, bless you, and multiply you. He will also bless the fruit of your womb and the fruit of your ground, your grain and your wine and your oil, the increase of your herds and the young of your flock, in the land that he swore to your fathers to give you. You shall be blessed above all peoples. There shall not be male or female barren among you or among your livestock."*
>
> Deuteronomy 7:12-14

Israel's God was not merely Lord of storm or sea; He had created the heavens and the earth. All was His. The land was His, to give and to bless. But God was not capricious in His blessings; He desired right behavior from His children.

> *"But the land that you are going over to possess is a land of hills and valleys, which drinks water by the rain from heaven, a land that the LORD your God cares for. The eyes of the LORD your God are always upon it, from the beginning of the year to the end of the year.*
>
> *"And if you will indeed obey my commandments that I command you today, to love the LORD your God, and to serve him with all your heart and with all your soul, he will give the rain for your land in its season, the early rain and the later rain, that you may gather in your grain and your wine and your oil. And he will give grass in your fields for your livestock, and you shall eat and be full. Take care lest your heart be deceived, and you turn aside and serve other gods and worship them; then the anger of the LORD will be kindled against you, and he will shut up the heavens, so that there will be no rain, and the land will yield no fruit, and you will perish quickly off the good land that the LORD is giving you."*
>
> Deuteronomy 11:11-17

Because of the threat of polytheism Moses instructed Israel to take radical protective measures:

> *"When the LORD your God brings you into the land that you are entering to take possession of it, and clears away many nations before you, the Hittites, the Girgashites, the Amorites, the Canaanites, the Perizzites, the Hivites, and the Jebusites, seven nations more numerous and mightier than you, and when the LORD your God gives them over to you, and you defeat them, then you must devote them to complete destruction. You shall make no covenant with them and show no mercy to them. You shall not intermarry with them, giving your daughters to their sons or taking their daughters for your sons, for they would turn away your sons from following me, to serve other gods. Then the anger of the LORD would be kindled against you, and he would destroy you quickly. But thus shall you deal with them: you shall break down their altars and dash in pieces their pillars and chop down their Asherim and burn their carved images with fire.*
>
> *"For you are a people holy to the LORD your God. The LORD your God has chosen you to be a people for his treasured possession, out of all the peoples who are on the face of the earth."*
>
> Deuteronomy 7:1-7

What God had done to Pharaoh in Egypt and at the Red Sea, He could do again to any people or power in the Promised Land. Yet His children were not to become arrogant, thinking God favored them because of their righteousness. God had chosen and loved them in their weakness, not their strength (Deut. 7:7-11). They had endured the wilderness only by the provisions of His word, not by their own ingenuity. God had used the rigors of the wilderness to prepare them for entering the Promised Land (Deut. 8).

Christians recognize that the successful today often bow to false gods, offering lies, bribery, and cheating in sacrifice to the idols of power and greed. The true God, however, the Father of Jesus Christ, is the only source of life and well-being. While the trappings of success may for the moment be worn by the polytheist, the one true God shall in His time accomplish His good will of blessing. Meanwhile, His people must honor Him by loyalty to Him and loving neighbor while fleeing the "gods" of fortune, fertility, and success.

> *"And now, Israel, what does the LORD your God require of you, but to fear the LORD your God, to walk in all his ways, to love him, to serve the LORD your God with all your heart and with all your soul, and to keep the commandments and statutes of the*

LORD, which I am commanding you today for your good? Behold, to the LORD your God belong heaven and the heaven of heavens, the earth with all that is in it. Yet the LORD set his heart in love on your fathers and chose their offspring after them, you above all peoples, as you are this day. Circumcise therefore the foreskin of your heart, and be no longer stubborn. For the LORD your God is God of gods and Lord of lords, the great, the mighty, and the awesome God, who is not partial and takes no bribe. He executes justice for the fatherless and the widow, and loves the sojourner, giving him food and clothing."

Deuteronomy 10:12-18

Joshua

During the time of Moses a certain Israelite named Nun reared a remarkable son. His son proved himself to be a leader among leaders. He willingly accepted and executed dangerous spy missions. He demonstrated fearlessness in the face of powerful opposition. He was courageous in telling his own people unpopular truths. He endured forty years wandering in a wilderness, watching older friends and family members die one by one. But most remarkable of all, this son of Nun was able to succeed the great hero Moses in leading Israel into the Promised Land (Joshua 1:16-18).

Joshua, the son of Nun, was a strong and courageous man (1:1-9). The book of Joshua records his important role in leading the Israelites into Canaan.

More than about the man, the book is about the faithfulness and integrity of Joshua's God—the LORD God of Israel. Long before, God had led Abraham through this same place, promising him not only countless descendants but the land as well.

Now in Joshua's time, God begins to give Israel this land—ground she had not plowed, cities she had not built, vineyards she had not planted (24:13). The story of God's giving and Israel's possessing is the story of the book of Joshua.

Unlike the generation at Sinai, this second generation does not retreat at the borders of the Promised Land. Joshua, the master spy, now sends out two spies himself to investigate the first stronghold across the Jordan River, the walled city of Jericho. The spies are not impressed by the strength of the city. Instead, they are impressed with the city's fear of Israel's God, the God who had dried up the Red Sea (2:10, 24).

God now dries up the Jordan River, permitting the people to cross over to the plains of Jericho (Joshua 4). The wilderness wanderings have ceased. No more manna!

All the sons born in the wilderness are circumcised. And Joshua is confronted with the true commander-general of the troops of Israel:

> *When Joshua was by Jericho, he lifted up his eyes and looked, and behold, a man was standing before him with his drawn sword in his hand. And Joshua went to him and said to him, "Are you for us, or for our adversaries?" And he said, "No; but I am the commander of the army of the LORD. Now I have come." And Joshua fell on his face to the earth and worshiped and said to him, "What does my lord say to his servant?" And the commander of the LORD's army said to Joshua, "Take off your sandals from your feet, for the place where you are standing is holy." And Joshua did so.*
>
> Joshua 5:13-15

What follows is Israel's conquest of certain Canaanite cities and defeat of 31 kings. The fall of Jericho, its walls collapsing at the noise of trumpets and shouting, is indicative of the victories God gives to faithful Israel:

> *So Joshua struck the whole land, the hill country and the Negeb and the lowland and the slopes, and all their kings. He left none remaining, but devoted to destruction all that breathed, just as the LORD God of Israel commanded. And Joshua struck them from Kadesh-barnea as far as Gaza, and all the country of Goshen, as far as Gibeon. And Joshua captured all these kings and their land at one time, because the LORD God of Israel fought for Israel. Then Joshua returned, and all Israel with him, to the camp at Gilgal.*
>
> Joshua 10:40-43

God's requirement of absolute destruction indicates the seriousness of His warnings against idolatry and intermarriage with polytheists (Joshua 6). When Israel violates the ban, she suffers swift and tragic consequences (Joshua 7).

After entering Canaan, Joshua allots the land to Israel according to her tribes for an inheritance. At last, the people have rest from forty years of desert wandering. They have relied on God. They are enjoying food and settled life. But there is a problem.

Not all the inhabitants of the land have been driven out as God commanded (15:63; 16:10; 17:12). Joshua warns the people that this remnant can become a thorn in their eyes:

> *"Be very careful, therefore, to love the LORD your God. For if you turn back and cling to the remnant of these nations remaining among you and make marriages with them, so that you associate with them and they with you, know for certain that the LORD your God will no longer drive out these nations before you, but they shall be a snare and a trap for you, a whip on your sides and thorns in your eyes, until you perish from off this good ground that the LORD your God has given you."*
>
> Joshua 23:11-13

In his *last will and testament*, Joshua pleads with the people to serve the God who has brought them into this good land rather than the gods of Canaan.

> *"Now therefore fear the LORD and serve him in sincerity and in faithfulness. Put away the gods that your fathers served beyond the River and in Egypt, and serve the LORD. And if it is evil in your eyes to serve the LORD, choose this day whom you will serve, whether the gods your fathers served in the region beyond the River, or the gods of the Amorites in whose land you dwell. But as for me and my house, we will serve the LORD."*
>
> Joshua 24:14-15

For first-century Jews who believed in Jesus as Messiah, the land promised to Abraham was no longer an expectation. The Christians had turned to a new Joshua, Jesus Christ, who would lead them to a quite different rest—a rest begun on the seventh day of creation when God ceased His work; a rest in the presence of God available through Jesus' high priesthood; a rest complete only after a Day of universal judgment—in the new Jerusalem (Hebrews 4:11).

Judges

In the exodus from Egypt and conquest of Canaan Israel was blessed to have the leadership of two great men of God—Moses and Joshua. The story of Israel's life after Joshua's death is told in the book of Judges. The last sentence of Judges describes this period in disturbing ways:

> *In those days there was no king in Israel. Everyone did what was right in his own eyes.*

This portrayal of Israel prompts us to ask an important question: "What is the best kind of government for people to have?"

Is it better to have a tightly structured, highly centralized form of government, headed by a powerful leader to whom people turn over individual freedoms for the common good? Or is it better to have a decentralized form of government—one that stresses local leadership and maximum personal freedom?

Before we take up this issue directly, let us consider how Israel lived and was governed in the land God had given her.

Settled into their allotted portion of land, each of the twelve tribes developed its own self-rule. There was no centralized bureaucracy. Local individuals called elders functioned as the real leaders, with an occasional individual called a judge interpreting and administering civil and religious law among the tribes.

As long as Israel was loyal to God's laws, and as long as no foreign group attacked her, this system worked well. But, according to the book of Judges, the reality was that Israel frequently and flagrantly ignored God's will.

> *And the people of Israel did what was evil in the sight of the LORD and served the Baals. And they abandoned the LORD, the God of their fathers, who had brought them out of the land of Egypt. They went after other gods, from among the gods of the peoples who were around them, and bowed down to them. And they provoked the LORD to anger. They abandoned the LORD and served the Baals and the Ashtaroth.*
>
> Judges 2:11-13

God, in turn, allowed foreign invaders to oppress Israel. Then, when Israel cried out in penitence for relief, God raised up special persons called "judges" to lead the militia and deliver His people from their enemies. The stories of six of these Spirit-filled judges—Othniel, Ehud, Deborah, Gideon, Jephthah, and Samson—comprise the core of the book.

Israel's tribal confederacy, with its decentralized, highly individualistic structure, would have worked well had Israel remained faithful to God. But she did not. Time after time, one crisis was barely over before Israel forgot God again. And another crisis began.

After the judgeship of Samson, the situation became even worse. There was idolatry, personal and sexual abuse of all kinds, and civil war among the tribes. There was no king in Israel; everyone did what was right in his own eyes.

In the next generation, in the days of Samuel, things changed. Israel demanded a king, and in spite of Samuel's protests and warnings, God gave her a king. Now there was a central government, a standing army, and eventually a capital city, Jerusalem—with a temple for God and a palace for the king. When the king was righteous and wise, all was well. But more often than not, the king was neither righteous nor wise, and the people suffered.

So, which is best? Maximum individual freedom and local authority or a strong centralized government with a single powerful leader? The answer from the time of the judges, and beyond, is this: The form of government is not the primary concern. The ultimate issue is who rules in the hearts of the people. Gideon said it so well when the people wanted to make him a permanent leader:

> *Then the men of Israel said to Gideon, "Rule over us, you and your son and your grandson also, for you have saved us from the hand of Midian." Gideon said to them, "I will not rule over you, and my son will not rule over you; the LORD will rule over you."*
>
> Judges 11:22-23

God can work within any number of political systems if the people obey *Him* and do not trust in the government or its leaders for security, salvation, and well-being. The book of Judges tells us that even when we make choices that God knows are not the best, He will be patient and work through the actions we take—allowing us to make mistakes and to suffer the consequences—without abandoning us. And why?

IN SINCERE APPRECIATION…

Our friend and brother, David Worley, exemplified the motto by which he shaped his life, and by which he stood as an example to others : "*thelese*" – "if God wills". His love and service to and for the church stand as a lasting memorial to a heart given to God. In his death he continues to point the way for a deepening of faith, of strengthening the bonds of love and fellowship, and seeking God's Will in each and every facet of our lives.

David frequently prayed the prayer of Paul, found in the 3rd chapter of Ephesians:

"I bow my knees before the Father, from whom every family in heaven and on earth derives its name, that He would grant you according to the riches of His glory, to be strengthened with power through His Spirit in the inner man, so that Christ may dwell in your hearts through faith and that you, being rooted and grounded in love, may be able to comprehend with all the saints what is the breadth and length and height and depth, and to know the love of Christ which surpasses knowledge, that you may be filled up to all the fullness of God. Now to Him who is able to do far more abundantly beyond all that we ask or think according to the power that works within us, to Him be the glory in the church and in Christ Jesus to all generations forever and ever. Amen."

This book is only one small footprint of those left by David in the sands of the time of his life. As he said in the closing paragraph of his preface: "May this guide strengthen the desire to prayerfully read the Scripture with fellow believers, so to walk worthily of the Lord, fully pleasing to him, bearing fruit and increasing in understanding of God." (Col. 1:20).

For 36 years David and his family have been faithful members of the fellowship at Brentwood Oaks Church of Christ in Austin, Texas. For half that time he served as one of the shepherds for the congregation, leading the way for developing thoughtful, deliberate ways of shaping worship services and being involved in meaningful outreach, missions and benevolent activity. David's desire for his legacy, his heritage, is underscored by one of the verses in the Hymn *Find Us Faithful:*

"O may all who come behind us find us faithful,
May the fire of our devotion light their way.
May the footprints that we leave, lead them to believe,
And the lives we live inspire them to obey.
O may all who come behind us find us faithful."

As God said to Israel in Joshua's day, "I will never break my covenant with you." God's unwavering purpose is to establish His rule in our hearts, our homes, and our lands.

This is precisely the message of Jesus. "The time has come," He said. "The kingdom of God is near. Repent and believe the good news!"

God's kingdom is the one which will prevail over all human governments. God has vested ultimate authority, not in nations or governments, but in His Son, Jesus Christ. Isaiah the prophet spoke of this Son when he said,

For to us a child is born,
to us a son is given;
and the government shall be upon his shoulder,
and his name shall be called
Wonderful Counselor, Mighty God,
Everlasting Father, Prince of Peace.

Of the increase of his government and of peace
there will be no end,
on the throne of David and over his kingdom,
to establish it and to uphold it
with justice and with righteousness
from this time forth and forevermore.
The zeal of the LORD of hosts will do this.

Isaiah 9:6-7

We may live, for better or worse, under any number of human political systems. The only passport we really need is the one God has given us in the gift of His own Spirit—the guarantee of our citizenship in the new heaven and the new earth, which one day we will inherit for eternity.

Ruth

Only two of the sixty-six books in the Bible have the names of women in the title—Ruth and Esther—both in the Old Testament.

More remarkable than this, one of the two women is not even an Israelite. She is a Moabite who worshiped foreign gods. Why then is her story included in Holy Scripture?

Ruth lived during the time of the Judges. Israel had not been faithful in driving out the native peoples from the Promised Land. As a result, Israel was tempted to accommodate herself to the practices and mythology of the local culture. Through the intimacies of intermarriage, many Israelites followed the gods of the Canaanites, the gods of fertility and storm, in an effort to ensure prosperity through their crops.

In His anger, God allowed enemies to defeat the various tribes. In His mercy, God raised up warrior-rulers called judges to deliver Israel from her oppressors. Still, God's people turned to other gods.

Jewish society was in distress. There was anarchy and chaos. "Everyone was doing what was right in their own eyes." As a result of this national malaise and God's withdrawal of blessings, there was famine in the land. As with their forefathers, certain Israelites ventured into foreign territory seeking food. In the case of one family, a couple and their two sons, the search led south to Moab.

In Moab the two sons married native women, one of whom was named Ruth. Tragically, all the men of the family died. The mother, Naomi, who had left the village of Bethlehem "full" was now "empty"—having lost her husband and both sons (Ruth 1:20-21). She had only two daughters-in-law to comfort her.

Naomi decided to leave Moab and return home to Bethlehem in Judah. She said farewell to her daughters-in-law. That is when the remarkable happened:

> *Then they lifted up their voices and wept again. And Orpah kissed her mother-in-law, but Ruth clung to her.*
>
> *And she said, "See, your sister-in-law has gone back to her people and to her gods; return after your sister-in-law." But Ruth said, "Do not urge me to leave you or to return from following you. For where you go I will go, and where you lodge I will lodge. Your people shall be my people, and your God my God. Where you die I will die, and there will I be buried. May the LORD do so to me and more also if anything but death parts me from you."*
>
> Ruth 1:14-17

Ruth decided to embrace Naomi's God, the LORD God of Israel. In stark contrast to the disastrous results of intermarriage in Judges—when the

Israelites took foreign spouses and foreign gods (Judges 3:5, 6)—the foreign wife Ruth comes to worship the God who redeemed alien Israel from the land of Egypt.

Ruth is indeed an extraordinary woman. She gleans among the ears of wheat as an outsider, following the Israelites who reap first, in order to gather food for herself and Naomi (Ruth 2). She "happens" into the field of a wealthy man named Boaz, who is aware of her newfound faith. He compares her actions to the trust of Abraham who had left his father's homeland and gods:

> *But Boaz answered her, "All that you have done for your mother-in-law since the death of your husband has been fully told to me, and how you left your father and mother and your native land and came to a people that you did not know before. The LORD repay you for what you have done, and a full reward be given you by the LORD, the God of Israel, under whose wings you have come to take refuge!" Then she said, "I have found favor in your eyes, my lord, for you have comforted me and spoken kindly to your servant, though I am not one of your servants."*
>
> Ruth 2:11-13

It turns out that Boaz is a close relative of Ruth's dead husband—with a responsibility to him as next-of-kin. Boaz must marry his widow Ruth and raise children in the first husband's name. In this way the land inheritance will remain in the original family lineage (see Deut. 25:5-6; Ruth 4:10). And so Boaz marries Ruth, and God gives them a son, Obed.

Why then is one of the sixty-six books of the Bible about a non-Israelite woman and her Israelite relatives? As we are told, the son of Ruth becomes the grandfather of King David, a man after God's own heart. How could Ruth, a stranger in a new land, know that she would be the great grandmother of Israel's greatest king?

The lesson is clear: God indeed works His will, often through people unknown, in places obscure, and in circumstances unexpected. His eyes and ears are attuned to the hearts and cries of the righteous in every land who seek to do good. No matter the political unrest, the violence and lawlessness, God works among individuals and families in quiet, unobtrusive ways, disciplining His children through tests, advancing His plan for reconciling the world to Himself.

And in the town of Bethlehem centuries later, a descendant of Obed would be born, sent to save His people from their sins—Immanuel, the son of David, Jesus Christ.

1 Samuel 1-8

We now follow the story of God and Israel in 1-2 Samuel and 1-2 Kings. These four books cover a period of 500 years, from the first to the final king of Israel, from the time of Israel's slavery to its own king (1Samuel 8:17) to the time of Israel's slavery to a foreign king (2 Kings 25:27-30).

The story in 1 Samuel begins with a woman named Hannah who is in bitter distress. She is infertile. She wants so much to have a child that she makes a dangerous bargain with God. Like Abraham before, Hannah is willing to offer up her son in sacrifice. Unlike Abraham, Hannah initiates the proposal and will eventually give away her firstborn son to the service of God.

From a woman of such earnest prayer, it is perhaps not surprising to find one of her petitions recorded in Scripture. The prayer is at once autobiographical, expressing Hannah's joy at God's intervention, while at the same time biographical of Israel's experiences with the Holy God.

Hannah's prayer, as our own prayers, will impact generations to come. Early in the first century AD, her prayer became a resource for theological understanding and confident hope to a young, unmarried Jewish girl who found herself pregnant. Mary, the mother of Jesus, repeated Hannah's prayer as she awaited delivery of her own first child (Luke 1:46-55). Since Mary, many other women have remembered Hannah's prayer and drawn fresh courage from its words.

After weaning him, Hannah left her son Samuel with the priest Eli as she had promised. Samuel grew up in the sanctuary at Shiloh during a time when God's direct speech to His chosen servants was extremely rare (1 Sam. 3:1). During this time, Israel accepted all too easily the thinking of her polytheistic neighbors. For many years, God had rescued Israel from her travails by raising up warrior-leaders called "judges."

Early in 1 Samuel, Israel faced another crisis when she attempted to use the ark of the covenant as a kind of magical protection against the

Philistines. The plan, however, backfired. The unthinkable happened. The ark was captured in battle, the priest's sons were killed, and Israel was in shock. Hearing the news, Eli collapsed and broke his neck (1 Samuel 4).

But the Philistines had their hands full with the captured ark (1 Samuel 5). Tumors afflicted the residents in the cities where the sacred chest resided. Ironically, the Philistine god, Dagon, could not stand on his pedestal even overnight next to the ark. Each morning he was found face down. Finally, Dagon lost both head and hands!

The true God could not be contained in a box. The Divine One could not be manipulated by human strategies. Eventually the Philistines decided that the God who had afflicted Egypt was not to be trifled with. The Philistines sent the ark back where it came from (1 Samuel 6).

Such problems in Israel were the result in part of the failed leadership of Eli and his two impudent sons. Samuel grew up in this family observing Eli's parenting every day. In spite of such poor sibling behavior, Samuel gained remarkable wisdom and would become Israel's last judge. Unhappily, perhaps because of Eli's parenting, Samuel too was unable to train his own sons in honesty and justice before God. The situation became so serious that the elders of Israel finally had to talk to Samuel about his sons, making an unsettling request.

Sadly, Israel wanted to be like her neighbors, having an earthly king—a king to take control, a king to do the thinking, a king to fight the battles, a king to represent God. How Samuel reacts and what God decides are critical for the future of Israel.

1 Samuel 9-15

From the beginning in Genesis, God is King over His creation. He speaks and the elements obey. He delegates regal authority to humans to rule in the creation. He later selects one family to be a "kingdom of priests" under His exclusive sovereignty with a mission to the nations of the world.

But something goes terribly wrong: Israel chooses to reject God as King.

God sends a man to the prophet Samuel whom he is to anoint as the first king of Israel (9:16). God expresses confidence that the tall, handsome young man named Saul will be able to save Israel from her enemies.

God's choice is a surprise, however, because Saul is a shy, inexperienced fellow from the small tribe of Benjamin, who even views himself as insignificant.

Despite his humble pedigree, Saul is empowered by God's Spirit to meet his first military test. The Philistines, Israel's perennial enemies, are defeated. God promises wellbeing to Israel if she and her king will follow Him, even though her demand for a king was wicked in His sight (12:14-17).

Tragically, despite the opportunities and strengths laid before him, Saul disobeys God. On one occasion, impatient and pressured by the people, Saul initiates a sacrifice before battle in direct violation of God's command to wait for Samuel.

On another occasion, Saul spares the king and choice animals of the Amalekites for a sacrifice he planned "for the LORD"—again in direct violation of God's command to utterly destroy everything. Samuel's response is simple and profound:

> *"Has the LORD as great delight in burnt offerings and sacrifices,*
> *as in obeying the voice of the LORD?*
> *Behold, to obey is better than sacrifice,*
> *and to listen than the fat of rams.*
> *For rebellion is as the sin of divination,*
> *and presumption is as iniquity and idolatry.*
> *Because you have rejected the word of the LORD,*
> *he has also rejected you from being king."*
>
> 1 Samuel 15:22-23

Samuel himself cuts the Amalekite king into pieces (15:33). Why then, with such opportunities and power available, did Saul disobey the LORD? The narrator of 1 Samuel does not say. Why do *we* disobey God?

Certainly Saul's reactions and judgment in other situations can be criticized—as when he decided to deprive his troops of nourishment, forcing them to eat food with blood, a violation of Torah (14:32-35; Lev. 19:26). And he needlessly placed his own son Jonathan under a curse of death. All this, Jonathan realized, was imprudent:

> *Then Jonathan said, "My father has troubled the land. See how my eyes have become bright because I tasted a little of this honey. How much better if the people had eaten freely today of*

the spoil of their enemies that they found. For now the defeat among the Philistines has not been great."

1 Samuel 14:29-30

Saul's poor judgment, however, does not explain or excuse his failure to honor God's sovereignty.

Saul said to Samuel, "I have sinned, for I have transgressed the commandment of the LORD and your words, because I feared the people and obeyed their voice. Now therefore, please pardon my sin and return with me that I may bow before the LORD."

1 Samuel 15:24-25

Despite his penitence and confession, the kingship of Israel is torn from Saul's family. What is truly tragic is that Saul's honorable and good son, Jonathan, is deprived of any possible future as king. The Spirit departs from Saul and comes mightily upon a young man from the tribe of Judah (16:13-14). Jonathan will grow to love in deep friendship the son of Jesse—David, the next ruler of Israel.

Jonathan will live to save David from the evil of Saul. The hero of that tale is not the powerful king, but his son, Jonathan.

1 Samuel 16 – 2 Samuel 24

In the 10th century BC, the empires along the Nile and the Tigris-Euphrates Rivers were undergoing a period of weakness and decline. For Israel, this weakness was a welcome relief. Not surprisingly, the story covering this period in 1-2 Samuel involves Israel's largest occupation of the Promised Land.

But the story is about much more. Most of all, it is about the way God's Spirit came upon a young boy with beautiful eyes named David.

In 1 Samuel 16, God sends Samuel to Jesse, David's father, in Bethlehem.

And Jesse made seven of his sons pass before Samuel. And Samuel said to Jesse, "The LORD has not chosen these." Then Samuel said to Jesse, "Are all your sons here?" And he said, "There remains yet the youngest, but behold, he is keeping the sheep." And Samuel said to Jesse, "Send and get him, for we will not sit down till he comes here." And he sent and brought him in. Now he was ruddy and had beautiful eyes and was handsome. And the LORD said, "Arise, anoint him, for this is he." Then Samuel took the horn of oil and anointed him in the midst of his brothers. And the Spirit of the LORD rushed upon David from that day forward. And Samuel rose up and went to Ramah.

1 Samuel 16:10-13

As an adolescent shepherd boy David exhibited remarkable courage and physical prowess, killing lions and bears who attacked his flock (17:34). But David took no pride in his natural reflexes. In meeting and killing the great Philistine warrior Goliath, David did not call on his own agility and muscles, but on "the armies of the living God" (17:27).

When Saul heard the local songs praising David's exploits (18:7), the king turned against him in relentless pursuit, seeking his death. On two different occasions, however, David had opportunity to kill Saul. But he refused—not wanting to slay the LORD's anointed (1 Samuel 24 and 26). When finally David heard the news of Saul's death, he refused to rejoice; instead, he tore his clothes, mourned, wept, fasted, and lamented:

"You daughters of Israel, weep over Saul,
who clothed you luxuriously in scarlet,
who put ornaments of gold on your apparel.

"How the mighty have fallen
in the midst of the battle!

"Jonathan lies slain on your high places.
I am distressed for you, my brother Jonathan;
very pleasant have you been to me;
your love to me was extraordinary,
surpassing the love of women.

"How the mighty have fallen,
and the weapons of war perished!"

2 Samuel 1:24-27

Through his many days of evading Saul, David was being prepared to lead and rule all Israel. He learned firsthand the ways of the Philistines (1 Samuel 27). He learned to adapt to changing circumstances and alliances (1 Sam. 21:25). He learned how to enlist the aid of mercenaries.

But it was the poetic, emotional, and musical side of David's personality which was most deepened. A profound depth of thought and emotion is clearly evident in the Psalms he composed. Through all these experiences David was equipped to be king, not only for Judah but for all Israel (2 Samuel 5).

David chose to establish his capital in a "neutral" area—the captured Jebusite city of Jerusalem. Eventually he would bring the ark of the LORD there (2 Samuel 6). It was also in Jerusalem that God made a great promise to David through the prophet Nathan:

> *"When your days are fulfilled and you lie down with your fathers, I will raise up your offspring after you, who shall come from your body, and I will establish his kingdom. He shall build a house for my name, and I will establish the throne of his kingdom forever. I will be to him a father, and he shall be to me a son. When he commits iniquity, I will discipline him with the rod of men, with the stripes of the sons of men, but my steadfast love will not depart from him, as I took it from Saul, whom I put away from before you. And your house and your kingdom shall be made sure forever before me. Your throne shall be established forever.'"*
>
> *In accordance with all these words, and in accordance with all this vision, Nathan spoke to David.*
>
> 2 Samuel 7:12-17

This promise would be fulfilled in Jesus, who came as the son of David for an eternal throne.

But even in the life of great King David there was tragedy. He did what was evil, despising the word of the LORD. He took another man's wife (a violation of the commandment not to commit adultery) and had the woman's husband killed in battle (a violation of the commandment not to murder).

When the prophet Nathan confronted the king, David confessed he had indeed sinned against the LORD.

David's children experience the consequence of his sin. The baby of Bathsheba, the wife of Uriah, dies. Soon thereafter, rape and murder ensue within the family (2 Samuel 13) until Absalom, the son whom David so loved, seizes power from his father. David finds himself fleeing

Jerusalem (2 Samuel 15ff). But Absalom comes to a bitter end, stabbed and beaten while hanging in a tree.

David deeply mourned his son's death. He returned to power but he was never the same man. At the end of his life he is cared for by a nurse, while his family vies for succession to the throne (1 Kings 1-2).

David's last words are a stirring reminder of the source of his success. They remind us of the words of a later Son of David who gave sight to the blind, healing to the lame, and deliverance to Israel.

> *"The Spirit of the LORD speaks by me;*
> *his word is on my tongue.*
> *The God of Israel has spoken;*
> *the Rock of Israel has said to me:*
> *When one rules justly over men,*
> *ruling in the fear of God,*
> *he dawns on them like the morning light,*
> *like the sun shining forth on a cloudless morning,*
> *like rain that makes grass to sprout from the earth.*
>
> *"For does not my house stand so with God?*
> *For he has made with me an everlasting covenant,*
> *ordered in all things and secure.*
> *For will he not cause to prosper*
> *all my help and my desire?"*

2 Samuel 23:2-5

1 Kings 1-11

The twelve tribes of Israel were able to rally behind a single king for only a brief period of time, just 80 years. After the reigns of Saul, David, and Solomon, the monarchy irrevocably split into two kingdoms: ten tribes in the north and two tribes in the south. The story of the last king of a united Israel, King Solomon, and Israel's tragic division is told in 1 Kings 1-12.

As David's death approached, it was not at all clear who would succeed him to the throne (1 Kings 1). However, through the intervention of Bathsheba David finally pronounced their son Solomon as the next king.

After his anointing, Solomon created a series of situations which effectively neutralized any internal threats to his early kingship (1 Kgs. 2). Solomon's glorious reign, mentioned even by Jesus, was not the result, however, of any political skill.

God confronted Solomon at the beginning of his reign in a dream—not with a command (as He had with Abraham) nor with the Spirit's influence (as He had with David). He confronted Solomon with a question.

> *At Gibeon the LORD appeared to Solomon in a dream by night, and God said, "Ask what I shall give you." And Solomon said, "You have shown great and steadfast love to your servant David my father, because he walked before you in faithfulness, in righteousness, and in uprightness of heart toward you. And you have kept for him this great and steadfast love and have given him a son to sit on his throne this day. And now, O LORD my God, you have made your servant king in place of David my father, although I am but a little child. I do not know how to go out or come in. And your servant is in the midst of your people whom you have chosen, a great people, too many to be numbered or counted for multitude. Give your servant therefore an understanding mind to govern your people, that I may discern between good and evil, for who is able to govern this your great people?"*
>
> 1 Kings 3:5-9

God is well pleased with Solomon's request and lavishes wisdom upon the new monarch. He became renowned for judicial wisdom, deciding between conflicting parties and interests, the classic case being his judgment regarding a child who was claimed by two prostitutes (3:16-28).

> *Now when the queen of Sheba heard of the fame of Solomon concerning the name of the LORD, she came to test him with hard questions. She came to Jerusalem with a very great retinue, with camels bearing spices and very much gold and precious stones. And when she came to Solomon, she told him all that was on her mind. And Solomon answered all her questions; there was nothing hidden from the king that he could not explain to her. And when the queen of Sheba had seen all the wisdom of Solomon, the house that he had built, the food of his table, the seating of his officials, and the attendance of his servants, their clothing, his cupbearers, and his burnt offerings that he offered at the house of the LORD, there was no more breath in her.*

And she said to the king, "The report was true that I heard in my own land of your words and of your wisdom, but I did not believe the reports until I came and my own eyes had seen it. And behold, the half was not told me. Your wisdom and prosperity surpass the report that I heard.

1 Kings 10:1-7

Solomon became renowned for his practical wisdom in the organization of massive construction projects. David had no doubt impressed upon his son the responsibility to build a house for God's name. Not only did Solomon oversee its completion, but he also built a palace for himself as well as fortifications for Jerusalem and other cities (1 Kings 5-7).

Solomon also became renowned for his commercial and mercantile success, developing alliances with suppliers, accessing the necessary materials for magnificent buildings.

Thus King Solomon excelled all the kings of the earth in riches and in wisdom. And the whole earth sought the presence of Solomon to hear his wisdom, which God had put into his mind. Every one of them brought his present, articles of silver and gold, garments, myrrh, spices, horses, and mules, so much year by year.

1 Kings 10:23-25

But Solomon's greatest wisdom was his understanding of God's willingness to listen to prayer. In the dedication of the temple, Solomon pleaded with the LORD to hear Israel in her various crises and to forgive (1 Kings 8).

Solomon's decision to seek wisdom instead of riches, honor, or long life has forever influenced believers as to priorities in prayer. In the New Testament, James echoes Solomon's example in this instruction to the church: "If any of you lacks wisdom, let him ask God, who gives generously to all without reproach, and it will be given him" (James 1:5).

Though many of his 700 marriages were unions of diplomatic convenience (to foster peaceful relations with surrounding neighbors), Solomon also understood romantic love. Solomon's *Song of Songs* is one the world's great love songs.

In an effort to please his foreign wives, Solomon built sacrificial places for their various foreign gods—in direct disobedience to his covenant with the LORD. To build these projects involved forcing his kinsmen into slave labor. Solomon became known for placing a "heavy yoke" and hard service upon his fellow Israelites (1 Kings 12:4). Discontent was further fostered by his tampering with old tribal boundaries in the interest of forming new economic districts.

It comes as no surprise, then, when a prophet announces that the kingdom will be torn from him (1 Kings 11:30-39). And so it is: Ten tribes are removed from the dynasty of David's house.

Solomon's kingdom was truly the glorious zenith of Israel's appearance on the world stage.

But the story of Solomon is also a clear reminder of the exclusive loyalty demanded by the God of Abraham, Moses, and David: that the LORD God will not tolerate other gods before Him; that He loves His creation and His people; that He expects loyal love in return—especially from the wisest ruler of all, King Solomon.

1 Kings 12 – 2 Kings 2

Solomon's rich wisdom brought great benefit to the kingdom of Israel. Everyone had plenty to eat and drink. Happiness abounded (1 Kgs. 4:20).

But happiness, as happiness does, proved to be short-lived: The forced labor practices in the massive construction projects of Jerusalem led to unrest and rebellion in the northern sector of his kingdom (12:4).

Far more serious, however, was Solomon's unwise use of resources in building altars to his wives' gods. His idolatrous practices led to the most grievous sins in Israel, resulting finally in the dissolution and exile of the ten northern tribes some 200 years later.

In the consequent divided kingdom, Israel in the north had the advantage of better land and larger population. Judah's rugged topography in the south, however, gave her better protection from invasion.

More importantly, Judah had the true sanctuary, the temple in Jerusalem, and cherished the promise made to David of a continuous line of descendants on the throne. Indeed, through the years greater stability existed in Judah than in North Israel with its frequent change of kings.

The political volatility in the north was the occasion for two of the most powerful and colorful prophets of God in the Bible—Elijah and Elisha. The story of Elijah dominates the second half of 1 Kings.

Elijah's appearance in Israel occurred during the reign of Ahab in the mid-ninth century BC. The ethos and allegiances of Israel's rulers had already been set, however, in the reign of her first king. Jeroboam I fashioned golden calves to worship in the sanctuaries at the towns of Bethel and Dan (12:28ff). The judgment of God on Jeroboam was severe:

> *"[B]ut you have done evil above all who were before you and have gone and made for yourself other gods and metal images, provoking me to anger, and have cast me behind your back, therefore behold, I will bring harm upon the house of Jeroboam and will cut off from Jeroboam every male, both bond and free in Israel, and will burn up the house of Jeroboam, as a man burns up dung until it is all gone. Anyone belonging to Jeroboam who dies in the city the dogs shall eat, and anyone who dies in the open country the birds of the heavens shall eat, for the LORD has spoken it."*
>
> 1 Kings 14:9-11

Some fifty years later there arose in Israel a powerful king named Omri. He is remembered most for establishing Samaria in the north as a rival capital to Jerusalem in the south. Yet, Omri's accomplishments could not compensate for his blatant unfaithfulness to the LORD God.

> *Omri did what was evil in the sight of the LORD, and did more evil than all who were before him. For he walked in all the way of Jeroboam the son of Nebat, and in the sins that he made Israel to sin, provoking the LORD, the God of Israel, to anger by their idols.*
>
> 1 Kings 16:25-26

His defiance, however, would pale in comparison to that of his son, Ahab.

As with the diplomatic marriages of Solomon before, King Ahab also married a foreign princess whose name was Jezebel. But none of Solomon's wives was like Jezebel. She was a tireless, ruthless supporter of Baalism, the worship of the Canaanite storm god (16:31-33).

Elijah came challenging the mythology that Baal provided the annual cycles of rain for the crops. No. The LORD God of Israel controlled the rain—not Baal! Elijah announced a three year drought. No rain. No dew

(1 Kings 17). The drought began. Such trauma, however, did not stop the Baal industry and its prophets.

In a great dramatic moment, Elijah challenges the 450 prophets of Baal to meet at Mount Carmel to see which deity, Yahweh or Baal, really controls the elements of nature. The contest is simple: which God will consume a sacrificial bull by fire?

First, the prophets of Baal cry all day to their god to swoop down and take the bull. When nothing happens, Elijah sarcastically suggests that perhaps their god is on vacation, or taking a nap, or maybe going to the toilet (18:27). Then Elijah soaks the firewood, altar, and bull with water, and calls upon the God of Abraham, Isaac, and Jacob.

In an instant everything is consumed by fire from the LORD God (18:38).

But Jezebel is not swayed by such displays. She goes after Elijah with full force. Surprisingly, Elijah runs away in the direction of Sinai (Horeb). At the mountain, Elijah shows his own humanity, thinking he is a lone survivor, the only faithful one left (19:10).

Suddenly there sweeps past Elijah a tornado. Then an earthquake. Then a storm fire. And then an eerie silence (19:11-14). God does not deliver new commandments at a new Sinai. Instead, He mildly rebukes Elijah, telling him to get back to Israel—for God has new leaders and a new prophet to replace him. And 7,000 who were not worshipping Baal (19:15-18). Elijah's self-absorption is clear.

With his leather belt and hairy body, Elijah was truly a striking figure during his life, and all the more at the end, awaiting chariots and horses of fire for his ascension to heaven (2 Kings 1:8; 2:11f).

In the first century, Elijah was expected to return. After Moses, Abraham, and David, Elijah is the most frequently mentioned Old Testament personality in the Gospels.

Some Jews saw a return of Elijah in Jesus. Indeed, many actions of Jesus reminded people of the prophet's life. The real Elijah did appear with Moses at the transfiguration of Jesus, conversing with the Lord about His impending death.

But another came in the likeness of Elijah, preparing the way for Jesus. His name was John the Baptist.

2 Kings 3-25

In 2 Kings we witness the collapse of the northern kingdom of Israel, followed by the southern kingdom of Judah. The heartbreaking deportations of God's people to foreign lands were avoidable events! Even though God had warned His people of the dangers of having a king (1 Samuel 8:11ff), God had promised stability to the kings if they would worship Him and Him alone.

> *And I will take you, and you shall reign over all that your soul desires, and you shall be king over Israel. And if you will listen to all that I command you, and will walk in my ways, and do what is right in my eyes by keeping my statutes and my commandments, as David my servant did, I will be with you and will build you a sure house, as I built for David, and I will give Israel to you.*
>
> 1 Kings 11:37-38

God had graciously empowered two remarkable prophets, Elijah and Elisha, to turn His people and their leaders away from serving Baal toward worshipping the LORD. Despite the warnings of the prophets and the valiant efforts of one king, Jehu, to rid Israel of all traces of the worship of Baal introduced by Ahab and Jezebel (2 Kings 9-10), the distress of Israel continued as the people offered sacrifices to foreign gods on the high places (15:4).

In 721 BC, the world of northern Israel (or Samaria) finally came crashing down. The king of Assyria invaded, captured the capital, deported the Israelites (17:5f), and brought foreigners into Samaria's cities (17:24). Why did the LORD God permit this?

> *This occurred because the people of Israel had sinned against the LORD their God, who had brought them up out of the land of Egypt from under the hand of Pharaoh king of Egypt, and had feared other gods and walked in the customs of the nations whom the LORD drove out before the people of Israel, and in the customs that the kings of Israel had practiced. ... And they did wicked things, provoking the LORD to anger, and they served idols, of which the LORD had said to them, "You shall not do this." Yet the LORD warned Israel and Judah by every prophet and every seer, saying, "Turn from your evil ways and keep my commandments and my statutes, in accordance with all the Law that I commanded your fathers, and that I sent to you by my servants the prophets."*

But they would not listen, but were stubborn, as their fathers had been, who did not believe in the LORD their God. They despised his statutes and his covenant that he made with their fathers and the warnings that he gave them. They went after false idols and became false, and they followed the nations that were around them, concerning whom the LORD had commanded them that they should not do like them. ... And they burned their sons and their daughters as offerings and used divination and omens and sold themselves to do evil in the sight of the LORD, provoking him to anger.

2 Kings 17:7-17

Assyria also appeared as a threat to the southern kingdom. However, in Judah there was a faithful king, Hezekiah, who trusted in the LORD God and prayed frequently, listening to the counsel of the prophet Isaiah (2 Kings 18-19). On one occasion Hezekiah's fervent prayer led to an extension to his own life by 15 years (20:1-7).

Unhappily, Hezekiah's son, Manasseh reversed the good his father had done, again erecting altars to the storm god Baal and carving images of Asherah (21:1-9). The die had been cast: the LORD would use another nation to wipe out even Jerusalem (21:10-15).

Even though nothing could now stop the judgment of God (22:16f), a young king named Josiah was not deterred in his attempt to eliminate the abominations which had arisen in Judah and Jerusalem (2 Kings 22-23). It was a remarkable attempt at reformation, spurred on by the discovery of a lost book in the temple.

And Hilkiah the high priest said to Shaphan the secretary, "I have found the Book of the Law in the house of the LORD." And Hilkiah gave the book to Shaphan, and he read it. And Shaphan the secretary came to the king, and reported to the king, "Your servants have emptied out the money that was found in the house and have delivered it into the hand of the workmen who have the oversight of the house of the LORD." Then Shaphan the secretary told the king, "Hilkiah the priest has given me a book." And Shaphan read it before the king.

When the king heard the words of the Book of the Law, he tore his clothes. And the king commanded Hilkiah the priest, and Ahikam the son of Shaphan, and Achbor the son of Micaiah, and

Shaphan the secretary, and Asaiah the king's servant, saying, "Go, inquire of the LORD for me, and for the people, and for all Judah, concerning the words of this book that has been found. For great is the wrath of the LORD that is kindled against us, because our fathers have not obeyed the words of this book, to do according to all that is written concerning us."

2 Kings 22:8-13

King Josiah did the right thing even though there appeared no prospect of altering God's decision to decimate Jerusalem. In 597 BC, the city was captured by King Nebuchadnezzar of Babylon, and except for the poorest people, the population was deported to Babylon (24:10-17). Eleven years later, the splendid temple built by Solomon was destroyed along with the palace and the city walls (25:8-12).

It is difficult to overstate the effect of these events on Israel's collective identity. Her faith was shaken to its very foundations. The visible signs of security and identity were gone. Ten tribes were dispersed forever. And the remaining tribe of Judah was living in a foreign land, Babylonia, surrounded by its architecture, gardens, and symbols of success.

Who was the real god? Who was the most powerful god?

In exile Israel was forced to focus on the reasons for her deportation. It was not because of God's inability to keep promises. Israel had chosen other gods to worship. Prophets were commissioned to encourage the people to endure the crucible.

But all nations belong to the God of Abraham, Isaac, and Jacob—not just Israel. And soon Assyria and Babylon fell under His judgment, as had Israel. Righteousness exalts a nation; sin corrupts and destroys.

Even today, a nation's ability to act with justice toward all and maintain integrity in its economy and markets is a result, not of destiny or human ideology, but of obedient trust in the one God—the God who created heaven and earth, the God who chose Israel for universal purposes, the God who sent His only Son to save the world from sin and the Evil One.

Leaders who pray like Hezekiah and listen to the Scripture like Josiah will bring blessings upon their people. And they will please the God who directs all things for His good purposes.

1 Chronicles

The first twelve books of the Old Testament tell the story of God from beginnings in creation to the exile in Babylon. The next two books, 1 and 2 Chronicles, tell the same story again but in a quite different way and from a different viewpoint.

1 Chronicles in fact collapses all the stories from creation to exile into nine chapters of genealogies! These lineages highlight the importance of the temple and its servants, the Levites (1 Chr. 6 and 9).

Indeed as the story unfolds, the spotlight shines on King David and his unswerving faithfulness, especially in making elaborate plans to build the temple. Amazingly, David's sin against Uriah, Bathsheba's husband, is not mentioned, nor are David's difficulties with his children. What receives primary attention is David's bringing the ark of God into Jerusalem and his preparation for the temple.

> *David commanded to gather together the resident aliens who were in the land of Israel, and he set stonecutters to prepare dressed stones for building the house of God. David also provided great quantities of iron for nails for the doors of the gates and for clamps, as well as bronze in quantities beyond weighing, and cedar timbers without number, for the Sidonians and Tyrians brought great quantities of cedar to David. For David said, "Solomon my son is young and inexperienced, and the house that is to be built for the LORD must be exceedingly magnificent, of fame and glory throughout all lands. I will therefore make preparation for it." So David provided materials in great quantity before his death.*
>
> *Then he called for Solomon his son and charged him to build a house for the LORD, the God of Israel. David said to Solomon, "My son, I had it in my heart to build a house to the name of the LORD my God. But the word of the LORD came to me, saying, 'You have shed much blood and have waged great wars. You shall not build a house to my name, because you have shed so much blood before me on the earth. Behold, a son shall be born to you who shall be a man of rest. I will give him rest from all his surrounding enemies. For his name shall be Solomon, and I will give peace and quiet to Israel in his days. He shall build a house*

> *for my name. He shall be my son, and I will be his father, and I will establish his royal throne in Israel forever.'"*
>
> 1 Chronicles 22:2-10

Why then does the narrator retell the familiar stories of King David? The old tales of David and Solomon are retold in new ways in order to make a single point. As God blessed the kings of Israel when they were faithful and punished them when they were not, so God will now do for the Jews when they return from captivity.

After deportation, the Jews had no king, no temple, no political independence. They could have these again, however, if they would be faithful to God as David had been faithful. For David this faithfulness was a constant *seeking for God.*

Frequently, the story in Chronicles says that David *sought the LORD.* By contrast, the first king of Israel, Saul, failed to seek the LORD:

> *So Saul died for his breach of faith. He broke faith with the LORD in that he did not keep the command of the LORD, and also consulted a medium, seeking guidance. He did not seek guidance from the LORD. Therefore the LORD put him to death and turned the kingdom over to David the son of Jesse.*
>
> 1 Chronicles 10:13-14

For David, seeking the LORD meant bringing the ark out of storage. It meant moving the capital to Jerusalem. It meant planning the construction of a magnificent temple. David lived to instill in his son, Solomon, the same intense search for the LORD:

> *"And you, Solomon my son, know the God of your father and serve him with a whole heart and with a willing mind, for the LORD searches all hearts and understands every plan and thought. If you seek him, he will be found by you, but if you forsake him, he will cast you off forever. Be careful now, for the LORD has chosen you to build a house for the sanctuary; be strong and do it."*
>
> 1 Chronicles 28:9-10

There is no exodus, no wilderness, no Sinai, no conquest retelling in 1 Chronicles. Rather everything moves toward a focus on the praise of God.

It was easy to connect David with the music of praise. David understood the power of music in affecting the spirit. His compositions in the Psalter reflect a heart for worship. His organization of musicians and administrators in the temple was natural to his spirit and instincts (1 Chron. 23-26).

The gravitational pull of 1 Chronicles to the temple and in this, to the praise of God, was the right and best story to tell Israelites exiled in distant lands. 1 Chronicles is a solemn reminder that wealth, education, standing armies, even sacred cathedrals are no sure security against harm. What remains as most important is that hearts and lips are ever being formed in praise to God.

> *Therefore David blessed the LORD in the presence of all the assembly. And David said: "Blessed are you, O LORD, the God of Israel our father, forever and ever. Yours, O LORD, is the greatness and the power and the glory and the victory and the majesty, for all that is in the heavens and in the earth is yours. Yours is the kingdom, O LORD, and you are exalted as head above all. Both riches and honor come from you, and you rule over all. In your hand are power and might, and in your hand it is to make great and to give strength to all. And now we thank you, our God, and praise your glorious name.*
>
> *"But who am I, and what is my people, that we should be able thus to offer willingly? For all things come from you, and of your own have we given you. For we are strangers before you and sojourners, as all our fathers were. Our days on the earth are like a shadow, and there is no abiding. O LORD our God, all this abundance that we have provided for building you a house for your holy name comes from your hand and is all your own. I know, my God, that you test the heart and have pleasure in uprightness. In the uprightness of my heart I have freely offered all these things, and now I have seen your people, who are present here, offering freely and joyously to you. O LORD, the God of Abraham, Isaac, and Israel, our fathers, keep forever such purposes and thoughts in the hearts of your people, and direct their hearts toward you.*
>
> 1 Chronicles 29:10-18

2 Chronicles

Whatever a person sows that he will also reap.

So is stated in the Bible the principle of retribution. People get what they deserve. The books of Chronicles are filled with examples of this principle through their depiction of the rulers of Judah. One king in particular is a striking example—Manasseh.

Manasseh was one of Judah's last kings. His story is told in both 2 Kings and 2 Chronicles. Both accounts depict Manasseh as the worst possible monarch. As Saul had failed to seek the LORD in all things, so Manasseh turned from God, slaughtering His prophets. As King Jeroboam II had introduced idolatry into Israel, so Manasseh multiplied idolatry throughout the land.

There was no king more evil in turning away from God than Manasseh. As bad as Israel had been earlier, under Manasseh deeds were done which made it impossible for God to be patient any longer. Judah's future became set: the Judeans would lose their land, their king, the temple, and go to Babylon because of the evil of Manasseh.

North Israel's history was characterized by rebellion against God. South Judah went into exile because of Manasseh's wickedness. Second Kings explains God's just action in bringing Judah to account for her sins. Second Chronicles deals with the same story as 2 Kings. As a direct result of Manasseh's sin, God brought the Assyrians against Judah and took Manasseh away in chains.

> *Manasseh was twelve years old when he began to reign, and he reigned fifty-five years in Jerusalem. And he did what was evil in the sight of the LORD, according to the abominations of the nations whom the LORD drove out before the people of Israel. For he rebuilt the high places that his father Hezekiah had broken down, and he erected altars to the Baals, and made Asheroth, and worshiped all the host of heaven and served them. And he built altars in the house of the LORD, of which the LORD had said, "In Jerusalem shall my name be forever." And he built altars for all the host of heaven in the two courts of the house of the LORD. And he burned his sons as an offering in the Valley of the Son of Hinnom, and used fortune-telling and omens and*

sorcery, and dealt with mediums and with necromancers. He did much evil in the sight of the LORD, provoking him to anger.

Manasseh led Judah and the inhabitants of Jerusalem astray, to do more evil than the nations whom the LORD destroyed before the people of Israel.

The LORD spoke to Manasseh and to his people, but they paid no attention. Therefore the LORD brought upon them the commanders of the army of the king of Assyria, who captured Manasseh with hooks and bound him with chains of bronze and brought him to Babylon.

2 Chronicles 33:1-6, 9-11

But the Chronicler is not primarily interested in the ruin of Judah. Rather, 2 Chronicles emphasizes the principle of retribution. Manasseh's sin brought swift punishment; but his repentance brought restoration and God's favor.

And when he was in distress, he entreated the favor of the LORD his God and humbled himself greatly before the God of his fathers. He prayed to him, and God was moved by his entreaty and heard his plea and brought him again to Jerusalem into his kingdom. Then Manasseh knew that the LORD was God.

Afterward he built an outer wall for the city of David west of Gihon, in the valley, and for the entrance into the Fish Gate, and carried it around Ophel, and raised it to a very great height. He also put commanders of the army in all the fortified cities in Judah. And he took away the foreign gods and the idol from the house of the LORD, and all the altars that he had built on the mountain of the house of the LORD and in Jerusalem, and he threw them outside of the city. He also restored the altar of the LORD and offered on it sacrifices of peace offerings and of thanksgiving, and he commanded Judah to serve the LORD, the God of Israel.

2 Chronicles 33:12-16

Yes, Manasseh "sowed" evil and reaped the punishment due his sin. But he repented, "sowed" deeds of righteousness, and was blessed by God. As it happens, the blessing on Manasseh was a long reign; he ruled longer than any other king of Israel or Judah.

But this is more than just a story of "sin punished and repentance rewarded." The Jews needed hope after the exile. They were few in number and their homeland was still devastated. The neighboring nations were antagonistic. How could they live and invoke God's blessings? How could they survive such adversity?

The answer was taken from Judah's history. In the past, when Judah's rulers and people were faithful, God blessed them and led them out of adversity. But when they were unfaithful and rebellious, they suffered the consequences.

So it would be in the period following the exile. If the Jews would heed the warnings and retributions of the past, God would keep them secure and bless them in the present.

In the book of Ezra we shall learn what happened to Judah when she returned home.

Ezra

The book of 2 Chronicles ends with the destruction of Jerusalem and the burning of God's temple. The LORD hands His people over to the Babylonian king, Nebuchadnezzar. Israel's situation appears hopeless.

But it is not!

Through His prophet Jeremiah, God had promised deliverance after seventy years of exile. The book of Ezra is the story of God's faithfulness to bring His people home and rebuild the temple. Ezra is also a witness to the sovereignty of God by which He accomplishes His purposes (2 Chron. 36:15-23; Jer. 29:10-14; Ezra 1:1-4).

The book is named after its author, Ezra, a priest and a descendant of Aaron (though the first six chapters are not about his life and work). Ezra is well-educated in the Law—devoted to studying, observing, and teaching its decrees. He is a contemporary of Nehemiah.

> *Now after this, in the reign of Artaxerxes king of Persia...Ezra went up from Babylonia. He was a scribe skilled in the Law of Moses that the LORD, the God of Israel, had given, and the king granted him all that he asked, for the hand of the LORD his God was on him.*

And there went up also to Jerusalem, in the seventh year of Artaxerxes the king, some of the people of Israel, and some of the priests and Levites, the singers and gatekeepers, and the temple servants. And Ezra came to Jerusalem in the fifth month, which was in the seventh year of the king. For on the first day of the first month he began to go up from Babylonia, and on the first day of the fifth month he came to Jerusalem, for the good hand of his God was on him. For Ezra had set his heart to study the Law of the LORD, and to do it and to teach his statutes and rules in Israel.

Ezra 7:1-10

Ezra's story of Israel's "second exodus" begins with the proclamation of Cyrus, king of Persia, permitting the people to return to Jerusalem and rebuild the temple. The sovereignty of Yahweh is on display in the pagan king's acknowledgment that it is the "God of heaven" who has given him power and instruction. Indeed, God used the pagan leader as He uses leaders today to accomplish His sovereign will.

In the first year of Cyrus king of Persia, that the word of the LORD by the mouth of Jeremiah might be fulfilled, the LORD stirred up the spirit of Cyrus king of Persia, so that he made a proclamation throughout all his kingdom and also put it in writing:

"Thus says Cyrus king of Persia: The LORD, the God of heaven, has given me all the kingdoms of the earth, and he has charged me to build him a house at Jerusalem, which is in Judah. Whoever is among you of all his people, may his God be with him, and let him go up to Jerusalem, which is in Judah, and rebuild the house of the LORD, the God of Israel—he is the God who is in Jerusalem. And let each survivor, in whatever place he sojourns, be assisted by the men of his place with silver and gold, with goods and with beasts, besides freewill offerings for the house of God that is in Jerusalem."

Ezra 1:1-4

Not every Jew could make the long journey. God knew those most fit for the challenge would be those whose hearts He could influence. And so "everyone whose heart God had moved" made the journey back (1:5-7).

Zerubbabel was the leader of the first remnant to return. Once home, they gave their money freely to fund the rebuilding of the temple, despite their fear of the peoples around them (2:68-69; 3:1-3). Zerubbabel began work on the temple by first building the altar of God. Soon the priest sacrificed burnt offerings. The next project was to lay the foundation of the temple. When this was completed, the people thanked the LORD in singing, "He is good; His love endures forever" (3:2-14).

But good is always met with opposition. And opposition soon surfaced. The resistance was so intense that the work stopped for approximately fourteen years, during the entire reign of Cyrus king of Persia (4:1-5).

Two prophets, Haggai and Zechariah, stepped forward to encourage the people to begin again. They encouraged them with more than words; the prophets helped them work!

But again, opposition arose.

In response, a letter on Israel's behalf was sent to the new king, Darius, explaining the original decree by Cyrus. Upon receiving the letter Darius decreed that the work begun many years before be continued—without hindrance, with abundant provisions, and with diligence.

God had not abandoned them!

Ezra chronicles the celebration following the completion of the house of the LORD:

> *And they kept the Feast of Unleavened Bread seven days with joy, for the LORD had made them joyful and had turned the heart of the king of Assyria to them, so that he aided them in the work of the house of God, the God of Israel.*
>
> Ezra 6:22

The remaining chapters of Ezra (7-10) describe the priest's role 81 years after Zerubbabel in rebuilding the people spiritually and morally. During the 58-year gap between chapters 6 and 7, the people fell into a confused spiritual condition. The people and even priests had intermarried with foreign women, something forbidden in Israel. Identifying with their sin, Ezra offered an intercessory prayer on their behalf (9:1-15).

The people responded by putting away their foreign wives. Confession and obedience to the word of God resulted in spiritual renewal in the land.

God had not deserted them!

Nehemiah

Political leaders in any county can be tempted to use their power and influence for personal gain. A nation is blessed when its leaders resist the temptation.

In the mid-fifth century BC, there lived a man who sought the welfare of his people without any gain for himself. He was a Jew living in the Persian capital, Susa. He was not a priest or prophet or politician. He was a wine taster for the king. His name was Nehemiah.

We learn about Nehemiah in a source unique to the Old Testament—an autobiography, his own first-person account of events.

Nehemiah begins his memoirs by relating the time when he first heard the disturbing news of his relatives' plight in Judah. When he learned that the city of David, Jerusalem, remained defenseless with its walls in burned rubble, he sat down, wept, and prayed (Nehemiah 1:1-11).

Nehemiah's swollen eyes did not escape the notice of the Persian king who asked why he was so sad.

> *I said to the king, "Let the king live forever! Why should not my face be sad, when the city, the place of my fathers' graves, lies in ruins, and its gates have been destroyed by fire?" Then the king said to me, "What are you requesting?" So I prayed to the God of heaven. And I said to the king, "If it pleases the king, and if your servant has found favor in your sight, that you send me to Judah, to the city of my fathers' graves, that I may rebuild it."*
>
> Nehemiah 2:3-5

The king gave Nehemiah passports to travel from Susa to Jerusalem and authorization to gather building materials for a new wall around the city (2:7-9).

However, Nehemiah's good-hearted efforts to do right were quickly met with equally strong opposition. Sanballat, governor of the neighboring Samaritan territory, saw Nehemiah's intentions as a threat to his own political security and influence. He mocked and ridiculed the Jews' efforts:

> *And he said in the presence of his brothers and of the army of Samaria, "What are these feeble Jews doing? Will they restore it*

for themselves? Will they sacrifice? Will they finish up in a day? Will they revive the stones out of the heaps of rubbish, and burned ones at that?" Tobiah the Ammonite was beside him, and he said, "Yes, what they are building—if a fox goes up on it he will break down their stone wall!"

Nehemiah 4:2-3

Nehemiah did not respond in kind, with vengeance, evil for evil. Rather, the man of God prayed and prayed and prayed. And the people continued to build.

Sanballat and his allies then threatened an armed attack on the city. Nehemiah relates his response:

From that day on, half of my servants worked on construction, and half held the spears, shields, bows, and coats of mail. And the leaders stood behind the whole house of Judah, who were building on the wall. Those who carried burdens were loaded in such a way that each labored on the work with one hand and held his weapon with the other.

So neither I nor my brothers nor my servants nor the men of the guard who followed me, none of us took off our clothes; each kept his weapon at his right hand.

Nehemiah 4:16-17, 23

If human opposition were not enough, Nehemiah soon felt the economic hardship of those who labored at the walls. Many personal sacrifices had been made. Some were going without bread. Others had mortgaged their fields for food. And some had their children enslaved (5:1-8).

Nehemiah was outraged. He scolded the wealthy for charging excessive interest. He reminded them that he had refused any special privileges while governor:

"Moreover, from the time that I was appointed to be their governor in the land of Judah, from the twentieth year to the thirty-second year of Artaxerxes the king, twelve years, neither I nor my brothers ate the food allowance of the governor.

"Now what was prepared at my expense for each day was one ox and six choice sheep and birds, and every ten days all kinds of wine in abundance. Yet for all this I did not demand the food

allowance of the governor, because the service was too heavy on this people."

Nehemiah 5:14, 18

Sanballat continued to create schemes for disrupting Nehemiah's concentration. But the rebuilding continued and the wall was completed in an amazing fifty-two days.

And when all our enemies heard of it, all the nations around us were afraid and fell greatly in their own esteem, for they perceived that this work had been accomplished with the help of our God.

Nehemiah 6:16

The walls were dedicated with great festivity:

And at the dedication of the wall of Jerusalem they sought the Levites in all their places, to bring them to Jerusalem to celebrate the dedication with gladness, with thanksgivings and with singing, with cymbals, harps, and lyres.

And they offered great sacrifices that day and rejoiced, for God had made them rejoice with great joy; the women and children also rejoiced. And the joy of Jerusalem was heard far away.

Nehemiah 12:27, 43

Nehemiah returned to the service of the king of Persia.

But while he was away, one of his opponents took up residence in an apartment within the temple complex. When Nehemiah returned to Jerusalem he spent little time in evicting the enemy from the sacred premises.

Far more disturbing, however, was the Jews' failure to be a people dedicated to God. They had built stone walls for protection, but they failed to honor God, the true source of security and life.

Then I confronted the nobles of Judah and said to them, "What is this evil thing that you are doing, profaning the Sabbath day?"

As soon as it began to grow dark at the gates of Jerusalem before the Sabbath, I commanded that the doors should be shut and gave orders that they should not be opened until after the

Sabbath. And I stationed some of my servants at the gates, that no load might be brought in on the Sabbath day.

Then I commanded the Levites that they should purify themselves and come and guard the gates, to keep the Sabbath day holy. Remember this also in my favor, O my God, and spare me according to the greatness of your steadfast love.

Nehemiah 13:17, 19, 22

Not only through business but also through marriage relations Israel was becoming unholy. Nehemiah rebuked the Jews for jeopardizing the worship of God by marrying the women of Ashdod, Ammon, and Moab:

"Did not Solomon king of Israel sin on account of such women? Among the many nations there was no king like him, and he was beloved by his God, and God made him king over all Israel. Nevertheless, foreign women made even him to sin. Shall we then listen to you and do all this great evil and act treacherously against our God by marrying foreign women?"

Nehemiah 13:26-27

Nehemiah did not seek human approval for his actions. He faced major opposition in his efforts to do good for his people. But God's gracious hand was upon him (2:7, 18). Nehemiah believed God was awesome and great (4:14). His autobiography is filled with prayers asking God not to forget him, even at the very end of his memoirs: "Remember me, O my God, for good" (13:31b).

God did remember Nehemiah, granting him favor and protection, even in the midst of economic distress and political opposition. Nehemiah prayed without ceasing, as must we in the distress of our time, asking that God will grant us leaders like Nehemiah.

Esther

The second telling of Israel's history begun in 1 Chronicles comes to an end with the story of Esther. Whereas the narrator in Chronicles has left us in little doubt as to God's direct movement through Judah, the narrator in Esther does not mention God's explicit activity among His people. However, in the seeming coincidences and chance meetings within the story, such remarkable things happen (as in our own lives!) that, though God is not mentioned by name, His presence can certainly be detected.

The story of Esther takes place a century after Judah's deportation, in the early fifth century BC, in the capital of Persia, Susa.

King Ahasuerus (Xerxes I, 486-465 BC) is giving an extravagant feast designed to impress the administrators of his vast empire (1:1-9). Without explanation, Queen Vashti refuses his request to appear at the grand feast. So that other wives in the empire not follow her example by showing contempt for their own husbands, Vashti is prohibited access to the king and her royal position is to be given to another (1:17-2:4).

Among the many virgins who are considered as the next queen, the most admired and attractive young woman turns out to be an orphan who was reared by her cousin. When the king meets this beautiful woman, Esther, he loves her and makes her queen.

As it happens, Esther is a Jew. But her cousin, Mordecai, instructs her to tell no one (2:1-18).

As Esther is elevated to royal status, Mordecai unknowingly becomes involved in a potential genocide of his own people! He had refused to bow before a Persian official named Haman, a descendant of Saul's enemy Agag (1 Samuel 15:8-33). Haman engineers an "unalterable" decree through the entire empire that every Jew—not just Mordecai—be killed on a day chosen by lot (Esther 3:1-15).

Mordecai urges a hesitant Esther to approach the king for help:

> *"For if you keep silent at this time, relief and deliverance will rise for the Jews from another place, but you and your father's house will perish. And who knows whether you have not come to the kingdom for such a time as this?"*
>
> Esther 4:14

Esther shrewdly invites the king *and* Haman to a feast. After some wine, the king promises Esther anything—up to half his kingdom. What would she like?

Esther makes no requests except to invite them to a second feast the next day (5:1-8). Haman, gloating at his seeming privileged position before both king and queen, determines to complete his desire by having Mordecai hanged (5:9-14).

That night, unable to sleep, Ahasuerus has bedtime stories read to him, which include Mordecai's subversion of a plot to assassinate the king. The next morning the Persian ruler asks Haman how best to honor a man favored by the king. Thinking Ahasuerus was referring to himself, Haman responds accordingly. When he learns that the king wanted to honor Mordecai, Haman realizes his days are numbered (6:1-13).

Indeed, at the queen's second party with Haman present, Esther requests that the king deliver the Jews, pointing to Haman as perpetrator of the lethal decree. In swift order, the enraged king has Haman hanged and assigns Mordecai Haman's palace position (7:1-8:2). Further, a letter is circulated through all 127 provinces of the empire allowing the Jews to defend themselves on the allotted 13th day.

When the fatal day arrives, the Jews defend themselves against their enemies. And in remembrance of this deliverance, a holiday is established called "Purim," named for the "Pur" or "lot" cast to decide the execution (turned deliverance) day.

Is this, then, merely a story about a nation's "lucky" day? Certainly not. True, God's hand is not mentioned anywhere in the narrative. But it is not mere "luck" that explains the coincidence of events. Made aware earlier in Scripture of God's movements through human events, our explanation for the curious set of circumstances in Esther and Mordecai's lives cannot rest at the door of "luck." Much less should we understand the occurrence of favorable events in our own lives as "good luck."

We trust and live not by "luck" but by our knowledge of an active Creator who is both Father and fatherly. To say then when we experience good circumstances "we are lucky" is to dishonor the gracious gifts of a loving Creator who sends His rain on the just and the unjust.

But how can we explain (if we can) the accumulation of bad events that come our way? Are they "bad luck"? Or are even "bad" circumstances within the circumference of God's involvement in the world? Our next two chapters will address these difficult issues as we hear the story and words of Job.

Job 1-31

Nothing forces us to ask questions about the meaning of life more quickly than experiences of trauma and suffering. Through the Biblical stories of two who suffered, Job and Jesus, we are encouraged to contemplate the meaning of life.

The book of Job lets us overhear conversations at first within Job himself and between Job and his friends (chaps. 1-31) and later between God and Job (chaps. 32-41).

Job was truly an impressive man, one who genuinely respected God (1:1). The fear of God was in many ways the centerpiece of his life.

Job was a man who at every turn does good and avoids evil (28:28). At home, Job sacrificed on behalf of his children (1:5) and showed kindness to his slaves (31:13). Outside home, Job gave generously to the poor, the widow, the orphan, the hungry, and the naked (31:16-23). In his heart, he avoided falsehood (31:29-34), adultery (31:12), greed (31:24-28), and vengeance (31:29-34).

In accordance with other Old Testament stories, such goodness and wisdom would normally be rewarded. Indeed as the story begins, the wealth and prosperity of Job are well attested: "There was a man in the land of Uz whose name was Job, and that man was blameless and upright, one who feared God and turned away from evil" (1:3).

But disaster suddenly strikes: His prosperity and posterity collapse around him. Robbers steal his animals and kill his servants. His ten children are crushed to death by a tornado (1:13-19). Remarkably, Job responds, "Naked I came from my mother's womb, and naked shall I return. The LORD gave, and the LORD has taken away; blessed be the name of the LORD" (1:21). And if tragic loss is not enough, Job contracts a loathsome skin disease.

When one suffers, spouse and comrade may comfort. In Job's case, however, wife and friends only serve to increase his suffering.

When his three friends, Eliphaz, Bildad, and Zophar, first see Job shaven and afflicted, they don't even recognize him. They sit in stunned silence for seven days. Then, one by one, they speak to Job and to each Job replies. Through three ever-shortening dialogues, they in turn answer.

At first the friends affirm Job's goodness and fear of God; they encourage his thoughtful patience through the trial:

"Behold, you have instructed many,
and you have strengthened the weak hands.
Your words have upheld him who was stumbling,
and you have made firm the feeble knees.
But now it has come to you, and you are impatient;
it touches you, and you are dismayed.
Is not your fear of God your confidence,
and the integrity of your ways your hope?
"Remember: who that was innocent ever perished?
Or where were the upright cut off?" (Eliphaz)

"If you will seek God
and plead with the Almighty for mercy,
if you are pure and upright,
surely then he will rouse himself for you
and restore your rightful habitation."

"Behold, God will not reject a blameless man,
nor take the hand of evildoers." (Bildad)

However with each response by Job, the three friends become increasingly more upset, especially since Job will not admit that somewhere, sometime, somehow he has sinned and deserves such suffering (11:2-6).

Job's various answers are understandably marked by extreme frustration:

"No doubt you are the people,
and wisdom will die with you.
But I have understanding as well as you;
I am not inferior to you.
Who does not know such things as these?
I am a laughingstock to my friends;
I, who called to God and he answered me,
a just and blameless man, am a laughingstock.
In the thought of one who is at ease there is contempt for misfortune;
it is ready for those whose feet slip."

"Have mercy on me, have mercy on me, O you my friends,
for the hand of God has touched me!
Why do you, like God, pursue me?
Why are you not satisfied with my flesh?"

Job 12:2-5; 19:21-22

Job concedes he may have sinned (7:20f; 10:14f), but he is unaware of what he has done wrong. Through the dialogues, Job increasingly directs his comments to God, not to his friends.

Job maintains that there is order, reason, and justice in the creation (12:13-25). He can therefore ask God to deliver him (13:20ff). He can ask God to meet him (9:16). At the same time, Job can ventilate his painful condition (16:7-17), remembering happier days of old (29:1-25). Job finds nothing in his past behavior to warrant his present misery. He can only hope for someone to vindicate his cause after death (19:25-27).

Job, however, is not aware of a dimension to his own story which the reader has been told. Unknown to Job, something quite dramatic has transpired in the heavens with great consequence.

God has mentioned Job's integrity to a heavenly being named the "adversary" (*Satan*), a being who finds fault with humans on earth. This opponent replies that Job fears God only out of self-interest, only because his circumstances are good. If tragedy were to strike Job, then he would curse God.

God allows the adversary to initiate turmoil and death in Job's life! (1:6-2:7) To the reader it is clear that Job's suffering is not the result of sinfulness. What then does this story imply about the trauma and tragedies of our own lives?

Certainly it tells us that suffering is not necessarily punishment for wrongdoing. Of course, if we do wrong we will eventually suffer. But suffering per se is not a symptom of sin. And bad circumstances in our lives are not crosses for us to bear. Denying oneself and taking up the cross is a voluntary decision, not one imposed on us by external events.

But if we respect God, why then should we have to suffer?

We have not finished Job's story. We do not yet have an answer to the question of suffering. What has been revealed to us from the heavenly throne room is that God can display great trust in our integrity—even to the point of submitting us to a power that can affect harm. From this we should not tremble in fear, awaiting the attack of Satan. Rather, we should remember God's confidence in us to endure—not just by our own strength, but through trust and respect for the God who hears us in our darkest moments, as we cry out in pain. We must remember Job's determination to believe in the justice of God.

Job 32-42

If Job had penned his own memoirs he might have encouraged his readers not to lose heart when friends fail in life's darkest moments. He might have advocated giving voice to perceived injustices and a willingness to relentlessly defend personal integrity.

But biography often tends to be more revealing, more truthful than autobiography. In this case Job's autobiography could never have imagined what only his biography can tell us. Namely, that his calamity was the result of conversations between God and a heavenly opponent named Satan, and that God permitted this celestial prosecutor to instigate catastrophic events in Job's life.

The narrative indicates that Job's motivations for serving God were under test and that God had amazing confidence in Job to meet his trials. Job's three friends failed to convince him that he had been anything but blameless in his life (32:1). In fact, the friends were guilty of a more serious mistake: they had professed a wrong-headed theology. God was angry that they had not spoken what was right about Him (42:7).

When the friends conclude their speeches, another person begins to address Job. Surprisingly, it is a young man whose very age might throw in doubt the wisdom of his words. The young man, Elihu, nevertheless speaks and his words prepare Job for an unexpected encounter.

> *"Hear this, O Job;*
> *stop and consider the wondrous works of God.*
> *Do you know how God lays his command upon them*
> *and causes the lightning of his cloud to shine?*
> *Do you know the balancings of the clouds,*
> *the wondrous works of him who is perfect in knowledge,*
> *you whose garments are hot*

when the earth is still because of the south wind?
Can you, like him, spread out the skies,
hard as a cast metal mirror?
Teach us what we shall say to him;
we cannot draw up our case because of darkness."

Job 37:14-19

The LORD speaks to Job out of a whirlwind. He does not address Job's declarations of innocence. Rather, and in characteristic fashion, God asks questions of Job. As He asked Adam of his whereabouts (Genesis 3:9), as He asked Satan of his origins (Job 1:7), so now God asks Job where he was at creation:

"Where were you when I laid the foundation of the earth?
Tell me, if you have understanding.
Who determined its measurements—surely you know!
Or who stretched the line upon it?

Job 38:4-5

Job had sought wisdom—an understanding of his own dilemma (28:12-28). God questions Job about his knowledge of creation—where wisdom abides. God enquires into Job's knowledge of meteorology and zoology.

"Where is the way to the dwelling of light,
and where is the place of darkness,
that you may take it to its territory
and that you may discern the paths to its home?

"Have you entered the storehouses of the snow,
or have you seen the storehouses of the hail,
which I have reserved for the time of trouble,
for the day of battle and war?
What is the way to the place where the light is distributed,
or where the east wind is scattered upon the earth?

"Who provides for the raven its prey,
when its young ones cry to God for help,
and wander about for lack of food?

"Do you give the horse his might?
Do you clothe his neck with a mane?
Do you make him leap like the locust?

"Is it by your understanding that the hawk soars
and spreads his wings toward the south?
Is it at your command that the eagle mounts up
and makes his nest on high?" (Job 38-39)

The faultfinder Satan had questioned God; now God questions the faultfinder Job (40:2).

Stunned, Job puts his hand on his mouth. But God is not through with him. The LORD continues, simplifying the question: Can you take care of the mammoth sea monsters, Behemoth and Leviathan? At this Job's pride evaporates and he says,

"I know that you can do all things,
and that no purpose of yours can be thwarted.
'Who is this that hides counsel without knowledge?'
Therefore I have uttered what I did not understand,
things too wonderful for me, which I did not know.
'Hear, and I will speak;
I will question you, and you make it known to me.'
I had heard of you by the hearing of the ear,
but now my eye sees you;
therefore I despise myself,
and repent in dust and ashes."

Job 42:2-6

What has happened?

Surprisingly, God does not tell Job anything about Satan's role. God says not a word about the man's suffering. Instead, He compares Job's power and understanding to His own. For Job, hearing becomes an overwhelming sensation of sight (42:5).

What has the LORD accomplished with Job?

Job's fear of God has led him to wisdom—wisdom concerning the limits of human capacity to understand or control creation and its attendant circumstances. Unable to process the visible, how can Job access the invisible?

Yet God allows Job in intercessory prayer to access the invisible heavenly realms from whence his troubles sprang (42:8-11). If his sufferings have been educative and disciplinary God does not say. What God does is to restore Job's prosperity in abundance, giving him again ten children, including three beautiful daughters.

And as it happens in the end, the fear of God does indeed have its reward.

As it happens, though, the fear of God can entail its own severe mercy.

Psalm 1

In the very middle of Holy Scripture is a hymnbook—the book of Psalms, a collection of 150 chants praising God. The songs express a remarkable range of emotions, passions, thoughts, and feelings before God—from sadness to joy, from disappointment to satisfaction. Through the Psalms there is a discernible anatomy of the human heart in its relationship to God.

In its five books, the 150 Psalms are largely attributed to King David—a man after God's own heart, a man of great strength and great contrition, the shepherd boy who could meet the giant Goliath in the name of God, the man who could play music to soothe the troubled heart of Israel's first king, the man who could follow his passions with tragic results. Many of the Psalms have a heading or title indicating the situation which gave rise to the Psalm.

The themes of the Psalter are introduced in the first two Psalms. Psalm 1 focuses on the theme of righteous living.

> *Blessed is the man*
> *who walks not in the counsel of the wicked,*
> *nor stands in the way of sinners,*
> *nor sits in the seat of scoffers;*
> *but his delight is in the law of the LORD,*
> *and on his law he meditates day and night.*
> *He is like a tree*
> *planted by streams of water*
> *that yields its fruit in its season,*
> *and its leaf does not wither.*
> *In all that he does, he prospers.*

The wicked are not so,
but are like chaff that the wind drives away.
Therefore the wicked will not stand in the judgment,
nor sinners in the congregation of the righteous;
for the LORD *knows the way of the righteous,*
but the way of the wicked will perish.

Psalm 1

Surprisingly, the introductory Psalm does not begin with "Hallelujahs" or rehearsals of God's acts at creation, the exodus, or Sinai. What we find is not God but humans in the spotlight—with blessings pronounced. The Psalter opens with life's daily choices, our choices about the company we keep, the friends we make. We are blessed if we do not walk, stand, or sit with the wicked.

Indeed, it so happens we at first ***walk*** with associates and listen to their advice. But this soon can become ***standing*** with them and listening more intently. Finally we may be ***sitting*** with them at meal, laughing at their jokes or gossip. "Bad company corrupts good morals" (1 Corinthians 15:33). God is praised not just by our prayers, but by our preference of friends and associates. Psalm 1 proscribes being with people who always scoff or ridicule.

By contrast, the psalmist recommends we linger with the instruction of the LORD. Our delight should not be in the entertainment of associates who talk crudely or gossip or speak evil of others. True joy comes in hearing and understanding the voice of God.

The Psalm functions as a kind of therapy for our desires, challenging us through repetition aloud to seek delight in the discipline of instruction, rather than the momentary satisfaction of evil companions.

Such careful listening to the Word of God gives deep nourishment.

Many Psalms remind us of the sound wisdom in making daily Bible reading a habit. Psalm 1 compares the person who receives God's instructions to a tree carefully planted by streams of water. The proximity to flowing waters supplies vital nourishment to the roots. When the time comes for fruit, there is plenty.

By contrast, the wicked disperse in the wind like chaff. A miserable outcome for the wicked is assured though their future may seem bright in the short run.

Why in praising God should there be any mention of judgment for the wicked? It may appear to human eyes that the ungodly are prospering, that it might be good to walk, stand, and sit with the wicked in order to prosper. Psalm 1 is a reminder to wait on God, to see how God sees the situation. For a moment the godless may appear to be the winners, to be most powerful. Psalm 1 reminds us to believe and to live knowing the way of the wicked *will* perish while the way of the righteous will prosper.

God is praised when each day we avoid people who are wicked and embrace the wisdom of Scripture. We become as the strongest trees with the deepest roots, able to withstand the severest winds, bearing fruit in season, with verdant sheltering leaf.

Vengeance is to be rejected. The wicked will have a bitter end, someday, not through our hands but through the judgment of God.

Like the teacher's hand who guides the child in writing, the Psalms provide words for us to repeat as we learn to praise the LORD. The Psalms are the grammar of praise. They may surprise us in what God accepts as praise. In Psalm 1 the LORD is honored by avoiding evil. The result is not our "happiness," the result is "blessedness."

Psalm 2

The apostle Paul told the first urban Christians they were appointed to live for the *praise of God's glory* (Eph. 1:11-12). How then does a person learn to "praise God"?

The 150 Psalms are the textbook for learning to "praise God." The title of the collection in Hebrew means "praises"; in the Greek translation "psalms" means "songs." In these "songs of praises," the Israelites and later the Christians were given words to chant which would please God. In singing these it was also understood that the singer's heart, emotions, and will would be transformed toward loving God and neighbor.

The first two Psalms are the overture for the "Psalms Symphony." Psalms 1-2 sound the two major themes which recur through the five "movements" (books) of the Psalms.

The *first major theme* is to shun the company of the wicked and choose the way of the righteous by delighting in God's instruction. The *second major theme* is to honor God as the only true King.

Why do the nations rage
  and the peoples plot in vain?
The kings of the earth set themselves,
  and the rulers take counsel together,
  against the LORD and against his Anointed, saying,
"Let us burst their bonds apart
  and cast away their cords from us."

He who sits in the heavens laughs;
  the LORD holds them in derision.
Then he will speak to them in his wrath,
  and terrify them in his fury, saying,
"As for me, I have set my King
  on Zion, my holy hill."

I will tell of the decree:
The LORD said to me, "You are my Son;
  today I have begotten you.
Ask of me, and I will make the nations your heritage,
  and the ends of the earth your possession.
You shall break them with a rod of iron
  and dash them in pieces like a potter's vessel."

Now therefore, O kings, be wise;
  be warned, O rulers of the earth.
Serve the LORD with fear,
  and rejoice with trembling.
Kiss the Son,
  lest he be angry, and you perish in the way,
  for his wrath is quickly kindled.
Blessed are all who take refuge in him.

Psalm 2

We can choose to avoid a wicked person. But how can we escape the consequences of evil decisions made by political leaders? Often we cannot. Psalm 2 provides perspective.

First, the Psalm states that God sees the schemes of earthly rulers. Usually, world leaders—whether kings, presidents, prime ministers, or generals—do not make decisions on their knees in prayer. At worst, heads of government claim such an exalted status that they reject what pleases the one true and living God. In the first century, King Herod lost his life by such an arrogant posture:

> *On an appointed day Herod put on his royal robes, took his seat upon the throne, and delivered an oration to them. And the people were shouting, "The voice of a god, and not of a man!" Immediately an angel of the Lord struck him down, because he did not give God the glory, and he was eaten by worms and breathed his last.*
>
> *But the word of God increased and multiplied.*
>
> Acts 12:21-24

Rarely, however, do we see such quick judgment from God.

What Psalm 2 reveals is that God's normal response to the arrogance of earth's leaders is laughter. Yes, laughter (vs. 3). It is not the laughter of pleasure, but the laughter of derision.

How could a tiny mortal made from clay, so dependent on air and food and love, ever think himself able to thwart the Creator God and His laws for life? "God sits in heaven and laughs."

This is not to say that political leaders do not have power. They do. It is not to say that we do not suffer from the abuse of that power. We do. To recite this Psalm, however, is to listen for God's laughter—for *His* perspective amidst all the words, promises, and threats of this world's demagogues.

It is also to listen to God's pronouncement: "I have appointed a King." And to hear this Anointed One say, "God has said to me: 'You are my Son. Ask me for your inheritance. Your inheritance is the nations of the earth.'"

In Acts 4, the first Christians remembered this Psalm when they prayed together, remembering both God's laughter and His appointment of the greatest leader of all—Jesus the Messiah.

> *And when they heard it, they lifted their voices together to God and said, "Sovereign Lord, who made the heaven and the earth and the sea and everything in them, who through the mouth of our father David, your servant, said by the Holy Spirit,*

"'Why did the Gentiles rage,
and the peoples plot in vain?
The kings of the earth set themselves,
and the rulers were gathered together,
against the Lord and against his Anointed'—

for truly in this city there were gathered together against your holy servant Jesus, whom you anointed, both Herod and Pontius Pilate, along with the Gentiles and the peoples of Israel, to do whatever your hand and your plan had predestined to take place. And now, Lord, look upon their threats and grant to your servants to continue to speak your word with all boldness, while you stretch out your hand to heal, and signs and wonders are performed through the name of your holy servant Jesus." And when they had prayed, the place in which they were gathered together was shaken, and they were all filled with the Holy Spirit and continued to speak the word of God with boldness.

Acts 4:24-31

The power wielded by this great leader was not the power of armies or weapons or wealth or taxation or enslavement. The power borne by this leader was the power of sacrificial love. He claimed no territory but the human heart—and that not finally for Himself, but for the God who appointed Him.

Yet a demand is made of all earth's political leaders. The Psalm without embarrassment calls upon every ruler to serve the Christ in wisdom and fear lest He be angry and they perish like Herod.

At one level, Psalm 2 (and others like it) reflect the experience and confidence gained by King David. David honored Saul as God's anointed king; David respected and relied upon God when he was anointed king.

Today, we hear the Psalm as announcing the possession of every nation and kingdom by the Messiah at the end of time. In the first century, such thought led to Jesus' execution, as His kingship was considered a threat to Roman rule and authority.

The followers of King Jesus did not seek the levers of political power to bring about progress. They rather "kissed the feet" of Christ in their service to neighbor and nation even as Jesus had washed the feet of His own disciples. Christians who have become political leaders know that all decisions must be made in prayer; all believers know as Paul told Timothy to pray daily for their leaders:

> *First of all, then, I urge that supplications, prayers, intercessions, and thanksgivings be made for all people, for kings and all who are in high positions, that we may lead a peaceful and quiet life, godly and dignified in every way.*
>
> 1 Timothy 2:1-2

As an introduction to this beloved hymnbook, Psalms 1 and 2 reflect what Jesus said in the Sermon on the Mount: "Seek first God's kingdom and His righteousness and everything else will be given to you" (Matt. 6:33).

Psalms in Books I-II

The Psalms radiate a "ring of truth" in large measure because of their composition by King David. Of the 73 Psalms attributed to David, twelve in the first two books describe extreme situations in the king's life—moments of peril, escape, sin, imprisonment, struggle, desolation.

These Psalms offer great insight into the way tragedy and grief can be faithfully expressed to God, without embarrassment, while maintaining firm confidence in God's hearing pleas for help. Their words have given distressed believers ways of coping with trauma and oppression for centuries.

In Psalm 3, for example, David is faced with an excruciating dilemma. His own son is in uncontrollable rebellion: Absalom has stolen away the hearts of many Israelites from his father. How could David sleep at night in such hostility? Psalm 3 records the sentiments David expressed to God during this struggle.

David begins by describing how he feels and imagines the situation, even repeating before God what his enemies are saying: "There is no help for you from the LORD." In this distress, David still declares confidence that God will respond to his plea. David internalizes this confidence so much he can sleep sweetly at night.

Nevertheless, David is bold enough to challenge God to act and to act quickly—to deliver him from the evil of Absalom, his own flesh and blood. David does not want to take action; he wants God to rescue him.

In Psalm 4, David expresses gratitude for God's answer: "You have put gladness in my heart, more than wine can give. I can now sleep at night for I know you alone provide security" (4:7, 8).

In one particular trio of Psalms—22, 23, 24—David expresses a wide spectrum of praise to God. In the beginning of Psalm 22, in words repeated later by Jesus on the cross, David expresses what so many believers have sometimes felt: "God, why have you abandoned me?!" God, of course, has not left David, but David (like we) felt that way.

David vacillates between two poles—hardy confidence in God and an acute awareness of enemy pressure. Having said what he feels, David quickly asserts what he believes: that God is holy and that He is the only true King. Still, David feels his own hurt *and* the disdain of others. He also knows God's care from birth. Yet he must express to God, as we must, his physical anguish. He is dispersed like water; he is disjointed; he is melted like wax; his mouth is dry; he is all skin and bones!

Like a walking skeleton he cries out to God, surrounded by threats of all kinds. And he praises God in the presence of other believers, inviting them to glorify the LORD, supremely confident that God listens in our supreme distress, declaring God's kingdom as absolute—claiming the worship of the dead and of future generations.

This Psalm, in its harshness and structure, places boundaries on feelings of abandonment and loneliness. As with every Psalm it creates a world for our emotions and feelings to inhabit before God legitimately. It ventilates anger and channels emotion in pathways of praise to the Lord.

Psalm 22 gives way to the incomparable, calm assurance of Psalm 23, in which David projects upon God the role of a shepherd—David's own experience!—who genuinely cares for the well-being of the sheep.

The LORD is my shepherd; I shall not want.
He makes me lie down in green pastures.
He leads me beside still waters.
He restores my soul.
He leads me in paths of righteousness
for his name's sake.

Even though I walk through the valley of the shadow of death,
I will fear no evil,

for you are with me;
your rod and your staff,
they comfort me.

You prepare a table before me
in the presence of my enemies;
you anoint my head with oil;
my cup overflows.
Surely goodness and mercy shall follow me
all the days of my life,
and I shall dwell in the house of the LORD
forever.

Psalm 23

In the Gospel of John, Jesus identifies Himself as the Good Shepherd.

The sharing of grief before God recorded in the Psalms can be summarized in the following way. First, the believer has full confidence to approach God, not by way of flattery but in honesty and humility, knowing His steadfast love. Second, without embarrassment the speaker can describe every trouble and fear; and with this, ask urgently for relief and deliverance, revering God for His previous interventions. Finally, the Psalmist-Singer claims assurance that God will answer the petition faithfully.

Modern psychologists and counselors have described and often prescribed speech patterns for expressing anxiety and grief, even desire to avenge. Long before the 21st century, however, the Psalms were providing words for the people of God to repeat—for directing disappointments, hurts, and fears before His throne. These words, spoken in the forms they were first uttered, have constituted a rhythm of understanding life under the ultimate reign of God. They have also solidified the resolve of believers in the way of righteousness, denying the seeming triumph of evil in God's world.

Psalms, Book III

Book II of the Psalms closes with the note, "The prayers of David, son of Jesse, are ended" (72:20). We continue with Book III, hymnody composed by Israelite musicians and singers—Asaph, Korah, and Ethan—men who felt deeply the presence of God with Israel, men who found words to express the struggles and expectations of their hearts before the LORD.

The "praise" expressed by Asaph in Psalm 73 is not so much a cry for escape from oppressors as it is a frustration that the arrogant rich have no trouble while those who try to be pure of heart have numerous troubles.

Truly God is good to Israel,
to those who are pure in heart.
But as for me, my feet had almost stumbled,
my steps had nearly slipped.
For I was envious of the arrogant
when I saw the prosperity of the wicked.

For they have no pangs until death;
their bodies are fat and sleek.
They are not in trouble as others are;
they are not stricken like the rest of mankind.
Therefore pride is their necklace;
violence covers them as a garment.
Their eyes swell out through fatness;
their hearts overflow with follies.
They scoff and speak with malice;
loftily they threaten oppression.
They set their mouths against the heavens,
and their tongue struts through the earth.
Therefore his people turn back to them,
and find no fault in them.
And they say, "How can God know?
Is there knowledge in the Most High?"
Behold, these are the wicked;
always at ease, they increase in riches.
All in vain have I kept my heart clean
and washed my hands in innocence.
For all the day long I have been stricken
and rebuked every morning.

Psalm 73:1-14

Who among us has not felt mistreated? Who among us has not wondered whether only cheating and lying bring success?

If I had said, "I will speak thus,"
I would have betrayed the generation of your children.
But when I thought how to understand this,
it seemed to me a wearisome task,
until I went into the sanctuary of God;

then I discerned their end.
Truly you set them in slippery places;
you make them fall to ruin.
How they are destroyed in a moment,
swept away utterly by terrors!
Like a dream when one awakes,
O LORD, when you rouse yourself, you despise them as phantoms.

Psalm 73:15-20

Jesus said, "Blessed are the pure in heart for they shall see God." Those who are pure in heart, those who seek to do good to others, are *not* immediately rewarded; in fact, they often face the most cruel injustice. Jesus says they are blessed, not with less trouble or less heartache; rather, they are sustained with a steady vision of God and His ways, with firm insight as to the end of the wicked.

For behold, those who are far from you shall perish;
you put an end to everyone who is unfaithful to you.
But for me it is good to be near God;
I have made the LORD God my refuge,
that I may tell of all your works.

Psalm 73:27-28

The Psalm suggests that it is better to confess to God our envy than to complain to friends and relatives about the prosperity of the wicked. If words are to be spoken to children and associates, better that they be of God's works and wonders in His world. In Psalm 78, Asaph does this at great length:

Give ear, O my people, to my teaching;
incline your ears to the words of my mouth!
I will open my mouth in a parable;
I will utter dark sayings from of old,
things that we have heard and known,
that our fathers have told us.
We will not hide them from their children,
but tell to the coming generation
the glorious deeds of the LORD, and his might,
and the wonders that he has done.

Psalm 78:1-4

In Psalm 78, Asaph retells the wonder of God dividing the sea, permitting His people to escape the power of Pharaoh; of God leading the Israelites through the desert by a cloud during the day and by a fiery light at night; of God making water come from rocks for drink.

Yet, in spite of His marvels and signs, they rebel against God and demand more food. In a memorable line the Israelites say, "Is God capable of making a sumptuous picnic in the wilderness?" (Psalm 78:19). It is a question the people of God have asked ever since: "In depravation will God provide for us?" In the wilderness God did and does give food.

Nevertheless, the people sinned. God brought punishment—but soon had compassion and forgave their sins. Still the people sinned, worshipping idols. So God withdrew His protection from Israel, giving His power and glory to the enemy:

He forsook his dwelling at Shiloh,
the tent where he dwelt among mankind,
and delivered his power to captivity,
his glory to the hand of the foe.
He gave his people over to the sword
and vented his wrath on his heritage.
Fire devoured their young men,
and their young women had no marriage song.
Their priests fell by the sword,
and their widows made no lamentation.

Psalm 78:60-64

Psalm 78 closes with the remembrance of God's choice of David to shepherd His people.

The final Psalm of Book III, Psalm 89, recalls God's promise to David of an everlasting kingdom.

I will sing of the steadfast love of the LORD, forever;
with my mouth I will make known your faithfulness to all generations.
For I said, "Steadfast love will be built up forever;
in the heavens you will establish your faithfulness."
You have said, "I have made a covenant with my chosen one;
I have sworn to David my servant:
'I will establish your offspring forever,
and build your throne for all generations.'" Selah

Let the heavens praise your wonders, O LORD,
your faithfulness in the assembly of the holy ones!

Psalm 89:1-5

After extolling God's superiority above all members of the heavenly council, the Psalmist continues his remembrance of God's anointing David as king:

I have found David, my servant;
with my holy oil I have anointed him,
so that my hand shall be established with him;
my arm also shall strengthen him.
The enemy shall not outwit him;
the wicked shall not humble him.
I will crush his foes before him
and strike down those who hate him.
My faithfulness and my steadfast love shall be with him,
and in my name shall his horn be exalted.
I will set his hand on the sea
and his right hand on the rivers.
He shall cry to me, 'You are my Father,
my God, and the Rock of my salvation.'
And I will make him the firstborn,
the highest of the kings of the earth.
My steadfast love I will keep for him forever,
and my covenant will stand firm for him.
I will establish his offspring forever
and his throne as the days of the heavens.

Psalm 89:20-29

But tragedy strikes. David's kingdom is torn apart. And the Psalmist identifies God as the ultimate source of this work: "You, LORD, have done all this."

You have exalted the right hand of his foes;
you have made all his enemies rejoice.
You have also turned back the edge of his sword,
and you have not made him stand in battle.
You have made his splendor to cease
and cast his throne to the ground.
You have cut short the days of his youth;
you have covered him with shame.

Psalm 89:42-45

The Psalm, surprisingly, ends with a question and a call to remember:

Lord, where is your steadfast love of old,
which by your faithfulness you swore to David?
Remember, O Lord, how your servants are mocked,
and how I bear in my heart the insults of all the many nations,
with which your enemies mock, O LORD,
with which they mock the footsteps of your anointed.

Psalm 89:49-51

Book III ends characteristically with a blessing (89:52).

Blessed be the LORD forever!
Amen and Amen.

The Psalms in Book III reflect a progression of thought and emotion beyond the earlier songs in Books I and II. Just as a transcript of our prayers ten years ago put alongside our petitions today would show growth in our understanding God's will, so the Psalms through this collection reveal a shift of emphasis *away from* hopes dependent upon an earthly king (with temple, with land) *to* hopes dependent on God as the only true King.

The final step in interpretation comes with the first followers of Jesus who understood in His resurrection that God finally kept His promise of an eternal kingdom, that Jesus as David's son is the true king of Israel—and not just of Israel, but king of all nations of the earth.

In our final chapter on the Psalms we will see how the last years of faithful living may prompt less self-preoccupation and more focused, unadorned adoration of God.

Psalms, Books IV-V

Crises often come at the midpoint of our lives. Our youth spent, our ambitions run, we face our mortality. We assess, perhaps for the last time in our life, which things really matter.

The Psalms, as a diary of praise, record the midlife crisis of the people of God. In the transition from Book III (Psalm 89) to Book IV (Psalm 90) we see a midlife crisis, a theological crisis:

How long, O LORD? Will you hide yourself forever?
How long will your wrath burn like fire?
Remember how short my time is!
For what vanity you have created all the children of man!
What man can live and never see death?
Who can deliver his soul from the power of Sheol?
Lord, where is your steadfast love of old,
which by your faithfulness you swore to David?
Remember, O Lord, how your servants are mocked,
and how I bear in my heart the insults of all the many nations,
with which your enemies mock, O LORD,
with which they mock the footsteps of your anointed.

Psalm 89:46-51

Who can intercede for God's people? None other than Moses! Book IV begins with a prayer of the greatest leader of Israel. But Moses does not pray for a recovery of youth:

For all our days pass away under your wrath;
we bring our years to an end like a sigh.
The years of our life are seventy,
or even by reason of strength eighty;
yet their span is but toil and trouble;
they are soon gone, and we fly away.
Who considers the power of your anger,
and your wrath according to the fear of you?
So teach us to number our days
that we may get a heart of wisdom.

Psalm 90:9-12

Nor does Moses pray for renewed national power. What he prays is that God in His own ways will manifest His work and in turn prosper the work of His people.

What follows in Book IV is the recurring reassurance that no matter the crises of life, trust in God remains the only true shelter and refuge.

For he will deliver you from the snare of the fowler
and from the deadly pestilence.
He will cover you with his pinions,
and under his wings you will find refuge;
his faithfulness is a shield and buckler.

You will not fear the terror of the night,
nor the arrow that flies by day,
or the pestilence that stalks in darkness,
nor the destruction that wastes at noonday.

Psalm 91:3-6

Such assurance leads to thanksgiving and praise that God's love is endless. No longer is well-being dependent on the political leadership of Israel. Only Yahweh's rule as king really matters.

The LORD reigns; he is robed in majesty;
the LORD is robed; he has put on strength as his belt.
Yes, the world is established; it shall never be moved.
Your throne is established from of old;
you are from everlasting.

The floods have lifted up, O LORD,
the floods have lifted up their voice;
the floods lift up their roaring.
Mightier than the thunders of many waters,
mightier than the waves of the sea,
the LORD on high is mighty!
Your decrees are very trustworthy;
holiness befits your house,
O LORD, forevermore.

Psalm 93

God's loyalty and justice are exalted. Such praise cannot be self-contained. It's infectious! It solicits the praise of others:

Oh sing to the LORD a new song;
sing to the LORD, all the earth!
Sing to the LORD, bless his name;
tell of his salvation from day to day.
Declare his glory among the nations,
his marvelous works among all the peoples!

Psalm 96:1-3

While the last four Psalms of Book IV build the momentum of blessings to God, the tendency toward disobedience is not forgotten amidst the exuberance and abandonment of adoration:

Both we and our fathers have sinned;
we have committed iniquity; we have done wickedness.
Our fathers, when they were in Egypt,
did not consider your wondrous works;
they did not remember the abundance of your steadfast love,
but rebelled by the sea, at the Red Sea.

Psalm 106:6-7

In the last pages of the Psalter's worship diary, Book V records the mature words of praise. In Psalm 107, God's loving deliverance of those in darkness, in sickness, in distress is extolled. One collection within the Book gathers songs that either begin or end with "praise God." These Psalms (111-117) are known as the Hallelujah Psalms.

Praise the LORD, all nations!
Extol him, all peoples!
For great is his steadfast love toward us,
and the faithfulness of the LORD endures forever.
Praise the LORD!

Psalm 117

The longest hymn in the Psalter, Psalm 119, is an extended rehearsal of the delight experienced in reciting God's instruction. It is remarkable in that it is an acrostic—each eight verses beginning with a sequential letter of the Hebrew alphabet.

Another collection, Psalms 120-134, is a series of hymns meant for singing while traveling—not just any travel, but pilgrimages to the dwelling of God.

The last five hymns, Psalms 146-150, bring the collection to a joyous conclusion. Struggles behind, cries for vengeance silent, the Psalmist can now enthrone God in unadorned adoration. Words go begging.

Praise the LORD!
Praise God in his sanctuary;
praise him in his mighty heavens!
Praise him for his mighty deeds;
praise him according to his excellent greatness!

Praise him with trumpet sound;
praise him with lute and harp!

Praise him with tambourine and dance;
praise him with strings and pipe!
Praise him with sounding cymbals;
praise him with loud clashing cymbals!
Let everything that has breath praise the LORD!
Praise the LORD!

Psalm 150

Proverbs

After the treasury of Psalms, there follows in the Old Testament three books by Solomon: Proverbs, Ecclesiastes, and the Song of Songs. The three works reflect what we know as the two strongest features of his life: his unsurpassed wisdom (2 Chronicles 9:22) and his love for foreign women (1 Kings 11:1). The influence of his father David and his mother Bathsheba can also be detected.

The centerpiece of Proverbs, chapters 10-30, is an extended collection of two-line proverbs. These pithy sayings are what we commonly associate with Solomon's prudent teaching. They include classic wisdom for easy memorization—for children learning from parents and princes learning to become good rulers.

The proverbs deal with a wide variety of topics: self-control; mastery of the tongue and anger; generosity; avoiding drunkenness, laziness and gossip; and various other bits of sound advice. The proverbs presuppose that actions have consequences. But the beginning chapters have a much more important presupposition in mind.

In Proverbs 1-9, Solomon makes clear that wisdom is not easy; it is not innate. It is only attained by those who eagerly seek it.

Yes, if you call out for insight
and raise your voice for understanding,
if you seek it like silver
and search for it as for hidden treasures,
then you will understand the fear of the LORD
and find the knowledge of God.

Proverbs 2:3-5

Solomon had wisdom because he sought it from God, asking for that above all else. Not surprisingly then, Solomon says that fearing God is *the* presupposition for wisdom (2:5-11). We should not expect God to give wisdom when calamity strikes *if* we have not beforehand sought to be wise in our quiet times (1:20-33). In calm moments, we should acknowledge Him and not be wise in our eyes (3:6f). Humility is a prerequisite for hearing and acquiring God's wisdom.

Solomon likens the pursuit of wisdom to the pursuit of an attractive, gracious woman:

> *"Get wisdom; get insight;*
> *do not forget, and do not turn away from the words of my mouth.*
> *Do not forsake her, and she will keep you;*
> *love her, and she will guard you.*
> *The beginning of wisdom is this: Get wisdom,*
> *and whatever you get, get insight.*
> *Prize her highly, and she will exalt you;*
> *she will honor you if you embrace her.*
> *She will place on your head a graceful garland;*
> *she will bestow on you a beautiful crown."*
>
> Proverbs 4:5-9

Lady Wisdom invites from her house of honor and life:

> *"Whoever is simple, let him turn in here!"*
> *To him who lacks sense she says,*
> *"Come, eat of my bread*
> *and drink of the wine I have mixed.*
> *Leave your simple ways, and live,*
> *and walk in the way of insight."*
>
> Proverbs 9:4-6

On the other hand, Solomon understands folly to have the same appeal as the wayward woman who entices a young man to spend the night while her husband is away:

> *And behold, the woman meets him,*
> *dressed as a prostitute, wily of heart.*
> *She is loud and wayward;*
> *her feet do not stay at home;*

now in the street, now in the market,
and at every corner she lies in wait.
She seizes him and kisses him,
and with bold face she says to him,
"I had to offer sacrifices,
and today I have paid my vows;
so now I have come out to meet you,
to seek you eagerly, and I have found you.
I have spread my couch with coverings,
colored linens from Egyptian linen;
I have perfumed my bed with myrrh,
aloes, and cinnamon.
Come, let us take our fill of love till morning;
let us delight ourselves with love.
For my husband is not at home;
he has gone on a long journey;
he took a bag of money with him;
at full moon he will come home."
With much seductive speech she persuades him;
with her smooth talk she compels him.
All at once he follows her,
as an ox goes to the slaughter,
or as a stag is caught fast
till an arrow pierces its liver;
as a bird rushes into a snare;
he does not know that it will cost him his life.

Proverbs 7:10-23

Dame Folly invites from her house of deception and death:

"Whoever is simple, let him turn in here!"
And to him who lacks sense she says,
"Stolen water is sweet,
and bread eaten in secret is pleasant."
But he does not know that the dead are there,
that her guests are in the depths of Sheol.

Proverbs 9:16-18

Solomon knew in his own life the attraction of foreign women. This led him to build structures for the worship of his wives' gods. He could only imagine what it would have been like to have had a single wife of wisdom as described in Proverbs 31:

An excellent wife who can find?
She is far more precious than jewels.
The heart of her husband trusts in her,
and he will have no lack of gain.
She does him good, and not harm,
all the days of her life.
She seeks wool and flax,
and works with willing hands.

Her children rise up and call her blessed;
her husband also, and he praises her:
"Many women have done excellently,
but you surpass them all."
Charm is deceitful, and beauty is vain,
but a woman who fears the LORD is to be praised.
Give her of the fruit of her hands,
and let her works praise her in the gates.

Proverbs 31:10-12, 28-31

Solomon understood that wisdom could be attained through life's hard experiences because wisdom was part of the very structure of creation.

"The LORD possessed me at the beginning of his work,
the first of his acts of old.
Ages ago I was set up,
at the first, before the beginning of the earth.
When there were no depths I was brought forth,
when there were no springs abounding with water.
Before the mountains had been shaped,
before the hills, I was brought forth,
before he had made the earth with its fields,
or the first of the dust of the world.
When he established the heavens, I was there.

Proverbs 8:22-27a

This understanding of wisdom as being with God at creation led early Christians to think of Jesus as the wisdom of God (1 Cor. 1:30). And to think of Jesus as the agent of creation (Col. 1:16). The first Christians, however, felt more comfortable calling Jesus God's *Word* in creation (John 1:1-4) than God's Wisdom in creation.

Ecclesiastes

We want to be happy. Our understanding of happiness and its importance, of course, changes as we grow older and experience "happiness."

In the Old Testament, one book presents the reflections of a man who pursued happiness with great vigor. Solomon, who had unrivaled access to wealth and wisdom, recorded his reflections on the pursuit of happiness in Ecclesiastes.

> *I said in my heart, "Come now, I will test you with pleasure; enjoy yourself." But behold, this also was vanity. I said of laughter, "It is mad," and of pleasure, "What use is it?" I searched with my heart how to cheer my body with wine—my heart still guiding me with wisdom—and how to lay hold on folly, till I might see what was good for the children of man to do under heaven during the few days of their life. I made great works. I built houses and planted vineyards for myself. I made myself gardens and parks, and planted in them all kinds of fruit trees. I made myself pools from which to water the forest of growing trees. I bought male and female slaves, and had slaves who were born in my house. I had also great possessions of herds and flocks, more than any who had been before me in Jerusalem. I also gathered for myself silver and gold and the treasure of kings and provinces. I got singers, both men and women, and many concubines, the delight of the sons of man.*
>
> *So I became great and surpassed all who were before me in Jerusalem. Also my wisdom remained with me. And whatever my eyes desired I did not keep from them. I kept my heart from no pleasure, for my heart found pleasure in all my toil, and this was my reward for all my toil. Then I considered all that my hands had done and the toil I had expended in doing it, and behold, all was vanity and a striving after wind, and there was nothing to be gained under the sun.*
>
> Ecclesiastes 2:1-11

No pleasure of the senses, no pride of possessions, brings lasting profit. Nor is anything new in life really new: "What has been, is what will be ... There is nothing new under the sun" (1:4-10).

In such conclusions Solomon is not recommending folly over wisdom: "Wisdom excels folly as light excels darkness" (2:13). Yet, he knew that the fool and the wise alike must die (2:14-16); that before death, the foolish and wicked sometimes receive rewards which rightly should go to the wise (7:15; 8:10-14); that after death, the memory and inheritance of both wise and fool will have unforeseen, incalculable results (2:16-23).

Solomon recommends wisdom as the priceless orientation to life. Wisdom teaches that one should daily enjoy the simple pleasures of life—eating, drinking, and working.

> *Behold, what I have seen to be good and fitting is to eat and drink and find enjoyment in all the toil with which one toils under the sun the few days of his life that God has given him, for this is his lot. Everyone also to whom God has given wealth and possessions and power to enjoy them, and to accept his lot and rejoice in his toil—this is the gift of God.*
>
> Ecclesiastes 5:18-19 (cf. 2:24; 3:13; 8:15; 9:7; 10:19)

Yet, enjoying the simple benefits of food and work should not divert one from accepting the sorrows of life as well.

> *It is better to go to the house of mourning*
> *than to go to the house of feasting,*
> *for this is the end of all mankind,*
> *and the living will lay it to heart.*
> *Sorrow is better than laughter,*
> *for by sadness of face the heart is made glad.*
> *The heart of the wise is in the house of mourning,*
> *but the heart of fools is in the house of mirth.*
>
> Ecclesiastes 7:2-4

Solomon intended his words as goads to the young, prodding the inexperienced to wisdom (12:11) through a sobering account of life's meaning (11:9-12:1).

When life is experienced in all its dimensions to the fullest, then at the end of wisdom's search, life may indeed appear empty: a "vanity of vanities" (1:2), with no "song of songs" to sing. Life can be described as the "greatest emptiness."

Solomon's words at first seem to be a frontal assault on the sage tradition that "the beginning of wisdom is the fear of God." Yet, on this very point we read at the close of the book, “The end of the matter; all has been heard. Fear God and keep his commandments, for this is the whole duty of man” (12:13).

In Ecclesiastes, Solomon suggests that “the end of wisdom is the fear of God.” When wisdom in life has been fully pursued and weighed in the balance, at the end of the day happiness cannot be the measure of life. As it turns out, our human ability to find the best and happiest way in life is doomed to failure. Wisdom points beyond itself to the Creator.

Who decides what is good in life? We do, every day. At least, we choose. But the good cannot truly be realized apart from knowing God, revering God, and keeping His instructions for life.

This is the conclusion the wisest man reached about life, and about our search for happiness. “The end of the matter; all has been heard. Fear God and keep his commandments, for this is the whole duty of man. For God will bring every deed into judgment, with every secret thing, whether good or evil” (12:13-14).

Song of Songs

King Solomon was a prolific author, composing 3,000 proverbs and 1,005 songs (1 Kings 4:32). His greatest song has been preserved in the Old Testament canon. It is a love song which forms the last book of his trilogy: Proverbs, Ecclesiastes, and Song of Songs. This song of songs is a passionate, poetic conversation between and about a beautiful young woman and her beloved man.

That Solomon should compose such a subtly erotic song is not surprising. He loved foreign women. In Ecclesiastes, he could speak openly of sexual pleasures (2:8). What is intriguing is the particular mix of wisdom and sexual desire in the singer’s heart.

In Proverbs, Solomon expressed the persuasion and provisions of “wisdom” in the image and voice of an attractive woman, and the power of “folly” in the speech and allure of a seductive woman. For Solomon, the personification of “wisdom” as a powerful woman was a natural and transparent connection to make.

But the “song of songs” makes a deeper and more subtle association of wisdom and sexuality. The song breathes the atmosphere of the first garden, the garden of Eden—the paradise where the first man and woman were placed, the oasis where they were not ashamed, the primal habitation where “wisdom” served God as His “master worker” (Prov. 8:30). The very creation of man and woman and their attraction to each other is part of the handiwork of God’s wisdom. No surprise then that the wisest man would narrate in the most appropriate form, a poetic song, the ways of a man with a woman (cf. Prov. 30:18-19), merging the garden into the very descriptions of sexual love.

The man touches the woman lovingly with his words.

Behold, you are beautiful, my love,
behold, you are beautiful!
Your eyes are doves
behind your veil.
Your hair is like a flock of goats
leaping down the slopes of Gilead.
Your teeth are like a flock of shorn ewes
that have come up from the washing,
all of which bear twins,
and not one among them has lost its young.
Your lips are like a scarlet thread,
and your mouth is lovely.
Your cheeks are like halves of a pomegranate
behind your veil.
Your neck is like the tower of David,
built in rows of stone;
on it hang a thousand shields,
all of them shields of warriors.
Your two breasts are like two fawns,
twins of a gazelle,
that graze among the lilies.

How beautiful are your feet in sandals,
O noble daughter!
Your rounded thighs are like jewels,
the work of a master hand.

Your head crowns you like Carmel,
and your flowing locks are like purple;

a king is held captive in the tresses.
How beautiful and pleasant you are,
O loved one, with all your delights!

Song of Songs 4:1-5; 7:1, 5-6

The man sees his bride as a wondrous garden of delight:

How beautiful is your love, my sister, my bride!
How much better is your love than wine,
and the fragrance of your oils than any spice!
Your lips drip nectar, my bride;
honey and milk are under your tongue;
the fragrance of your garments is like the fragrance of Lebanon.
A garden locked is my sister, my bride,
a spring locked, a fountain sealed.
Your shoots are an orchard of pomegranates
with all choicest fruits,
henna with nard,
nard and saffron, calamus and cinnamon,
with all trees of frankincense,
myrrh and aloes,
with all choice spices—
a garden fountain, a well of living water,
and flowing streams from Lebanon.

Song of Songs 4:10-15

The tanned, beautiful woman cannot contain her own loving words for her man.

My beloved is radiant and ruddy,
distinguished among ten thousand.
His head is the finest gold;
his locks are wavy,
black as a raven.
His eyes are like doves
beside streams of water,
bathed in milk,
sitting beside a full pool.
His cheeks are like beds of spices,
mounds of sweet-smelling herbs.
His lips are lilies,

dripping liquid myrrh.
His arms are rods of gold,
set with jewels.
His body is polished ivory,
bedecked with sapphires.
His legs are alabaster columns,
set on bases of gold.
His appearance is like Lebanon,
choice as the cedars.

Song of Songs 5:10-15

When he is absent, her heart races to find him:

I opened to my beloved,
but my beloved had turned and gone.
My soul failed me when he spoke.
I sought him, but found him not;
I called him, but he gave no answer.
The watchmen found me
as they went about in the city;
they beat me, they bruised me,
they took away my veil,
those watchmen of the walls.
I adjure you, O daughters of Jerusalem,
if you find my beloved,
that you tell him
I am sick with love.

Song of Songs 5:6-8

The wise man is compelled to trace the movements of love, because as he writes near the end of the song, "love is strong as death, passion is as powerful as the grave; it flashes as fire, the fire of Yahweh God" (8:6). Certainly human love—the intimacy of man and woman—is not an end in itself. God's wisdom in such creation must have some larger purpose and design.

Even the wisdom of Solomon could not conceive the ultimate design. Much later the apostle Paul reveals a deep secret: the intimacy of marital love is a preview and intimation of Christ's profound love for the church, determined before the creation of human love (Eph. 5:32f).

In Ecclesiastes, the specter of death, the great equalizer, had forced Solomon to acknowledge a "vanity" to life. In Song of Songs, Solomon senses a force greater than death—the power of love. Centuries later, Paul would also recognize the defining power of love—the love of the Father for His Son, the love of the Son for the church, the love of Christians for one another.

> *Love is patient and kind; love does not envy or boast; it is not arrogant or rude. It does not insist on its own way; it is not irritable or resentful; it does not rejoice at wrongdoing, but rejoices with the truth. Love bears all things, believes all things, hopes all things, endures all things.*
>
> *Love never ends. As for prophecies, they will pass away; as for tongues, they will cease; as for knowledge, it will pass away. For we know in part and we prophesy in part, but when the perfect comes, the partial will pass away. When I was a child, I spoke like a child, I thought like a child, I reasoned like a child. When I became a man, I gave up childish ways. For now we see in a mirror dimly, but then face to face. Now I know in part; then I shall know fully, even as I have been fully known.*
>
> *So now faith, hope, and love abide, these three; but the greatest of these is love.*
>
> 1 Corinthians 13:4-13

Isaiah 1-23

The last major section of the Old Testament consists of the prophetic books. The prophets spoke for God from the 8th to the 5th century BC, amidst the crises which led to the destruction of the northern kingdom and subjugation of the southern kingdom to foreign overlords. During this period, Jerusalem was captured and the temple destroyed. The glory days of David and Solomon became a faint memory. The prophetic books warn of these disasters, explain the reasons, and offer hope for the future.

The book of Isaiah reaches from the 8th to the 6th century. It provides a singular overview of the entire prophetic corpus. Through 66 chapters we see both the justice and love of the Holy One of Israel.

When Isaiah began his ministry in the 740s BC, the nation of Judah was experiencing "good times." Their prosperity, however, was short-lived. Assyria, a vast nation to the East, was reclaiming its superpower status, and Judah along with its neighbors was deciding how to respond: to pay tribute to Assyria or to be her enemy.

For Isaiah, God's spokesman, the issue was even more critical: would Judah's leader look to Yahweh for strength and salvation or seek security through political, military alliances?

In the first chapter of Isaiah, God brings a lawsuit against His people. The indictments against Judah are clear:

How the faithful city
has become a whore,
she who was full of justice!
Righteousness lodged in her,
but now murderers.
Your silver has become dross,
your best wine mixed with water.
Your princes are rebels
and companions of thieves.
Everyone loves a bribe
and runs after gifts.
They do not bring justice to the fatherless,
and the widow's cause does not come to them.

Isaiah 1:21-23

Still, Judah is offered help. Though their sins are like scarlet and crimson, the people can be cleansed if they will but obey the LORD and cease their rebellion (1:18-19).

It was God's plan that His people and His house would be a magnet drawing all nations of the world to Zion and be taught of Him (2:2-4). Judah's pride and arrogance, however, had hindered God's plan (2:5-17). God decided He must strip Judah naked to humble and teach her (3:1-17), even her proud women:

The LORD said:
Because the daughters of Zion are haughty
and walk with outstretched necks,
glancing wantonly with their eyes,
mincing along as they go,
tinkling with their feet,
therefore the Lord will strike with a scab

the heads of the daughters of Zion,
and the LORD will lay bare their secret parts.

Instead of perfume there will be rottenness;
and instead of a belt, a rope;
and instead of well-set hair, baldness;
and instead of a rich robe, a skirt of sackcloth;
and branding instead of beauty.

Isaiah 3:16-17, 24

Once the LORD had washed the filth away, the people who remained would be devoted to God (4:1-6).

Isaiah has to upbraid those who were heroes in wine drinking (5:22) but who were not heroes in their treatment of neighbor. They would soon become like an abandoned vineyard, without rain, overgrown with thorns (5:1-13).

In stark contrast to Judah's sin, Isaiah 6 records an exalted vision of God's kingship—the very reality to which Judah was blind. Isaiah can see only the hem of God's robe (so majestic is God!), yet it *alone* fills the temple. The seraphs have to cover themselves for protection, and indeed must cry out a warning of God's presence: "Holy, Holy, Holy!" The prophet is overcome, confessing his own unclean lips. A seraph responds by placing a hot coal on Isaiah's mouth to cleanse him. Now prepared to speak, he is told his message will fall on deaf ears, even as the apostle Paul would know so well many centuries later (Romans 9-11).

Not only the prophet's words, but his own family become signs to assure Judah's rulers of God's protection (Isaiah 8:18). Isaiah tells King Ahaz that he must not fear the provocations and threats of his neighbors. Before Isaiah's two children are weaned, the threatening nations will come to an end (7:1-8:15). God will use Assyria like a razor to shave off Judah's enemies (7:20). But great Assyria, like any superpower at any time which glories in its military strength rather than God, will itself one day face God's devouring fire (10:5-19). Isaiah holds not only Assyria, but other nations as well, accountable before the LORD God their Creator (Isaiah 13-23).

All God's movements among the nations of the earth are with purpose, toward an end. Isaiah is given glimpses of this grand goal. It focuses on the One who will occupy the throne of David.

For to us a child is born,
to us a son is given;
and the government shall be upon his shoulder,
and his name shall be called
Wonderful Counselor, Mighty God,
Everlasting Father, Prince of Peace.
Of the increase of his government and of peace
there will be no end,
on the throne of David and over his kingdom,
to establish it and to uphold it
with justice and with righteousness
from this time forth and forevermore.
The zeal of the LORD of hosts will do this.

Isaiah 9:6-7

This king will have wisdom far greater than Solomon's. This ruler will inaugurate a reign that restores paradise—an Eden of reconciliation between predator and prey, man and creation:

The wolf shall dwell with the lamb,
and the leopard shall lie down with the young goat,
and the calf and the lion and the fattened calf together;
and a little child shall lead them.
The cow and the bear shall graze;
their young shall lie down together;
and the lion shall eat straw like the ox.
The nursing child shall play over the hole of the cobra,
and the weaned child shall put his hand on the adder's den.
They shall not hurt or destroy
in all my holy mountain;
for the earth shall be full of the knowledge of the LORD
as the waters cover the sea.

Isaiah 11:6-9

Such a vision of the future, while utterly incredible, is ground for hope and for wonder.

You will say in that day:
"I will give thanks to you, O LORD,
for though you were angry with me,
your anger turned away,
that you might comfort me.

"Behold, God is my salvation;
I will trust, and will not be afraid;
for the LORD GOD is my strength and my song,
and he has become my salvation."

Isaiah 12:1-2

It is a future already begun in the resurrection and exaltation of Jesus to God's right hand.

Isaiah 24-66

During the last half of the 8th century BC, tragedy befell the northern kingdom, Israel (28:1-8). In 722, Assyria captured the capital Samaria, deporting the people and repopulating the city with refugees from other parts of the empire.

Twenty years later, Assyria marched against the capital of the southern kingdom, Jerusalem, devastating the countryside and torching 46 Judean cities. The Assyrian king bragged that Judah could not resist such an onslaught.

> *"Beware lest Hezekiah mislead you by saying, 'The LORD will deliver us.' Has any of the gods of the nations delivered his land out of the hand of the king of Assyria? ... Who among all the gods of these lands have delivered their lands out of my hand, that the LORD should deliver Jerusalem out of my hand?"*
>
> Isaiah 36:18, 20

In the south, however, Judah was being ruled by a king who prayed. In the face of overwhelming military odds, difficult to overstate, King Hezekiah turned to God in prayer:

> *"O LORD of hosts, God of Israel, enthroned above the cherubim, you are the God, you alone, of all the kingdoms of the earth; you have made heaven and earth. Incline your ear, O LORD, and hear; open your eyes, O LORD, and see; and hear all the words of Sennacherib, which he has sent to mock the living God. Truly, O LORD, the kings of Assyria have laid waste all the nations and their lands, and have cast their gods into the fire. For they were no gods, but the work of men's hands, wood and stone. Therefore they were destroyed. So now, O LORD our God, save us from his*

hand, that all the kingdoms of the earth may know that you alone are the LORD."

Isaiah 37:16-20

Isaiah reported to Hezekiah that Jerusalem would *not* fall to Assyria!

> *"Therefore thus says the LORD concerning the king of Assyria: He shall not come into this city or shoot an arrow there or come before it with a shield or cast up a siege mound against it. By the way that he came, by the same he shall return, and he shall not come into this city, declares the LORD. For I will defend this city to save it, for my own sake and for the sake of my servant David."*
>
> Isaiah 37:33-35

Soon after, the king was faced with his personal crisis, a terminal illness. His reaction to the news was characteristic:

> *Then Hezekiah turned his face to the wall and prayed to the LORD, and said, "Please, O LORD, remember how I have walked before you in faithfulness and with a whole heart, and have done what is good in your sight." And Hezekiah wept bitterly.*
>
> Isaiah 38:2-3

Isaiah delivered a word of the LORD in response to Hezekiah's prayer.

> *"Go and say to Hezekiah, Thus says the LORD, the God of David your father: I have heard your prayer; I have seen your tears. Behold, I will add fifteen years to your life. I will deliver you and this city out of the hand of the king of Assyria, and will defend this city.*
>
> *"This shall be the sign to you from the LORD, that the LORD will do this thing that he has promised: Behold, I will make the shadow cast by the declining sun on the dial of Ahaz turn back ten steps." So the sun turned back on the dial the ten steps by which it had declined.*
>
> Isaiah 38:5-8

Through prayer, an earthly king named Hezekiah submitted himself to a greater King, the LORD God. And through this person's prayer, a nation was delivered and an individual rescued from death. For Isaiah, however, the story of Hezekiah served another function: to depict the character of the Holy One of Israel—the Holy One who waits for His children to turn to Him, who cares for them deeply, who responds to prayer.

Isaiah gives full force to this picture of God in the last half of his book (40-66). No longer does Isaiah stop the ears and shut the eyes of God's people because of their rebellion (6:10). Now God commissions the prophet to comfort His people, speaking tenderly to Jerusalem (40:1-2).

Have you not known? Have you not heard?
The LORD is the everlasting God,
the Creator of the ends of the earth.
He does not faint or grow weary;
his understanding is unsearchable.
He gives power to the faint,
and to him who has no might he increases strength.
Even youths shall faint and be weary,
and young men shall fall exhausted;
but they who wait for the LORD shall renew their strength;
they shall mount up with wings like eagles;
they shall run and not be weary;
they shall walk and not faint.

For a brief moment I deserted you,
but with great compassion I will gather you.
In overflowing anger for a moment
I hid my face from you,
but with everlasting love I will have compassion on you,"
says the LORD, your Redeemer.

Isaiah 40:28-31; 54:7-8

Comfort certainly comes to Hezekiah in his acknowledgment of the true King. Judah could not receive God's comfort except through knowing His universal rule.

Thus says the LORD, the King of Israel
and his Redeemer, the LORD of hosts:
"I am the first and I am the last;
besides me there is no god.
Who is like me? Let him proclaim it.
Let him declare and set it before me,
since I appointed an ancient people.
Let them declare what is to come, and what will happen.
Fear not, nor be afraid;
have I not told you from of old and declared it?
And you are my witnesses!

Is there a God besides me?
There is no Rock; I know not any."

Isaiah 44:6-8

Ultimately, God controls all nations of the world. In His time, for His purposes, God uses the world's politicians and leaders as a potter uses clay. For a season He uses the superpower Assyria, then Babylon, then another. But all must finally be held accountable for their deeds—not before a human judge but before the judgment throne of God.

Come down and sit in the dust,
O virgin daughter of Babylon;
sit on the ground without a throne,
O daughter of the Chaldeans!
For you shall no more be called
tender and delicate.

Sit in silence, and go into darkness,
O daughter of the Chaldeans;
for you shall no more be called
the mistress of kingdoms.

You felt secure in your wickedness;
you said, "No one sees me";
your wisdom and your knowledge led you astray,
and you said in your heart,
"I am, and there is no one besides me."
But evil shall come upon you,
which you will not know how to charm away;
disaster shall fall upon you,
for which you will not be able to atone;
and ruin shall come upon you suddenly,
of which you know nothing.

Isaiah 47:1, 5, 10-11

God intended that His chosen people be *servants*—servants to the nations, a light to the nations, drawing nations to the only true and living God.

Thus says God, the LORD,
who created the heavens and stretched them out,
who spread out the earth and what comes from it,
who gives breath to the people on it
and spirit to those who walk in it:

"I am the LORD; I have called you in righteousness;
I will take you by the hand and keep you;
I will give you as a covenant for the people,
a light for the nations,
to open the eyes that are blind,
to bring out the prisoners from the dungeon,
from the prison those who sit in darkness.

Arise, shine, for your light has come,
and the glory of the LORD has risen upon you.
For behold, darkness shall cover the earth,
and thick darkness the peoples;
but the LORD will arise upon you,
and his glory will be seen upon you.
And nations shall come to your light,
and kings to the brightness of your rising.

Isaiah 42:5-7; 60:1-3

The comfort experienced by God's servants was to be extended to the world. But His people had forsaken their calling. So God had to use foreign leaders as His "servants" to discipline His people Israel.

I was ready to be sought by those who did not ask for me;
I was ready to be found by those who did not seek me.
I said, "Here I am, here I am,"
to a nation that was not called by my name.
I spread out my hands all the day
to a rebellious people,
who walk in a way that is not good,
following their own devices.

Isaiah 65:1-2

It would not be until the coming of the son of Judah named Jesus that the identity of the "servant" in Isaiah would be fully realized and understood.

He was despised and rejected by men,
a man of sorrows and acquainted with grief;
and as one from whom men hide their faces
he was despised, and we esteemed him not.
Surely he has borne our griefs
and carried our sorrows;
yet we esteemed him stricken,

smitten by God, and afflicted.
But he was pierced for our transgressions;
he was crushed for our iniquities;
upon him was the chastisement that brought us peace,
and with his wounds we are healed.
All we like sheep have gone astray;
we have turned—every one—to his own way;
and the LORD has laid on him
the iniquity of us all.
He was oppressed, and he was afflicted,
yet he opened not his mouth;
like a lamb that is led to the slaughter,
and like a sheep that before its shearers is silent,
so he opened not his mouth.

Isaiah 53:3-7

By this servant at last, in God's own timetable, a great light shone and the Spirit of God was poured out:

The Spirit of the Lord GOD is upon me,
because the LORD has anointed me
to bring good news to the poor;
he has sent me to bind up the brokenhearted,
to proclaim liberty to the captives,
and the opening of the prison to those who are bound;
to proclaim the year of the LORD's favor,
and the day of vengeance of our God;
to comfort all who mourn.

Isaiah 61:1-2

Jeremiah 1-25

Who likes delivering bad news? Who wants to tell somebody to give up, to quit? Nobody likes exposing weaknesses. Yet God called Jeremiah to do all this, and in the process to kill the dearest of his heart's desires.

The book of Jeremiah records the words and biography of this man born north of Jerusalem in the volatile seventh century BC. Babylon was rapidly becoming a superpower while Judah considered alliances with the two other declining powers, Assyria and Egypt, in a desperate attempt to maintain independence (2:18).

The reforms of King Josiah had brought a measure of optimism in the country. Perhaps, the people thought, God would preserve Judah.

It was not to be.

God called Jeremiah before he was born (1:5). Jeremiah did not want to be a prophet, especially a prophet to other countries. When he heard God's call, he objected that he was inarticulate and too young (1:8). God, however, touched his mouth and revealed the theme of his preaching: a boiling pot is tilting from the north ready to pour out its scalding contents on Judah.

"Behold, I am bringing against you
a nation from afar, O house of Israel,
declares the LORD.
It is an enduring nation;
it is an ancient nation,
a nation whose language you do not know,
nor can you understand what they say.
Their quiver is like an open tomb;
they are all mighty warriors.
They shall eat up your harvest and your food;
they shall eat up your sons and your daughters;
they shall eat up your flocks and your herds;
they shall eat up your vines and your fig trees;
your fortified cities in which you trust
they shall beat down with the sword."

Jeremiah 5:15-17 (cf. 1:13-16)

Judah would not escape exile. Jeremiah felt deeply the force of this message. He was not a mere casual observer.

My anguish, my anguish! I writhe in pain!
Oh the walls of my heart!
My heart is beating wildly;
I cannot keep silent,
for I hear the sound of the trumpet,
the alarm of war.
Crash follows hard on crash;
the whole land is laid waste.
Suddenly my tents are laid waste,
my curtains in a moment.
How long must I see the standard
and hear the sound of the trumpet?

Jeremiah 4:19-21

Jeremiah sees order devolving and chaos returning:

> *I looked on the earth, and behold, it was without form and void;*
> *and to the heavens, and they had no light.*
> *I looked on the mountains, and behold, they were quaking,*
> *and all the hills moved to and fro.*
> *I looked, and behold, there was no man,*
> *and all the birds of the air had fled.*
> *I looked, and behold, the fruitful land was a desert,*
> *and all its cities were laid in ruins*
> *before the LORD, before his fierce anger.*
>
> Jeremiah 4:23-26 (cf. 7:16)

What had Judah done to deserve such punishment? She had gone after the fertility gods (2:23; 5:7; 7:18; 9:14; 11:13; 19:5). She was like a bride who had forgotten her wedding dress and honeymoon (2:1, 32). And in the most stinging question Jeremiah asks:

> *Has a nation changed its gods,*
> *even though they are no gods?*
> *But my people have changed their glory*
> *for that which does not profit.*
> *Be appalled, O heavens, at this;*
> *be shocked, be utterly desolate,*
> *declares the LORD,*
> *for my people have committed two evils:*
> *they have forsaken me,*
> *the fountain of living waters,*
> *and hewed out cisterns for themselves,*
> *broken cisterns that can hold no water.*
>
> Jeremiah 2:11-13

How could this have happened? With deeply personal consequences, Jeremiah lays the blame partly at the feet of his own priestly heritage (1:1). Judah has had bad priests, bad prophets, and bad shepherds.

> *I have heard what the prophets have said who prophesy lies in my name, saying, 'I have dreamed, I have dreamed!' How long shall there be lies in the heart of the prophets who prophesy lies, and who prophesy the deceit of their own heart, who think to make my people forget my name by their dreams that they tell one another, even as their fathers forgot my name for Baal?*
>
> Jeremiah 23:25-27 (cf. 5:31; 8:10; 14:14-18; 23:11)

The leaders had said, "Peace, peace," when there was no prospect of peace (6:14; 8:11; 14:13; 16:5; 23:1). They had pointed to the presence of the temple as a sign of security, but theirs were deceptive words (7:3-14). Neither profession of wisdom nor possession of the law could save this people. They must return to living right and just lives, worshipping the only true God (8:8; 5:1).

Judah had crossed the line. The foe from the north was coming.

In a remarkable confirmation of this reality, God decreed that Jeremiah should not pray or intercede for Judah (7:16; 11:14; 14:11). Further, the prophet is neither to marry nor have a family. The times were perilous. Neither feasting nor mourning, events of normal human life, were to be visited. The times were desperate (16:1-13).

In a non-patriotic vein, Jeremiah advises surrender to the foe from the north (Jer. 21; 24:5ff). Not surprisingly, such seeming lack of loyalty brought hardship to God's messenger. His hometown threatened to kill him (11:18-33) as did others (18:18ff). The priest in charge of the temple police had Jeremiah arrested, beaten, and put in stocks (20:1-6). God, of course, remained with the prophet as He promised. Jeremiah was a "fortified wall of bronze."

> *And I, behold, I make you this day a fortified city, an iron pillar, and bronze walls, against the whole land, against the kings of Judah, its officials, its priests, and the people of the land. They will fight against you, but they shall not prevail against you, for I am with you, declares the LORD, to deliver you."*
>
> Jeremiah 1:18-19 (cf. 15:20)

In this darkest abyss Jeremiah offers signs of hope—a return to the land (3:15; 12:15; 16:15-19). For the moment, however, not Judah's king but a foreign king is God's servant—none other than the ruler of Babylon, Nebuchadrezzar (25:9).

Jeremiah's life helps us picture the apostle Paul's self-understanding. For like Jeremiah, he too sensed God's pre-natal choice; he too felt his own rhetorical inadequacies; he too perceived anxious times ahead warranting celibacy; he too experienced extreme hardships preaching God's word.

Put simply: *When God calls a man He calls him to die.*

Indeed in our own times, real security cannot be found in wealth, political influence, or military power. True strength is only in God the Creator, the Father of the Lord Jesus, who calls us to live kindly toward our neighbors and our enemies.

Jeremiah 26-52

It is terribly painful to watch the disintegration of a nation in a single generation. It is more difficult still to know the reasons for such decay and to be responsible for declaring those reasons to one's fellow citizens.

Jeremiah had the unenviable task of telling the priests, prophets, people, and kings of Judah that Jerusalem would be incinerated.

> *Therefore, thus says the LORD: Behold, I am giving this city into the hands of the Chaldeans and into the hand of Nebuchadnezzar king of Babylon, and he shall capture it. The Chaldeans who are fighting against this city shall come and set this city on fire and burn it, with the houses on whose roofs offerings have been made to Baal and drink offerings have been poured out to other gods, to provoke me to anger. For the children of Israel and the children of Judah have done nothing but evil in my sight from their youth. The children of Israel have done nothing but provoke me to anger by the work of their hands, declares the LORD.*
>
> Jeremiah 32:28-30

The people had proven faithless (35:15), enslaving their fellow Hebrews (34:8ff) and offering cakes to the false queen of heaven (44:19). Jeremiah suffered much for uttering God's word. The leaders wanted him executed (26:8ff). Another prophet, Uriah, was killed for such predictions (26:20-24). Jeremiah was thrown in a muddy cistern to die (38:4-6). But an Ethiopian eunuch rescued Jeremiah (38:7ff), presaging another Ethiopian eunuch who centuries later accepted the truth about the Son of God, who like Jeremiah did nothing deserving of death (Acts 8:26-40; cf. Jer. 39:16-18; 26:16ff).

Judah's king, Jehoiakim, hated Jeremiah's preaching. The king burned the scroll with Jeremiah's words (Jer. 36). These words—that God would give Judah (and even the wild animals!) to His "servant," the king of Babylon (27:1ff)—infuriated the false prophets in the king's court. When

Jeremiah donned a wooden yoke to visualize Judah's impending service to Babylon, the prophet Hananiah broke Jeremiah's yoke in anger (28:1ff).

The nation Judah had become so arrogant she did not appreciate that her God was in fact Lord of *all nations*. In his call, Jeremiah had been appointed a prophet to the *nations*, not to Judah alone (1:5). In his letter to the exiles (29:5ff), Jeremiah conveys God's command to settle down in Babylon, build houses, plant gardens, marry, have children, "seek the welfare of the city where I have sent you into exile, and pray to the LORD on its behalf, for in its welfare you will find your welfare" (29:7).

God's sovereignty over all nations (as even today!) did not exclude them from judgment, or release Jeremiah as "prophet to the nations" from proclaiming such condemnation. The book ends with oracles against ten nations (chaps. 46-51). Jeremiah announces God's punishment of all the nations, from Egypt to Babylon. The most devastating words are reserved for Babylon. Another foe from the north will wreak vengeance, making it a perpetual waste. The Creator will act, stirring up the Medes, punishing the god Bel, and the "sea will overtake Babylon!" (Jer. 50-51)

As it happens, Jeremiah chose to stay in Judah while others were carried into exile (40:1-6). His advice to the remaining survivors *not to go to Egypt* went unheeded. Tragically, Jeremiah himself was taken to Egypt (43:6f) where he eventually died.

But before the final exile, Jeremiah did a remarkable thing. He bought a piece of real estate, a field in his hometown—even as the Babylonian invaders overran Judah! He believed that one day Judah would return, and that houses, fields, and vineyards would again be bought in the land (32:1-15).

Jeremiah died without child, in a strange place, his people taken far away. Faithfulness did not bring him health, homeland, or happiness. Yet even in these tumultuous times the prophet knew the hope and promise of a completely new relationship with God.

> *"Behold, the days are coming, declares the LORD, when I will make a new covenant with the house of Israel and the house of Judah, not like the covenant that I made with their fathers on the day when I took them by the hand to bring them out of the land of Egypt, my covenant that they broke, though I was their husband, declares the LORD. For this is the covenant that I will make with the house of Israel after those days, declares the*

LORD: I will put my law within them, and I will write it on their hearts. And I will be their God, and they shall be my people. And no longer shall each one teach his neighbor and each his brother, saying, 'Know the LORD,' for they shall all know me, from the least of them to the greatest, declares the LORD. For I will forgive their iniquity, and I will remember their sin no more."
Jeremiah 31:31-34

Christians believe that in the death of Christ this new relationship with God has been inaugurated, not for Israel alone but the entire world, promising forgiveness of every sin and cleansed memory from the debilitating habits of the heart (Hebrews 8-10).

All peoples of the earth are welcome to participate in this new relationship with God through the priesthood of Christ, so completing Jeremiah's mission to the nations.

Lamentations

Few events in human history are as heartrending as the blockade and starvation of a city. In the sixth century BC, Jerusalem faced starvation, defeat, and destruction at the hands of Babylon. Societal tragedies of this depth cry out for comfort, for healing, for explanation, for renewal.

In the short term, words must be spoken out of grief in order to cope with the experience. With such words emotions can find shape and run their course. But expressions of grief which effect healing are not spontaneous; they need a form which conveys the sense of loss yet contains that loss to its proper proportions.

The book of Lamentations expresses deep pain and sorrow over the destruction of Jerusalem. The grief is more intense because of the expectation that David's city would not, could not experience such devastation—for in it resided the temple of God. But the city fell.

The loss of Jerusalem is mourned in five carefully crafted laments. Four of the five are composed as acrostics, poems in which each stanza begins with the next letter of the Hebrew alphabet. Such literary intention indicates both the deftly expressed emotion of the poetry as well as a sense of progress and completion of the grief experience.

In the first lament, Jerusalem is pictured as a widow, weeping, with no one to comfort her. The city also speaks in the first person, calling out in remorse and pain. The grieving process begins with the cries of the exposed, raw nerve of anguish.

"Look, O LORD, for I am in distress;
my stomach churns;
my heart is wrung within me,
because I have been very rebellious.
In the street the sword bereaves;
in the house it is like death.
They heard my groaning,
yet there is no one to comfort me.
All my enemies have heard of my trouble;
they are glad that you have done it.
You have brought the day you announced;
now let them be as I am."

Lamentations 1:20-21

In the second lament, the Source of destruction is magnified.

How the Lord in his anger
has set the daughter of Zion under a cloud!
He has cast down from heaven to earth
the splendor of Israel;
he has not remembered his footstool
in the day of his anger.
The Lord has swallowed up without mercy
all the habitations of Jacob;
in his wrath he has broken down
the strongholds of the daughter of Judah;
he has brought down to the ground in dishonor
the kingdom and its rulers.

Lamentations 2:1-2

Palace, temple, altar, walls, and gates have all been torn down by the LORD. Grief pleads with *all* sufferers to cry out in the night to God.

Look, O LORD, and see!
With whom have you dealt thus?
Should women eat the fruit of their womb,
the children of their tender care?
Should priest and prophet be killed

in the sanctuary of the Lord?
In the dust of the streets
lie the young and the old;
my young women and my young men
have fallen by the sword;
you have killed them in the day of your anger,
slaughtering without pity.

Lamentations 2:20-21

In the third lament, at the very moment the affliction and loss seem unbearable, hope breaks through:

Remember my affliction and my wanderings,
the wormwood and the gall!
My soul continually remembers it
and is bowed down within me.
But this I call to mind,
and therefore I have hope:
The steadfast love of the LORD never ceases;
his mercies never come to an end;
they are new every morning;
great is your faithfulness.
"The LORD is my portion," says my soul,
"therefore I will hope in him."
The LORD is good to those who wait for him,
to the soul who seeks him.
It is good that one should wait quietly
for the salvation of the LORD.

Lamentations 3:19-26

There is the calm assurance that God has heard. The plea that He should avenge those who destroyed Jerusalem is not held back (3:64-66).

Renewed strength for endurance does not mean, of course, that grief is erased. In the fourth lament, the inhumanity of the starvation is described vividly:

The hands of compassionate women
have boiled their own children;
they became their food
during the destruction of the daughter of my people.

Lamentations 4:10

The LORD has poured out his anger on all. Yet there is hope the exile will come to an end (4:22).

In the final lament, the LORD is asked to consider their disgrace: "We are homeless, orphans, aliens, widows; we are weary, slaves rule over us, the jackals prowl." Yet the confession rings through: "You, O LORD, reign forever" (5:19).

The five poems of Lamentations offer exercises in the bearing and sharing of grief. God's people are allowed to express the full range of emotions, frustrations, disappointments, confusion, and to ask God for judgment on those who oppress. But in the catharsis, faith increases so that endurance can see God's steadfast love which never comes to an end.

Ezekiel 1-24

In 701 BC, Jerusalem narrowly escaped destruction at the hands of the Assyrians. A century later, Jerusalem again barely escaped destruction at the hands of the Babylonians. But this time at a heavy cost. In 598 BC, the leading citizens of Jerusalem were deported to Babylon. Among those relocated was a priest named Ezekiel.

At an abandoned village near an irrigation canal where Ezekiel and others had been settled, life was a mixture of deep disorientation and cautious hope: *hope* that Jerusalem would not be destroyed because of God's promises, yet *disorientation* with having to live in an alien culture apart from God's sacred temple.

In 593 BC, five years after the deportation, the exiled priest experienced the extraordinary; he beheld visions of God. The heavens opened and Ezekiel saw "something like" the throne of God, incredibly mobile, accompanied by wings and wheels!

> *As I looked, behold, a stormy wind came out of the north, and a great cloud, with brightness around it, and fire flashing forth continually, and in the midst of the fire, as it were gleaming metal. And from the midst of it came the likeness of four living creatures. And this was their appearance: they had a human likeness, but each had four faces, and each of them had four wings.*

Now as I looked at the living creatures, I saw a wheel on the earth beside the living creatures, one for each of the four of them.

And when the living creatures went, the wheels went beside them; and when the living creatures rose from the earth, the wheels rose. Wherever the spirit wanted to go, they went, and the wheels rose along with them, for the spirit of the living creatures was in the wheels.

Ezekiel 1:4-6, 15, 19-20

Ezekiel is overcome by the radiance and the splendor.

And above the expanse over their heads there was the likeness of a throne, in appearance like sapphire; and seated above the likeness of a throne was a likeness with a human appearance. And upward from what had the appearance of his waist I saw as it were gleaming metal, like the appearance of fire enclosed all around. And downward from what had the appearance of his waist I saw as it were the appearance of fire, and there was brightness around him. Like the appearance of the bow that is in the cloud on the day of rain, so was the appearance of the brightness all around.

Such was the appearance of the likeness of the glory of the LORD. And when I saw it, I fell on my face, and I heard the voice of one speaking.

Ezekiel 1:26-28

In His glory, God transforms Ezekiel from a priest to a prophet—a spokesman to His rebellious people (2:1-3:11). God confines Ezekiel to his own house, not permitting him to speak anything other than words He might give (3:24-27).

In silence Ezekiel acts out various dramas to impress upon his fellow exiles the bad news awaiting Jerusalem. He creates a miniature battle scene about Jerusalem. He restricts his diet to that of blockade rations. He divides his cut hair into parts representing a sundered, scattered, slain population. He digs a hole through a wall and carries out an exile's bag (chaps. 4-5; 12). With his body Ezekiel attempts to make visually, dramatically real to the leaders in exile Jerusalem's inevitable destruction.

Most amazingly, a year after his call Ezekiel is taken up by the Spirit in a vision to the entrance of the temple in Jerusalem (8:1-4). There Ezekiel witnesses great abominations (8:5-18). God announces the rescue of only those who sigh and groan about such practices (9:4-11).

Then the unimaginable, the unthinkable happens before Ezekiel's eyes: the glory of God leaves the temple (8:6), pausing at the threshold (9:3) before departing the city.

> *Then the glory of the* LORD *went out from the threshold of the house, and stood over the cherubim. And the cherubim lifted up their wings and mounted up from the earth before my eyes as they went out, with the wheels beside them. And they stood at the entrance of the east gate of the house of the* LORD, *and the glory of the God of Israel was over them.*
>
> *Then the cherubim lifted up their wings, with the wheels beside them, and the glory of the God of Israel was over them. And the glory of the* LORD *went up from the midst of the city and stood on the mountain that is on the east side of the city.*
>
> Ezekiel 10:18-19; 11:22-23

How could God abandon Jerusalem, Judah, and the temple? Judah had not merely worshipped graven images; she had taken false gods into her *heart* (14:1-5). She acted like an ungrateful daughter or a faithless wife.

> *"And when I passed by you and saw you wallowing in your blood, I said to you in your blood, 'Live!' I said to you in your blood, 'Live!'*
>
> *"When I passed by you again and saw you, behold, you were at the age for love, and I spread the corner of my garment over you and covered your nakedness; I made my vow to you and entered into a covenant with you, declares the Lord* GOD, *and you became mine.*
>
> *"But you trusted in your beauty and played the whore because of your renown and lavished your whorings on any passerby; your beauty became his.*
>
> *"And in all your abominations and your whorings you did not remember the days of your youth, when you were naked and bare, wallowing in your blood.*

"You played the whore also with the Assyrians, because you were not satisfied; yes, you played the whore with them, and still you were not satisfied. You multiplied your whoring also with the trading land of Chaldea, and even with this you were not satisfied.

"How sick is your heart, declares the Lord GOD, because you did all these things, the deeds of a brazen prostitute."

Ezekiel 16:6, 8, 15, 22, 28-30

Judah's two sisters were Samaria and Sodom! (16:46-58)

The word of the Lord interprets Israel's experiences of exodus and wilderness as episodes of rebellion. God spared Israel time and again because He did not want His name profaned before the nations (Ezek. 20). What God desired above all else was that He be known truly among His children (20:42). But by and large they chose ignorance and faithlessness, though a few embraced righteousness and repentance. For the obedient there was life (18:26-32).

Ezekiel also experienced a great personal tragedy. His wife died, the delight of his eyes. God prohibited Ezekiel from any public display of sorrow so that his fellow exiles might be jolted awake to the heartbreak awaiting Jerusalem.

Then I said to them, "The word of the LORD came to me: 'Say to the house of Israel, Thus says the Lord GOD: Behold, I will profane my sanctuary, the pride of your power, the delight of your eyes, and the yearning of your soul, and your sons and your daughters whom you left behind shall fall by the sword. And you shall do as I have done; you shall not cover your lips, nor eat the bread of men. Your turbans shall be on your heads and your shoes on your feet; you shall not mourn or weep, but you shall rot away in your iniquities and groan to one another. Thus shall Ezekiel be to you a sign; according to all that he has done you shall do. When this comes, then you will know that I am the Lord GOD.'"

Ezekiel 24:20-24

The book of Ezekiel, however, does not end on this tragic note. For the future there is a vision of hope.

Ezekiel 25-48

Before the destruction of Jerusalem, the prophet Ezekiel had the unenviable task of impressing upon his fellow exiles that the loss of the temple was inevitable. Judah had been rebellious and unrepentant. The first half of the book of Ezekiel is heavy with this sad news.

And the other nations of the world who rebel against God? In chapters 25-32, Ezekiel delivers a series of oracles against foreign peoples who had acted arrogantly or vengefully against Judah. All are accountable to the God of Abraham—Ammon, Moab, Edom, Philistia, Sidon—nations who had applauded Judah's hardships. But especially Tyre, the wealthy island seaport, who had welcomed Judah's plunder for the commercial advantage it might bring (chaps. 26-28).

Ezekiel's strongest rebuke, however, is reserved for Egypt and her Pharaoh who had boasted, "The Nile is mine; I made it" (29:9).

> *I will put hooks in your jaws,*
> *and make the fish of your streams stick to your scales;*
> *and I will draw you up out of the midst of your streams,*
> *with all the fish of your streams*
> *that stick to your scales.*
> *And I will cast you out into the wilderness,*
> *you and all the fish of your streams;*
> *you shall fall on the open field,*
> *and not be brought together or gathered.*
> *To the beasts of the earth and to the birds of the heavens*
> *I give you as food.*
>
> Ezekiel 29:4-5

God's punishment of the nations is not, however, merely vengeful. As His creation, God desires that all people know Him as the only LORD (25:5, 7, 11, 17; 16:6; 28:21, 26; 29:6, 8, 16, 21; 30:8, 19, 26; 33:29; 35:4, 9, 15; 36:11, 23).

When Ezekiel hears that Jerusalem has fallen, he is able to speak again to his fellow exiles (33:21). He feels a keen responsibility to speak as a watchman over a city must speak, warning that disaster is approaching (33:1-9). Ezekiel delivers a powerful rebuke to the shepherds who have not cared for the flock but have rather fed only themselves.

The weak you have not strengthened, the sick you have not healed, the injured you have not bound up, the strayed you have not brought back, the lost you have not sought, and with force and harshness you have ruled them.

Ezekiel 34:4

In a moving passage, God declares that He alone will be their shepherd.

As a shepherd seeks out his flock when he is among his sheep that have been scattered, so will I seek out my sheep, and I will rescue them from all places where they have been scattered on a day of clouds and thick darkness. And I will bring them out from the peoples and gather them from the countries, and will bring them into their own land. And I will feed them on the mountains of Israel, by the ravines, and in all the inhabited places of the country. I will feed them with good pasture, and on the mountain heights of Israel shall be their grazing land. There they shall lie down in good grazing land, and on rich pasture they shall feed on the mountains of Israel. ... I will seek the lost, and I will bring back the strayed, and I will bind up the injured, and I will strengthen the weak, and the fat and the strong I will destroy. I will feed them in justice.

Ezekiel 34:12-14, 16

In the New Testament, Jesus comes as the Good Shepherd.

God will rescue Judah from exile but it will not be because of her goodness:

"But when they came to the nations, wherever they came, they profaned my holy name, in that people said of them, 'These are the people of the LORD, and yet they had to go out of his land.' But I had concern for my holy name, which the house of Israel had profaned among the nations to which they came."

"Therefore say to the house of Israel, Thus says the Lord GOD: It is not for your sake, O house of Israel, that I am about to act, but for the sake of my holy name, which you have profaned among the nations to which you came. And I will vindicate the holiness of my great name, which has been profaned among the nations, and which you have profaned among them. And the nations will know that I am the LORD, declares the Lord GOD, when through you I vindicate my holiness before their eyes."

Ezekiel 36:20-23

Salvation can only come through a radical heart transplant:

> *And I will give you a new heart, and a new spirit I will put within you. And I will remove the heart of stone from your flesh and give you a heart of flesh. And I will put my Spirit within you, and cause you to walk in my statutes and be careful to obey my rules.*
>
> Ezekiel 36:26-27

Then and only then may they enter the garden of Eden again (36:35).

God's restoration of His people will be nothing short of a resurrection or second creation! Ezekiel in fact is shown a valley of very dry bones. Oddly, the prophet begins prophesying to bones!

> *So I prophesied as I was commanded. And as I prophesied, there was a sound, and behold, a rattling, and the bones came together, bone to its bone.*
>
> Ezekiel 37:7

In flesh and blood the slain come to life!

> *Then he said to me, "Son of man, these bones are the whole house of Israel. Behold, they say, 'Our bones are dried up, and our hope is lost; we are indeed cut off.' Therefore prophesy, and say to them, Thus says the Lord GOD: Behold, I will open your graves and raise you from your graves, O my people. And I will bring you into the land of Israel.*
>
> Ezekiel 37:11-12

But will God's people encounter His presence again in the land? Didn't God's glory leave Jerusalem? In the final part of his book (chaps. 40-48), Ezekiel is brought in visions to the land. He sees a man in appearance like shining bronze, carefully measuring the structures of a new temple. No word is offered until the man suddenly speaks, "This is the most holy place" (41:4). The measuring continues with special concern for ways of access to the holy.

Then, unexpectedly, the glory of God comes from the east and fills the temple (43:1-5). The outer gate closes. The LORD has entered. Admission is now restricted (44:1-14).

Ezekiel then sees something striking coming from the temple. A small stream flows toward the east, getting ever wider and deeper until it becomes a river deep enough to swim (47:1-6). Stranger still, the river transforms the stagnant sea it enters into a fresh habitat for life to flourish (47:7-12).

As the source of living waters, Jesus enacts in his own life (and in his fishing) the abundance and flourishing of fish available to catch! Finally, Ezekiel hears that Jerusalem will be renamed Jahwehsham, "The LORD is There" (48:35).

The book of Ezekiel closes in expectation and hope. God has not abandoned His own. But His holiness demands a people of new heart and spirit. And God will provide an even better way to His presence, not in animal sacrifices or human priests, but through His only Son Jesus, the great High Priest, whose own entrance into the heavenly temple has completely opened our access in prayer to the Father of glory.

Daniel

When the children of Israel found themselves in foreign lands under pagan rulers, typically a few individuals would emerge who displayed deep faith and unswerving wisdom under trial. Sometimes such stalwarts rose to positions of great influence within the new regimes. Joseph in Egypt, for example, suffered the slander of Potiphar's wife, but eventually rose to manage Pharaoh's entire kingdom.

In the sixth century BC, a Judean exile named Daniel was promoted to positions of power in both Babylon and Persia. The stories about Daniel and his faithful friends have been collected in the book bearing his name. This text forms the transition between the three larger prophetic books (Isaiah, Jeremiah, Ezekiel) and the twelve smaller prophetic books which close the Old Testament.

Daniel had been handpicked, along with three other young Judean men, to receive the best education in arts and sciences available in Babylon. The four excelled in literature and wisdom, and each found a place in the king's court (1:3-21). Soon, however, they along with every other sage in Babylon faced execution if none could recount and interpret the king's ever troubling dreams (2:1-16).

God chose to reveal the dream and its interpretation to Daniel, who in turn related its meaning to King Nebuchadnezzar (2:17-45). For this the king gave Daniel authority over the entire province of Babylon. Great dangers, however, lay ahead for Daniel and his friends.

King Nebuchadnezzar commissioned a giant statute of himself to be built. It was decreed that whoever failed to worship this image would be thrown into a furnace of blazing fire. Daniel's three close friends steadfastly refused to worship the golden figure:

> *"If this be so, our God whom we serve is able to deliver us from the burning fiery furnace, and he will deliver us out of your hand, O king. But if not, be it known to you, O king, that we will not serve your gods or worship the golden image that you have set up."*
>
> Daniel 3:17-18

Quickly bound with their clothes still on, the young men (Shadrach, Meshach, and Abednego) were thrown into the fire—the heat so intense that the guards who had brought them instantly died (3:1-23).

Then the king was absolutely astonished to see four men standing unbound, unhurt in the heart of the fire! The three friends emerged from the furnace without a trace of smoke or flame. And the king acknowledged the protection and primacy of the God of Shadrach, Meshach, and Abednego (3:24-30).

But Nebuchadnezzar continued to have troubling dreams. Daniel interpreted them, explaining that the king would give up his humanity, devolving into the animal world, eating grass, growing hair like an eagle's and nails like a bird's (4:1-33).

It happened. But when his humanity was restored, the king praised God:

> *"At the end of the days I, Nebuchadnezzar, lifted my eyes to heaven, and my reason returned to me, and I blessed the Most High, and praised and honored him who lives forever,*
> *for his dominion is an everlasting dominion,*
> *and his kingdom endures from generation to generation;*
> *all the inhabitants of the earth are accounted as nothing,*
> *and he does according to his will among the host of heaven*
> *and among the inhabitants of the earth;*
> *and none can stay his hand*
> *or say to him, 'What have you done?'"*
>
> Daniel 4:34-35

Daniel's gifts and faith continued to be tested by powerful officials. During a royal banquet, Daniel interpreted handwriting inscribed by a bodiless hand on the palace wall. The message was bad news for the regent: his kingdom was at an end (5:1-30).

But Daniel was yet to face the greatest danger to his life.

When the next king came to power, Daniel's gifts were soon recognized and he was on his way to the top administrative post in the kingdom. However, the jealousy of others led to the publication of an interdict prohibiting prayer for 30 days! But Daniel continued to pray three times a day. As a result, to the king's dismay, Daniel was ordered to die in the teeth of hungry lions! (6:1-18)

The king, whose name was Darius, fasted all night. At dawn's early light, to his great relief, the fearful ruler found his subject alive.

> *Then Daniel said to the king, "O king, live forever! My God sent his angel and shut the lions' mouths, and they have not harmed me, because I was found blameless before him; and also before you, O king, I have done no harm."*
>
> Daniel 6:21-22

The king acknowledged and praised the God of Daniel (6:25-28).

The remainder of the book relates dreams which Daniel had and their interpretation. These visions are of various beasts and creatures which represent world powers and which vie for the control of people and realms (chaps. 7-12). The dreams indicate that no matter the surprise, the horror, the violence wrought by rulers and despots, the living God sees all, directs all, and judges all: that the only God is working a plan through the vagaries of life that His kingdom shall finally encompass all; that presidents and rulers today should fall down on their knees in prayer before Him who moves through the ordinary and extraordinary moments, accomplishing His will; that the battles on earth mirror conflicts in the heavenlies beyond our control, conflicts between angels and princes of the air over nations and empires (10:13-11:1); that prayer to the Ancient One on His throne is ever our best defense (7:9-10; 9:1-19).

Daniel encourages us to trust in the *Son of Man* who at one time walked the earth and one day is coming again on the clouds.

"I saw in the night visions,
and behold, with the clouds of heaven
there came one like a son of man,
and he came to the Ancient of Days
and was presented before him.
And to him was given dominion
and glory and a kingdom,
that all peoples, nations, and languages
should serve him;
his dominion is an everlasting dominion,
which shall not pass away,
and his kingdom one
that shall not be destroyed."

Daniel 7:13-14

Hosea

Of all the prophets of ancient Israel, none speaks with more passion than Hosea. He takes us into the very heart of God, where we encounter a depth of emotion that is almost beyond comprehension.

Hosea reveals to us God's affection for Israel as the ardent love of a devoted husband, the tender love of a compassionate father. Hosea shows us God's heart-wrenching anguish over Israel's unfaithful, scornful response to that love. Hosea's ability to communicate God's message so earnestly springs from the experience of life to which God called him.

When the LORD began to speak through Hosea, He commanded, "Go, take to yourself a wife of whoredom and have children of whoredom, for the land commits great whoredom by forsaking the LORD" (1:2). Hosea's own life becomes a mirror image of his prophecy, lending a piercing authenticity to his words.

Hosea's ministry spanned the last 25 years of North Israel's existence as a state, before her capital city of Samaria fell to the Assyrians in 722 BC. During this quarter century of decline, her political system, a monarchy for which she had asked, increasingly ignored the true King. Israel departed from the pure worship of the one holy God. Israel confused God with Baal, accumulating rituals of Baal-worship, many sexual in nature.

God says of His unfaithful wife Israel,

"Plead with your mother, plead—
for she is not my wife,
and I am not her husband—
that she put away her whoring from her face,
and her adultery from between her breasts.

"Upon her children also I will have no mercy,
because they are children of whoredom.
For their mother has played the whore;
she who conceived them has acted shamefully.
For she said, 'I will go after my lovers,
who give me my bread and my water,
my wool and my flax, my oil and my drink.'

"And she did not know
that it was I who gave her
the grain, the wine, and the oil,
and who lavished on her silver and gold,
which they used for Baal."

Hosea 2:2, 4-5, 8

The LORD separates from this people. He vows,

"Therefore I will take back
my grain in its time,
and my wine in its season,
and I will take away my wool and my flax,
which were to cover her nakedness.

"And I will lay waste her vines and her fig trees,
of which she said,
'These are my wages,
which my lovers have given me.'
I will make them a forest,
and the beasts of the field shall devour them.
And I will punish her for the feast days of the Baals
when she burned offerings to them
and adorned herself with her ring and jewelry,
and went after her lovers
and forgot me, declares the LORD."

Hosea 2:9, 12-13

God's anger and sense of betrayal are indisputable. But His love is unwavering. Throughout Israel's unfaithfulness, God's foremost desire is reconciliation. His yearning to win her back is undisguised:

"Therefore, behold, I will allure her,
and bring her into the wilderness,
and speak tenderly to her.
And there I will give her her vineyards."

Hosea 2:14-15a

Why would a God of infinite power and majesty concern Himself with wooing a people of such persistent disloyalty and faithlessness? Because as He later affirms, "I am God, and not man, the Holy One among you" (11:9).

While capable of feeling the full range of emotions as we know them, God is not bound by the limits of humanness. He feels and loves perfectly. So He continues.

"And I will betroth you to me forever. I will betroth you to me in righteousness and in justice, in steadfast love and in mercy. I will betroth you to me in faithfulness. And you shall know the LORD.

"And in that day I will answer, declares the LORD,
... and I will sow her for myself in the land.
And I will have mercy on No Mercy,
and I will say to Not My People, 'You are my people';
and he shall say, 'You are my God.'"

Hosea 2:19-21a, 23

Hosea next turns to another facet of God's character—His justice:

Hear the word of the LORD, O children of Israel,
for the LORD has a controversy with the inhabitants of the land.
There is no faithfulness or steadfast love,
and no knowledge of God in the land;
there is swearing, lying, murder, stealing, and committing adultery;
they break all bounds, and bloodshed follows bloodshed.

Hosea 4:1-2

A just God cannot close His eyes to evil. Sin demands punishment.

What shall I do with you, O Ephraim?
What shall I do with you, O Judah?
Your love is like a morning cloud,
like the dew that goes early away.
Therefore I have hewn them by the prophets;
I have slain them by the words of my mouth,
and my judgment goes forth as the light.

Hosea 6:4-5

We later hear God's anguish: "I long to redeem them but they speak lies against me" (7:13b). God's desire to rescue His people is profound, but He will not, He cannot, redeem a people who refuse to recognize Him. He charges:

To me they cry,
"My God, we—Israel—know you."
Israel has spurned the good;
the enemy shall pursue him.
They made kings, but not through me.
They set up princes, but I knew it not.
With their silver and gold they made idols
for their own destruction.

Hosea 8:2-4

Finally, Hosea shows us God as a loving father. With poignant tenderness the LORD recalls:

When Israel was a child, I loved him,
and out of Egypt I called my son.

Yet it was I who taught Ephraim to walk;
I took them up by their arms,
but they did not know that I healed them.
I led them with cords of kindness,
with the bands of love,
and I became to them as one who eases the yoke on their jaws,
and I bent down to them and fed them.

Hosea 11:1, 3-4

God's heart is pierced by Israel's determined refusal to repent. Yet He says, "How can I give you up, Ephraim? How can I hand you over, Israel? My heart is changed within me; all my compassion is aroused" (11:8). God the compassionate Father cannot bear to punish His beloved child. But at the same time, perfect in justice and love, He cannot bear not to. Israel will not escape punishment nor be spared pain and grief.

So I am to them like a lion;
like a leopard I will lurk beside the way.
I will fall upon them like a bear robbed of her cubs;
I will tear open their breast,
and there I will devour them like a lion,
as a wild beast would rip them open.

Hosea 13:7-8

God will execute justice, but His judgment will not mean annihilation. Beyond that terrible moment will come restoration and renewal. He says, "I will ransom them from the power of the grave; I will redeem them from death" (13:14a).

How could Israel claim this redemption? What ultimate act of penance could make up for her grievous sins? God asks only one thing.

Return, O Israel, to the LORD your God,
for you have stumbled because of your iniquity.
Take with you words
and return to the LORD;
say to him,
"Take away all iniquity;
accept what is good,
and we will pay with bulls
the vows of our lips."

Hosea 14:1-2

God responds to such sincere, single-hearted confession with infinite compassion. "I will heal their waywardness and love them freely" (14:4a).

This God who absolutely will not stand for Israel's sin, yet who also will forgive and restore those whom He has punished, is the very same God known and proclaimed by Jesus Christ. Jesus speaks of the Father's uncompromising demand for loyalty: "Love the Lord your God with all your heart and with all your soul and with all your mind and with all your strength" (Mark 12:30). He speaks of God's forgiving, redeeming love: "For God so loved the world that he gave his only begotten son, that whoever believes in him shall not perish but have eternal life" (John 3:16).

Through both his words and life, Hosea opens the door for us to this God.

Joel

The hardships on a nation unleashed by agricultural disasters—whether through drought, war or pestilence—are not easily forgotten. The memory is deeper yet when the calamity has struck the vineyards of a country, depriving its people of the intoxication of wine. The book of Joel is concerned with just such a catastrophe in the Promised Land.

No date is given for the disaster. What happened, however, had been terrifying—a tale to tell one's children and one's children's children.

A swarm, successive waves of locusts, had devastated the countryside.

> *The fields are destroyed,*
> *the ground mourns,*
> *because the grain is destroyed,*
> *the wine dries up,*
> *the oil languishes.*
> *Be ashamed, O tillers of the soil;*
> *wail, O vinedressers,*
> *for the wheat and the barley,*
> *because the harvest of the field has perished.*
> *The vine dries up;*
> *the fig tree languishes.*
> *Pomegranate, palm, and apple,*
> *all the trees of the field are dried up,*
> *and gladness dries up*
> *from the children of man.*

Joel 1:10-12

In dramatic images, enough to make one's skin crawl, Joel recounts the overwhelming assault of the locust hordes.

> *A day of darkness and gloom,*
> *a day of clouds and thick darkness!*
> *Like blackness there is spread upon the mountains*
> *a great and powerful people;*
> *their like has never been before,*
> *nor will be again after them*
> *through the years of all generations.*
> *Fire devours before them,*
> *and behind them a flame burns.*

The land is like the garden of Eden before them,
but behind them a desolate wilderness,
and nothing escapes them.
Their appearance is like the appearance of horses,
and like war horses they run.
As with the rumbling of chariots,
they leap on the tops of the mountains,
like the crackling of a flame of fire
devouring the stubble,
like a powerful army
drawn up for battle.
Before them peoples are in anguish;
all faces grow pale.
Like warriors they charge;
like soldiers they scale the wall.
They march each on his way;
they do not swerve from their paths.
They do not jostle one another;
each marches in his path;
they burst through the weapons
and are not halted.
They leap upon the city,
they run upon the walls,
they climb up into the houses,
they enter through the windows like a thief.
The earth quakes before them;
the heavens tremble.
The sun and the moon are darkened,
and the stars withdraw their shining.

Joel 2:2-10

Surprisingly, Joel announces that it is the LORD who has led these troops (2:11). It has been "the day of the LORD." Weeping and mourning are in order.

Joel does not accuse the people of any specific sins; they realize their guilt.

"Yet even now," declares the LORD,
"return to me with all your heart,
with fasting, with weeping, and with mourning;
and rend your hearts and not your garments."
Return to the LORD your God,

for he is gracious and merciful,
slow to anger, and abounding in steadfast love;
and he relents over disaster.
Who knows whether he will not turn and relent,
and leave a blessing behind him,
a grain offering and a drink offering
for the LORD your God?

Joel 2:12-14

The LORD graciously promises to send grain, wine, and oil; and food for the animals (2:18-24). God then makes an unexpected promise:

"And it shall come to pass afterward,
that I will pour out my Spirit on all flesh;
your sons and your daughters shall prophesy,
your old men shall dream dreams,
and your young men shall see visions.
Even on the male and female servants
in those days I will pour out my Spirit.

"And I will show wonders in the heavens and on the earth, blood and fire and columns of smoke. The sun shall be turned to darkness, and the moon to blood, before the great and awesome day of the LORD comes. And it shall come to pass that everyone who calls on the name of the LORD shall be saved. For in Mount Zion and in Jerusalem there shall be those who escape, as the LORD has said, and among the survivors shall be those whom the LORD calls.

Joel 2:28-32

There follows the prediction of a great gathering in a valley called "Jehoshaphat," a place where God would judge the nations—all who had plundered Judah, treating her cruelly (3:1-17).

When, then, did God pour out His Spirit and judge such a world assembly?

Fifty days after Jesus' resurrection, the apostle Peter announced on the day of Pentecost that the prediction of Joel was taking place.

Jesus had released the Holy Spirit (Acts 2:16-21, 33). There was no sound of thundering locusts' wings, but the sound of God's Spirit rushing from heaven. There was no fire ravaging crops, but the flaming tongues of manifold languages both seen and heard (Joel 2:3-5; Acts 2:2-4). It was a time of momentous decision in Jerusalem, not only for the Jews but also for the nations. "For the promise is for you and for your children and for all who are far off, everyone whom the Lord our God calls to himself" (Acts 2:39).

God had made the crucified Jesus both Lord and Messiah by raising Him from the dead. His Spirit had inspired the prophecy that everyone who now called on the name of Jesus would be saved, calling upon Him in repentance and immersion in water.

Today, twenty centuries later, the apostle's words are still as penetrating to the human heart as they were then.

> *And Peter said to them, "Repent and be baptized every one of you in the name of Jesus Christ for the forgiveness of your sins, and you will receive the gift of the Holy Spirit. For the promise is for you and for your children and for all who are far off, everyone whom the Lord our God calls to himself." And with many other words he bore witness and continued to exhort them, saying, "Save yourselves from this crooked generation." So those who received his word were baptized, and there were added that day about three thousand souls.*
>
> *And they devoted themselves to the apostles' teaching and the fellowship, to the breaking of bread and the prayers.*
>
> Acts 2:38-42

Amos

A nation is in grave danger when its leaders conspire to restrict the free expression of truth by small groups, especially the prophetic speaking of outsiders or foreigners. Israel faced this danger in the eighth century BC before catastrophe struck.

Israel's priests, closely aligned with the ruling government, wanted to protect the country and sanctuary from any outside prophetic voice. The land was at peace and prosperity was at its peak. Further, public religion was popular. The people were bringing sacrifices to the national shrine at Bethel with great regularity and in great abundance.

One priest named Amaziah tried to persuade the government to prohibit any outsiders from speaking religious truth in Israel—in particular, one foreigner named Amos, a simple shepherd from the south, from Judah.

> *Then Amaziah the priest of Bethel sent to Jeroboam king of Israel, saying, "Amos has conspired against you in the midst of the house of Israel. The land is not able to bear all his words. For thus Amos has said,*
>
> *"'Jeroboam shall die by the sword,*
> *and Israel must go into exile*
> *away from his land.'"*
>
> *And Amaziah said to Amos, "O seer, go, flee away to the land of Judah, and eat bread there, and prophesy there, but never again prophesy at Bethel, for it is the king's sanctuary, and it is a temple of the kingdom."*
>
> Amos 7:10-13

Amos, however, was not dissuaded from speaking.

> *Then Amos answered and said to Amaziah, "I was no prophet, nor a prophet's son, but I was a herdsman and a dresser of sycamore figs. But the LORD took me from following the flock, and the LORD said to me, 'Go, prophesy to my people Israel.' Now therefore hear the word of the LORD.*
>
> *"You say, 'Do not prophesy against Israel,*
> *and do not preach against the house of Isaac.'*
> *Therefore thus says the LORD:*
>
> *"'Your wife shall be a prostitute in the city,*
> *and your sons and your daughters shall fall by the sword,*
> *and your land shall be divided up with a measuring line;*
> *you yourself shall die in an unclean land,*
> *and Israel shall surely go into exile away from its land.'"*
>
> Amos 7:14-17

The oracles and poems Amos spoke against Israel have been collected in the book with his name. Israel and her priests were totally unprepared to hear the message that God sent through Amos: "Your prosperity is illusory; it is based on dishonest practices. Your religion is totally unacceptable to God!"

The people were leading lives of idleness and immorality, even introducing cultic prostitution into their worship services. The wealthy were becoming richer by defrauding their impoverished neighbors. Amos even indicts the wives of Israel's leaders for inciting their husbands to expand their wealth at the expense of the poor. God would not accept sacrifices and offerings no matter how frequent or abundant, because the priests and people were unjust and unrighteous.

"I hate, I despise your feasts,
and I take no delight in your solemn assemblies.
Even though you offer me your burnt offerings and grain offerings,
I will not accept them;
and the peace offerings of your fattened animals,
I will not look upon them.
Take away from me the noise of your songs;
to the melody of your harps I will not listen.
But let justice roll down like waters,
and righteousness like an ever-flowing stream."

Amos 5:21-24

The people could not look forward to more peace and prosperity; death awaited the nation. Indeed, Amos imagines such loss in the form of a funeral dirge which he cites over them.

Hear this word that I take up over you in lamentation,
O house of Israel:
"Fallen, no more to rise,
is the virgin Israel;
forsaken on her land,
with none to raise her up."

Amos 5:1-2

Amos knew that Israel's priests were pretending to be righteous while in reality they were greedy, acquiring wealth by crushing the poor.

Hear this, you who trample on the needy
and bring the poor of the land to an end,
saying, "When will the new moon be over,
that we may sell grain?
And the Sabbath,
that we may offer wheat for sale,

that we may make the ephah small and the shekel great
and deal deceitfully with false balances,
that we may buy the poor for silver
and the needy for a pair of sandals
and sell the chaff of the wheat?"

Amos 8:4-6

Israel's religious rituals and festivals sickened God when injustice and evil were rampant. The prohibition of prophecy and the callous disregard of justice could only bring retribution.

"Behold, the days are coming," declares the Lord GOD,
"when I will send a famine on the land—
not a famine of bread, nor a thirst for water,
but of hearing the words of the LORD.
They shall wander from sea to sea,
and from north to east;
they shall run to and fro, to seek the word of the LORD,
but they shall not find it.

Behold, the eyes of the Lord GOD are upon the sinful kingdom,
and I will destroy it from the surface of the ground,
except that I will not utterly destroy the house of Jacob,"
declares the LORD.
"For behold, I will command,
and shake the house of Israel among all the nations
as one shakes with a sieve,
but no pebble shall fall to the earth.
All the sinners of my people shall die by the sword,
who say, 'Disaster shall not overtake or meet us.'"

Amos 8:11-12; 9:8-10

God calls us to repentance. First and foremost He desires inward faithfulness and outward righteousness. Only when we have devoted our hearts to Him and our hands to serving one another will our worship be pleasing and acceptable to God.

Take away from me the noise of your songs;
to the melody of your harps I will not listen.
But let justice roll down like waters,
and righteousness like an ever-flowing stream."

Amos 5:23-24

Obadiah

Brothers may be the dearest of friends or the worst of enemies. When relationships between siblings sour or worse become poisoned, the effect on future generations can be devastating.

The bitter rivalry between the sons of Isaac—Jacob and Esau—lasted for generations. The enmity between their descendants reached its zenith in the aftermath of Jerusalem's destruction in 587 BC. The smallest book in the Old Testament, Obadiah, reflects this sad chapter in the history of God's people.

Esau's descendants, the Edomites, lived south of the Dead Sea in the dry, arid land of Edom. They built striking structures in the bare red rock. Their spot under the sun was small indeed, a country measuring 25 by 110 kilometers. Many considered the Edomites to possess great wisdom. One of Job's friends came from a city in Edom. Perhaps Job himself lived there.

After the Exodus, when Israel desired to cross Edom to enter the Promised Land, its people refused passage (Num. 20:14-21). There were subsequent battles with Saul. Later, David would bring Edom under his control. In the sixth century BC, when Judah was attacked by Babylonia and Jerusalem was being destroyed, Edom stood by and watched, not lifting a finger to help. The people of Judah never forgot.

The prophets Jeremiah (chap. 49) and Ezekiel (chap. 25) both uttered harsh words against Edom. But the strongest denunciation would come from Obadiah. Who Obadiah was we do not know. His name means "servant of God." The book shows no interest in the prophet's personality; rather, it levels a series of severe oracles against Judah's brother. Why?

Edom had taken advantage of Judah in its most vulnerable moment. When Judah had all but been stripped and decimated by Babylonia, Edom came into Jerusalem grabbing spoils of the war for herself (vs. 13). Worse, when the citizens of Jerusalem fled south, seeking refuge in Edom, its inhabitants handed the refugee-survivors over to the enemy (vs. 14).

> *On the day that you stood aloof,*
> *on the day that strangers carried off his wealth*
> *and foreigners entered his gates*
> *and cast lots for Jerusalem,*

you were like one of them.
But do not gloat over the day of your brother
in the day of his misfortune;
do not rejoice over the people of Judah
in the day of their ruin;
do not boast
in the day of distress.

Obadiah 11-12

Obadiah has a stinging prediction about Edom:

For the day of the LORD is near upon all the nations.
As you have done, it shall be done to you;
your deeds shall return on your own head.

Obadiah 15

The nations will arise for battle against Edom (vs. 1) and she will know firsthand the plunder and betrayal she had inflicted upon Judah.

How Esau has been pillaged,
his treasures sought out!
All your allies have driven you to your border;
those at peace with you have deceived you;
they have prevailed against you;
those who eat your bread have set a trap beneath you—
you have no understanding.
Will I not on that day, declares the LORD,
destroy the wise men out of Edom,
and understanding out of Mount Esau?

Obadiah 6-8

Obadiah attacks Edom's arrogance as the root cause of her problem.

The pride of your heart has deceived you,
you who live in the clefts of the rock,
in your lofty dwelling,
who say in your heart,
"Who will bring me down to the ground?"
Though you soar aloft like the eagle,
though your nest is set among the stars,
from there I will bring you down,
declares the LORD.

Obadiah 3-4

The oracles of judgment against Edom remind us of God's *justice*. God orders the world according to justice and righteousness. All nations of the earth are held accountable by the Creator for wrongs done.

The world's tribunals are not the only or final courts of justice. God sees all and judges all. But siblings and fellow humans must look first to the true fountain of reconciliation, Jesus Christ, who in His death brought the only peace that endures—reconciliation to the One who made us and loves us still.

Jonah

In countries where religion enjoys official status, it is all too easy for religious leaders to equate being patriotic with being devout. When religion embraces nationalism, however, these leaders too easily feel the opportunity to ask the state to exclude alternative groups from enjoying full religious freedom.

In eighth century Israel, a prophet named Jonah delivered oracles to his home country which were highly nationalistic, promoting the expansion of the northern kingdom to boundaries reminiscent of the glory days of Solomon. Jonah's pride in his homeland also led him, along with his fellow countrymen, to abhor the power and intentions of their brutal enemy to the north, Assyria.

A strange and unexpected thing happened to Jonah, however.

> *Now the word of the LORD came to Jonah the son of Amittai, saying, "Arise, go to Nineveh, that great city, and call out against it, for their evil has come up before me."*
>
> Jonah 1:1-2

Often, God inspired His prophets to speak about foreign nations. In this instance, however, God tells Jonah to actually go to a foreign nation, Assyria, and its great city of 120,000 people, Nineveh.

But Jonah disobeyed God. He caught a boat heading in the opposite direction. The God of heaven, however, hurled a great wind on the sea and the ship threatened to break apart. Jonah understood that his disobedience was the cause of their distress and requested his fellow sailors throw him overboard. They at first refused, but soon realized they had no other choice. When the mariners threw Jonah into the sea, the storm ceased its raging.

> *Then the men feared the LORD exceedingly, and they offered a sacrifice to the LORD and made vows.*
> *And the LORD appointed a great fish to swallow up Jonah. And Jonah was in the belly of the fish three days and three nights.*
>
> Jonah 1:16-17

In the belly of the fish, Jonah prayed confidently of the LORD's deliverance. His prayer is conspicuous, however, for the absence of any confession of disobedience or repentance. Nevertheless, the LORD spoke to the fish and the fish spewed Jonah out—conveniently onto dry land rather than back into the sea (2:1-10).

Again the word of the LORD commanded Jonah to go to Nineveh and preach. This time he went.

> *Jonah began to go into the city, going a day's journey. And he called out, "Yet forty days, and Nineveh shall be overthrown!"*
>
> Jonah 3:4

Incredibly, the violent Ninevites responded. Not only the people, but the king himself repented, declaring a fast and a period of mourning for humans and animals alike (3:5-9). To Jonah's great displeasure (but not surprise), the LORD did not destroy Nineveh on Day 41.

> *When God saw what they did, how they turned from their evil way, God relented of the disaster that he had said he would do to them, and he did not do it.*
>
> *But it displeased Jonah exceedingly, and he was angry. And he prayed to the LORD and said, "O LORD, is not this what I said when I was yet in my country? That is why I made haste to flee to Tarshish; for I knew that you are a gracious God and merciful, slow to anger and abounding in steadfast love, and relenting from disaster. Therefore now, O LORD, please take my life from me, for it is better for me to die than to live."*
>
> Jonah 3:10-4:3

Jonah goes to the outskirts of the city and waits, either for Nineveh to return to its evil ways or for God to change His mind and proceed with the city's destruction (4:5).

As He had been gracious to Jonah in delivering him from the sea, so God is gracious again in providing him with shade from the heat of the day. Even this, however, occasions Jonah's anger when the shade bush withers the next morning (4:6-10). The book ends with God questioning Jonah's concerns and priorities.

> *And should not I pity Nineveh, that great city, in which there are more than 120,000 persons who do not know their right hand from their left, and also much cattle?"*
>
> Jonah 4:11

Jonah, like a good patriot/nationalist, did not want the enemy (in this case, Assyria) to win. Jonah wanted the God of Israel to take care of Israel, not other countries. Jonah understood God's character and knew that if Nineveh did repent He would not destroy them. Jonah wanted them overthrown and no longer to threaten Israel. Why should Jonah have to give a false prophecy if God would change His mind and void His warning?

Jonah was too parochial in his thinking. The God of Israel was not only God of heaven but also God of all nations of the earth. He was the true and only God of the seamen as well as the God of the Ninevites. Jonah's nationalism had blinded him to the love and care of God for His whole creation.

As it would happen, this immediate rescue of Nineveh did not bode well for Israel. A few years later, in 721 BC, the Assyrians destroyed Israel and took the people into captivity. Eventually Assyria would be defeated. But for the moment Jonah's preaching enabled Nineveh to survive and Assyria to be used by God against Israel.

Jonah's nationalism blinded him to God's sovereignty over all peoples of the earth. God desires all nations to repent of their wickedness and violence lest they face destruction. No religious leaders should ever equate patriotism with holiness or encourage a country to hate its strangers and aliens.

If God could be concerned about Nineveh's ignorance, so also must we be concerned that every land hears the news of the Man who stayed in the belly of the earth three days but was raised from the dead to give healing, hope, and salvation to the nations.

Micah

The prophet Micah lived during the last half of the eighth century BC, when Amos and Hosea were prophesying to the northern state of Israel and Isaiah along with Micah were active in the southern state of Judah. These were perilous times for both countries.

In 722 BC, the northern capital of Samaria fell to the Assyrians and Israel was no more. Judah was able to escape only because she was a satellite state of Assyria. Twenty years later Judah tried to rebel, only to see 46 fortified towns fall to the Assyrians. Jerusalem was besieged until King Hezekiah paid tribute.

Like Isaiah, Micah spoke in and around Jerusalem. Unlike Isaiah, Micah was a man of the countryside. He had lived, worked, and perhaps served as a civic leader in the small village of Moresheth-gath, a border town about 40 kilometers southwest of Jerusalem. As an outsider, Micah could perhaps see more clearly than the inhabitants of Jerusalem what was wrong with their city and their nation. In any case, Micah minced no words as he delivered God's words of judgment.

Corruption in Judah and Jerusalem started at the top, with both political and religious leaders always eager to accept a bribe.

> *Hear this, you heads of the house of Jacob*
> *and rulers of the house of Israel,*
> *who detest justice*
> *and make crooked all that is straight,*
> *who build Zion with blood*
> *and Jerusalem with iniquity.*
> *Its heads give judgment for a bribe;*
> *its priests teach for a price;*
> *its prophets practice divination for money;*
> *yet they lean on the LORD and say,*
> *"Is not the LORD in the midst of us?*
> *No disaster shall come upon us."*
> *Therefore because of you*
> *Zion shall be plowed as a field;*
> *Jerusalem shall become a heap of ruins,*
> *and the mountain of the house a wooded height.*

Micah 3:9-12

Prophets in particular would say anything you wanted, provided you paid them to say it.

Thus says the LORD concerning the prophets
who lead my people astray,
who cry "Peace"
when they have something to eat,
but declare war against him
who puts nothing into their mouths.
Therefore it shall be night to you, without vision,
and darkness to you, without divination.
The sun shall go down on the prophets,
and the day shall be black over them;
the seers shall be disgraced,
and the diviners put to shame;
they shall all cover their lips,
for there is no answer from God.

Micah 3:5-7

The politicians and judges acted as cannibals, devouring their own people!

Hear, you heads of Jacob
and rulers of the house of Israel!
Is it not for you to know justice?—
you who hate the good and love the evil,
who tear the skin from off my people
and their flesh from off their bones,
who eat the flesh of my people,
and flay their skin from off them,
and break their bones in pieces
and chop them up like meat in a pot,
like flesh in a cauldron.

Micah 3:1b-3

A gruesome description of life in the Jerusalem of Micah's day! Even individual family units were not safe from the infiltration of evil.

Put no trust in a neighbor;
have no confidence in a friend;
guard the doors of your mouth
from her who lies in your arms;
for the son treats the father with contempt,

the daughter rises up against her mother,
the daughter-in-law against her mother-in-law;
a man's enemies are the men of his own house.

Micah 7:5-6

The summation of God's charges against His people comes in Micah 6:1-8, a passage that many have called the high-water mark of all Israelite prophecy. The scene is set in a courtroom that the LORD enters, bringing His case against Israel. God is the plaintiff, Israel is the defendant, and the mountains and hills are both witnesses and jury.

God presents His case, which rests on all that He has done for His people. Israel has no answer except to imply, through sarcastic suggestions of exorbitant offerings, that God demands too much. The jury announces its verdict: God does not require unreasonable sacrifice. He does expect His people to keep their covenant with Him and with one another:

Hear what the LORD says:
Arise, plead your case before the mountains,
and let the hills hear your voice.
Hear, you mountains, the indictment of the LORD,
and you enduring foundations of the earth,
for the LORD has an indictment against his people,
and he will contend with Israel.
"O my people, what have I done to you?
How have I wearied you? Answer me!
For I brought you up from the land of Egypt
and redeemed you from the house of slavery,
and I sent before you Moses,
Aaron, and Miriam.
O my people, remember what Balak king of Moab devised,
and what Balaam the son of Beor answered him,
and what happened from Shittim to Gilgal,
that you may know the righteous acts of the LORD."

"With what shall I come before the LORD,
and bow myself before God on high?
Shall I come before him with burnt offerings,
with calves a year old?
Will the LORD be pleased with thousands of rams,
with ten thousands of rivers of oil?
Shall I give my firstborn for my transgression,

the fruit of my body for the sin of my soul?"
He has told you, O man, what is good;
and what does the LORD require of you
but to do justice, and to love kindness,
and to walk humbly with your God?

Micah 6:1-8

God still demands this—as Jesus Himself said to those who tithed the smallest herbs of their gardens while ignoring God's fundamental expectations.

> *"Woe to you, scribes and Pharisees, hypocrites! For you tithe mint and dill and cumin, and have neglected the weightier matters of the law: justice and mercy and faithfulness. These you ought to have done, without neglecting the others."*
>
> Matthew 23:23

Given the stubborn resistance of his countrymen to God's commands, Micah knew that punishment was inevitable:

Therefore I strike you with a grievous blow,
making you desolate because of your sins.
You shall eat, but not be satisfied,
and there shall be hunger within you;
you shall put away, but not preserve,
and what you preserve I will give to the sword.
You shall sow, but not reap;
you shall tread olives, but not anoint yourselves with oil;
you shall tread grapes, but not drink wine.

Micah 6:13-15

Micah was also shown that beyond the darkness of judgment there would come the dawn of peace.

It shall come to pass in the latter days
that the mountain of the house of the LORD
shall be established as the highest of the mountains,
and it shall be lifted up above the hills;
and peoples shall flow to it,
and many nations shall come, and say:
"Come, let us go up to the mountain of the LORD,
to the house of the God of Jacob,

that he may teach us his ways
and that we may walk in his paths."
For out of Zion shall go forth the law,
and the word of the LORD from Jerusalem.
He shall judge between many peoples,
and shall decide disputes for strong nations far away;
and they shall beat their swords into plowshares,
and their spears into pruning hooks;
nation shall not lift up sword against nation,
neither shall they learn war anymore;
but they shall sit every man under his vine and under his fig tree,
and no one shall make them afraid,
for the mouth of the LORD of hosts has spoken.

Micah 4:1-4

This God who was like none other would pardon their iniquities out of His profound compassion for them.

Who is a God like you, pardoning iniquity
and passing over transgression
for the remnant of his inheritance?
He does not retain his anger forever,
because he delights in steadfast love.
He will again have compassion on us;
he will tread our iniquities underfoot.
You will cast all our sins
into the depths of the sea.

Micah 7:18-19

And how would this forgiveness and restoration be accomplished? By a new and righteous ruler who would establish God's peace.

But you, O Bethlehem Ephrathah,
who are too little to be among the clans of Judah,
from you shall come forth for me
one who is to be ruler in Israel,
whose coming forth is from of old,
from ancient days.
Therefore he shall give them up until the time
when she who is in labor has given birth;
then the rest of his brothers shall return
to the people of Israel.

And he shall stand and shepherd his flock in the strength of the
LORD,
in the majesty of the name of the LORD his God.
And they shall dwell secure, for now he shall be great
to the ends of the earth.
And he shall be their peace.

Micah 5:2-5a

In God's good time that Ruler would come, born in Bethlehem, giving His very life to establish the kingdom of God, over which He rules today and until the end of time—Jesus, the Messiah.

Nahum

Assyria, the superpower on the world's stage in the seventh century BC, was renown in the ancient Near East—not for its high culture but for its military ruthlessness. When Jonah walked through the capital proclaiming its destruction in 40 days, the city did not debate its guilt or cruelty or violent ways. On behalf of its people, the king of Nineveh responded, leading a national movement of repentance (Jonah 3:1-10). God changed His mind and spared Nineveh. Repentance, however, can be short lived!

Later, another prophet named Nahum also announced judgment oracles against the city. Nineveh's destruction was inescapable. There would be no rescue.

The book of Nahum begins with theology: God is a jealous God who avenges wrongdoing. He is slow to take irreversible action. He had given opportunity earlier for Nineveh to repent. But He will eventually deal with guilt—even the guilt of mighty Assyria and its capital city.

Nineveh was large, impressive, and fortified. Records indicate that it was 10 km in circumference and within its ramparts could hold a population of 300,000 people. It seemed impregnable with its dense wall and surrounding moats.

Nahum declared, however, that the earth itself was helpless and defenseless before the presence and movement of God.

The LORD will by no means clear the guilty.
His way is in whirlwind and storm,

and the clouds are the dust of his feet.
He rebukes the sea and makes it dry;
he dries up all the rivers;
Bashan and Carmel wither;
the bloom of Lebanon withers.
The mountains quake before him;
the hills melt;
the earth heaves before him,
the world and all who dwell in it.
Who can stand before his indignation?
Who can endure the heat of his anger?
His wrath is poured out like fire,
and the rocks are broken into pieces by him.

Nahum 1:3b-6

In Nineveh, the kings of Assyria have plotted against the God of Israel (1:9). The end is sure. Their carved idols will be destroyed (1:14). Judah can take comfort in the prospect of Assyria's downfall (1:15).

With penetrating vision Nahum can already see Nineveh under siege. The floodgates are open. Nineveh will be plundered as it has so often plundered others (2:1-9).

In her grand carvings, Assyria envisioned herself in lionesque images. Like lions, Assyria had chosen and eaten its prey. But no longer; Assyria's prey will be cut off (2:10-13). Nahum depicts the audible and visual aspects of Nineveh's doom.

The crack of the whip, and rumble of the wheel,
galloping horse and bounding chariot!
Horsemen charging,
flashing sword and glittering spear,
hosts of slain,
heaps of corpses,
dead bodies without end—
they stumble over the bodies!
And all for the countless whorings of the prostitute,
graceful and of deadly charms,
who betrays nations with her whorings,
and peoples with her charms.
Behold, I am against you,
declares the LORD of hosts,

and will lift up your skirts over your face;
and I will make nations look at your nakedness
and kingdoms at your shame.
I will throw filth at you
and treat you with contempt
and make you a spectacle.
And all who look at you will shrink from you and say,
"Wasted is Nineveh; who will grieve for her?"
Where shall I seek comforters for you?

Nahum 3:2-7

On one occasion Assyria had taken impenetrable Thebes, the capital of Egypt. Does she really think she is less vulnerable than Thebes (3:8-11)? No. Assyria's troops are like weak women. The gates of Nineveh are open to enemy legions.

Nineveh may try to fortify itself (3:14-15). When the battle rages, however, the generals will flee like grasshoppers on a hot day (3:15-17). Already her leaders are asleep. Already Nineveh is mortally wounded (3:18-19).

Nineveh, indeed, falls in 622 BC. God had used Assyria to punish His people in the past. But Assyria had overstepped her bounds. Assyria must be punished. She is.

Nahum, whose name means "comfort," delivered a message of God's justice which comforted Judah. God was the Lord of Assyria as even today He is Lord over every nation on the face of the earth. Today as then, God sees and judges the nations according to equity, justice, and righteousness—that His kingdom may come more fully and His will be done on earth as it is done in heaven.

Habakkuk

A true prophet was more than a mechanical mouthpiece for God. A true prophet took seriously the word of God for his own life with all the strain and complications it might bring, both for consistent thinking and for honest living.

Habakkuk was such a prophet. He apparently lived in the late seventh century BC, the time of Assyria's decline and Babylon's ascendancy.

Whatever the immediate situation, Habakkuk found himself overwhelmed with the sheer weight and breadth of violence and lawlessness in his homeland. Because Habakkuk believed God was just and justice would prevail, he cried out in perplexity at the absence of divine intervention:

O LORD, how long shall I cry for help,
and you will not hear?
Or cry to you "Violence!"
and you will not save?
Why do you make me see iniquity,
and why do you idly look at wrong?
Destruction and violence are before me;
strife and contention arise.
So the law is paralyzed,
and justice never goes forth.
For the wicked surround the righteous;
so justice goes forth perverted.

Habakkuk 1:2-4

He surely was not prepared to hear God's response to his dilemma:

"Look among the nations, and see;
wonder and be astounded.
For I am doing a work in your days
that you would not believe if told.
For behold, I am raising up the Chaldeans,
that bitter and hasty nation,
who march through the breadth of the earth,
to seize dwellings not their own."

Habakkuk 1:5-6

It was an absolute shock that God would suggest using evil Babylon to right wrongs! How could God even gaze at the impure Babylonians? How could God be involved with the tactics the enemy employed in treating captives? (1:12-17) Habakkuk prefers to retreat to a solitary watchtower and wait there for God's response (2:1).

God's response does not reveal why God's reaction time is not man's. Rather, He reminds the prophet that the righteous always live by faithfulness (2:4). The faithful remember that

If it seems slow, wait for it;
it will surely come; it will not delay.

Habakkuk 2:3b

The righteous must remember what will happen finally to the treacherous. Five “woes” are pronounced on such people. These woes effect judgment on the unrighteous while at the same time give warning to the righteous.

Woes *will* befall those who have needlessly accumulated goods in pledge (2:7-8).

Woes *will* befall those who have built houses through dishonest means (2:9-11).

Woes *will* befall those who build cities and communities through bloodshed and iniquity (2:12-14).

Woes *will* befall those who induce neighbors into drunkenness only to manipulate them (2:15-17).

Woes *will* befall those who trust idols to instruct them in truth (2:18-19).

Like Job’s response after God encountered him, Habakkuk too reacts with awe to God’s instruction and revelation.

> *O Lord, I have heard the report of you,*
> *and your work, O Lord, do I fear.*
> *In the midst of the years revive it;*
> *in the midst of the years make it known;*
> *in wrath remember mercy.*
> *God came from Teman,*
> *and the Holy One from Mount Paran.*
> *His splendor covered the heavens,*
> *and the earth was full of his praise.*
> *His brightness was like the light;*
> *rays flashed from his hand;*
> *and there he veiled his power.*
> *Before him went pestilence,*
> *and plague followed at his heels.*
> *He stood and measured the earth;*
> *he looked and shook the nations;*
> *then the eternal mountains were scattered;*
> *the everlasting hills sank low.*
> *His were the everlasting ways.*
>
> *I hear, and my body trembles;*
> *my lips quiver at the sound;*
> *rottenness enters into my bones;*

my legs tremble beneath me.
Yet I will quietly wait for the day of trouble
to come upon people who invade us.

Habakkuk 3:2-6, 16

How then should we respond to violence? How should we respond to undeserved hurt and hardship?

Habakkuk's response was first to cry out to God, not to man, with honest dismay about the situation. Following this, we, with Habakkuk may well receive a word of God we do not expect or want. The prophet, however, teaches us to persevere with God's word while continuing to express incomprehension or even dismay.

What Habakkuk finally had to hear very closely and learn very deeply is the lesson we too must learn well: "the righteous live by faithfulness." The righteous must wait and wait and wait. But Paul's use of this passage in his letter to the Christians at Rome amplifies its meaning for us.

> *For I am not ashamed of the gospel, for it is the power of God for salvation to everyone who believes, to the Jew first and also to the Greek. For in it the righteousness of God is revealed from faith for faith, as it is written, "The righteous shall live by faith."*
>
> Romans 1:16-17

The power to endure violence and suffering comes finally through seeing and understanding the faithfulness and vindication of the One whose sufferings are the very gospel message itself.

Zephaniah

From the beginning paradise was not to last very long. In the ten generations from Adam to Noah wickedness increased exponentially on earth. Such evil grieved God deeply, so much so that He said, "I will blot out man whom I have created from the face of the land, man and animals and creeping things and birds of the heavens, for I am sorry that I have made them" (Genesis 6:7).

In the first half of the seventh century BC, wickedness again filled the earth. God declared, in words reminiscent of Noah's day,

"I will utterly sweep away everything
from the face of the earth," declares the LORD.
"I will sweep away man and beast;
I will sweep away the birds of the heavens
and the fish of the sea,
and the rubble with the wicked.
I will cut off mankind
from the face of the earth," declares the LORD.

These words come from the prophet Zephaniah, the first in a line of great men including Jeremiah who declared to Judah the judgment she was facing. Zephaniah delivered his message in the early days of Josiah, king of Judah. Josiah, taking his words to heart, tried fervently to reverse Judah's evil ways and idolatry. He made progress but his reforms were cut short by a tragic early death.

What Josiah faced and Zephaniah opposed was the continued presence of Baal devotees in Judah (1:4)—a terrible offense to the One who had blessed His people so often with rain and crops! Not only Baal, but the gods of Judah's neighbors (Milcom for example, 1:6) found their names on the lips of God's people. Such scandalous conditions were the result of depraved leaders.

Her officials within her
are roaring lions;
her judges are evening wolves
that leave nothing till the morning.
Her prophets are fickle, treacherous men;
her priests profane what is holy;
they do violence to the law.

Zephaniah 3:3-4

Evil had brought prosperity to greedy traders and merchants. Since violence and fraud apparently brought success, at least near-term success, and since wickedness appeared to go unpunished, many were beginning to say, "The LORD will not do good, nor will he do ill" (1:12b).

Zephaniah announces that God has come to the end of His patience. He will pick up a flashlight and go into the darkest night to search and find the lazy drunks who now believe He no longer cares. But God does care. God declares the "day is near."

The great day of the LORD is near,
near and hastening fast;
the sound of the day of the LORD is bitter;
the mighty man cries aloud there.
A day of wrath is that day,
a day of distress and anguish,
a day of ruin and devastation,
a day of darkness and gloom,
a day of clouds and thick darkness,
a day of trumpet blast and battle cry
against the fortified cities
and against the lofty battlements.

Zephaniah 1:14-16

In the middle of such hopeless words, Zephaniah reminds Judah that there are still those who are ashamed of their sinful condition before God and still able to turn to Him.

Seek the LORD, all you humble of the land,
who do his just commands;
seek righteousness; seek humility;
perhaps you may be hidden
on the day of the anger of the LORD.

Zephaniah 2:3

While judgment begins at the household of God, God still holds the other nations of the world accountable—as He does today. So, Zephaniah proclaims the destruction of Philistia (2:4-7), of Moab and Ammon with their scoffing pride (2:8-11), of Ethiopia, and finally of Assyria and Nineveh.

This is the exultant city
that lived securely,
that said in her heart,
"I am, and there is no one else."
What a desolation she has become,
a lair for wild beasts!
Everyone who passes by her
hisses and shakes his fist.

Zephaniah 2:15

But God's actions in response to sin are never merely retributive. God always has a larger purpose in mind, a plan for rescuing His creation. And in Zephaniah's message God announces a reversal of Babel:

> *"For at that time I will change the speech of the peoples*
> *to a pure speech,*
> *that all of them may call upon the name of the* LORD
> *and serve him with one accord."*

Zephaniah 3:9

What God promises for the future seems too good to be true.

> *"But I will leave in your midst*
> *a people humble and lowly.*
> *They shall seek refuge in the name of the* LORD,
> *those who are left in Israel;*
> *they shall do no injustice*
> *and speak no lies,*
> *nor shall there be found in their mouth*
> *a deceitful tongue.*
> *For they shall graze and lie down,*
> *and none shall make them afraid.*
>
> *"The* LORD *your God is in your midst,*
> *a mighty one who will save;*
> *he will rejoice over you with gladness;*
> *he will quiet you by his love;*
> *he will exult over you with loud singing.*
> *I will gather those of you who mourn for the festival,*
> *so that you will no longer suffer reproach."*

Zephaniah 3:12-13, 17-18

Jerusalem would be destroyed. Judah would be deported. But the people would one day return from exile, back to the land of promise.

Yet things would never be the same until another King, not of this earth but from above, would walk among the masses, telling the poor in spirit of their blessed inheritance and inviting all to seek first His kingdom and His righteousness that they might enjoy the delights of a kingdom prepared before the universe itself was created.

A return to paradise.

Haggai

Finding food for hungry mouths, staying warm in cold winters, providing relief from life's diseases, securing protection from thieves—such efforts consume our energies. But do they bring us satisfaction?

The prophet Haggai asked this question in 520 BC of the Judean leaders who had returned to Jerusalem from exile in Babylonia.

> *Now, therefore, thus says the LORD of hosts: Consider your ways. You have sown much, and harvested little. You eat, but you never have enough; you drink, but you never have your fill. You clothe yourselves, but no one is warm. And he who earns wages does so to put them into a bag with holes.*
>
> Haggai 1:5-6

Earlier in 538 BC, excitement had filled the air when the exiles had been released by Persian edict to return home. Expectations ran high. But now, 18 years later, when Haggai begins to speak the word of the LORD in August 520 BC, the economy and living conditions of Judah are in poor shape. Haggai reveals this as the direct result of God's intervening hand:

> *"Therefore the heavens above you have withheld the dew, and the earth has withheld its produce. And I have called for a drought on the land and the hills, on the grain, the new wine, the oil, on what the ground brings forth, on man and beast, and on all their labors."*
>
> Haggai 1:10-11

Why? The prophet explains:

> *"Is it a time for you yourselves to dwell in your paneled houses, while this house lies in ruins?*
> *"You looked for much, and behold, it came to little. And when you brought it home, I blew it away. Why? declares the LORD of hosts. Because of my house that lies in ruins, while each of you busies himself with his own house."*
>
> Haggai 1:4, 9

As it happened, the leaders had busied themselves satisfying their own desires while neglecting God's desire that His people rebuild His house, the temple, which had been burned to the ground 67 years earlier.

Haggai's message, however, effects a change. The leaders, the governor Zerubbabel, and the high priest Joshua obey the voice of God. Their spirits are aroused to action and work begins again on the house of the LORD (1:12-15).

As the building starts to take shape, however, discouragement sets in. The older returnees remember the splendor and wealth of Solomon's temple. The present house looks so meager and modest by comparison. Haggai admonishes the people to take courage.

> *For thus says the LORD of hosts: Yet once more, in a little while, I will shake the heavens and the earth and the sea and the dry land. And I will shake all nations, so that the treasures of all nations shall come in, and I will fill this house with glory, says the LORD of hosts. The silver is mine, and the gold is mine, declares the LORD of hosts. The latter glory of this house shall be greater than the former, says the LORD of hosts. And in this place I will give peace, declares the LORD of hosts.'"*
>
> Haggai 2:6-9

A consecrated place for receiving offerings will mean fruitfulness in the field (2:10-19). What God blesses in the land, however, is but a small sample of what He will do in the political realm. Haggai declares that the line of kingship through David has not come to an end (2:20-23). Indeed, through the lineage of Zerubbabel is eventually born in Bethlehem of Judea, Jesus the Messiah, the son of David (Matthew 1:1, 13, 16).

The rebuilding of the temple, then, was God's way of awakening His people to their misplaced priorities. Today, ever since the resurrection of Jesus, God is pleased to dwell by His Spirit in the church, the body of Christ—not in a building, but in a holy people. What pleases God is believers meeting together regularly for prayer, singing, encouragement, eating, the reading of Scripture, and fellowship.

At Jesus' death the curtain in the temple was ripped apart. Forty years later, His prediction that the temple would be destroyed came true. Paul reminded the Corinthian Christians (and us) that it is the people of God who form His temple:

> *Do you not know that you are God's temple and that God's Spirit dwells in you?*

What agreement has the temple of God with idols? For we are the temple of the living God; as God said,

"I will make my dwelling among them and walk among them,
and I will be their God,
and they shall be my people."

1 Corinthians 3:16; 2 Corinthians 6:16

So returning to our first question, is facing and meeting the harsh realities of life all that we should expect in life? Haggai says no.

Our best efforts seem always to fall short. And they will continue to fall short until our ears hear the news about Jesus and our hearts are touched by God's love for His creation and His love for the church which His Son died to save, to create, to sanctify, to commission, to build—until the time God once more shakes the cosmos, not to bring the nations' wealth to Jerusalem, but to leave standing the unshakable kingdom, in which we share even now as we give thanks to God (Hebrews 12:25-29).

Zechariah

In the Old Testament, God conveyed His messages directly (unmediated) to His servants the prophets. In the case of one prophet, however, the LORD communicated His message quite differently.

With Zechariah, God used an angel to interpret a series of eight visions the prophet saw in the night—visions and oracles he then revealed to the returned exiles. These have been collected in the book of Zechariah, the next to last book in the Old Testament.

How we imagine life is how we live it. Our imaginations about reality, whether true or false, engage our spirits and our enthusiasms, our likes and dislikes, our pursuits and our fears. The exiles who returned from Babylonia carried with them imaginations filled with stories about the destruction of Jerusalem. How then to reimagine the future? What could they see to give them hope amid burned buildings and foreign rule?

The prophet Haggai had reasoned with them, urging and chiding them to have courage and stamina in rebuilding the temple. Zechariah approaches the spirit of the people differently. Zechariah attempts to recharge and reshape their imaginations to see the present and the future in a new light. He does so by retelling the visions he had seen in the night.

In the first and last visions, the imagination is to envision horses and chariots from God patrolling the earth:

> *"I saw in the night, and behold, a man riding on a red horse! He was standing among the myrtle trees in the glen, and behind him were red, sorrel, and white horses. Then I said, 'What are these, my lord?' The angel who talked with me said to me, 'I will show you what they are.' So the man who was standing among the myrtle trees answered, 'These are they whom the LORD has sent to patrol the earth.' And they answered the angel of the LORD who was standing among the myrtle trees, and said, 'We have patrolled the earth, and behold, all the earth remains at rest.'"*
>
> Zechariah 1:8-11

God is watching, aware of all activities of all nations. He has permitted other peoples to punish Judah, but they have gone too far. And now God has stopped the foes from the north. Jerusalem will be comforted.

In another vision, Zechariah sees horns about to be beaten by the blacksmith's hammer. The powers who scattered Judah and Israel will themselves be shattered (1:18-21). Again Zechariah looks up and sees a young man ready to measure the dimensions of Jerusalem. But an angel says it cannot be done:

> *"Run, say to that young man, 'Jerusalem shall be inhabited as villages without walls, because of the multitude of people and livestock in it. And I will be to her a wall of fire all around, declares the LORD, and I will be the glory in her midst.'"*
>
> Zechariah 2:4-5

Zechariah is shown the high priest Joshua in filthy clothes, being accused by Job's old adversary Satan. Is the priesthood so dirty as to be beyond cleansing and renewal? No. Joshua is given clean clothes and festal apparel (3:1-10).

In the fifth vision, Zechariah is shown a tall oil lamp continually supplied with oil from two olive trees (4:1-14). God provides and is the only true light in the world. But it is two of His anointed servants who have a vital role in providing the fuel for effecting God's plans.

> *Then I said to him, "What are these two olive trees on the right and the left of the lampstand?" And a second time I answered*

and said to him, "What are these two branches of the olive trees, which are beside the two golden pipes from which the golden oil is poured out?" He said to me, "Do you not know what these are?" I said, "No, my lord." Then he said, "These are the two anointed ones who stand by the Lord of the whole earth."

Zechariah 4:11-14

In the seventh vision, Zechariah sees a strange thing: A woman in a basket with a leaden cover is being borne aloft by two winged females who transport the basket to the land of Babel, the land of confused languages, the land of Babylon. The woman is Wickedness contained, captured, and removed from Judah's presence (5:5-11).

Through these eight visions God attempts to convey to shattered imaginations new imaginings of future possibilities. Reasoning is not enough; the pictures of the heart have to be repainted.

This done, the book proceeds to various oracles and promises intended to promote endurance in the people who have recently returned to Judah.

Thus says the LORD *of hosts: Old men and old women shall again sit in the streets of Jerusalem, each with staff in hand because of great age. And the streets of the city shall be full of boys and girls playing in its streets. Thus says the* LORD *of hosts: If it is marvelous in the sight of the remnant of this people in those days, should it also be marvelous in my sight, declares the* LORD *of hosts? Thus says the* LORD *of hosts: Behold, I will save my people from the east country and from the west country, and I will bring them to dwell in the midst of Jerusalem. And they shall be my people, and I will be their God, in faithfulness and in righteousness."*

Zechariah 8:4-8

God will deal with the foreign nations, inducing even in them the desire to seek God's presence among God's people. It begins with a most humble event:

Rejoice greatly, O daughter of Zion!
Shout aloud, O daughter of Jerusalem!
Behold, your king is coming to you;
righteous and having salvation is he,
humble and mounted on a donkey,

on a colt, the foal of a donkey.
I will cut off the chariot from Ephraim
and the war horse from Jerusalem;
and the battle bow shall be cut off,
and he shall speak peace to the nations;
his rule shall be from sea to sea,
and from the River to the ends of the earth.

Zechariah 9:9-10

Jesus indeed enters Jerusalem on a donkey. He becomes King of Kings through the vindication of resurrection from the dead.

Zechariah's words encompass a grand landscape. They take the breath away with the strength and conviction of their imagination. All our exciting dreams and selfish visions pale in comparison with the true revelation Zechariah sees—the day which will be like no other, the last day which ends the counting of days.

> *On that day there shall be no light, cold, or frost. And there shall be a unique day, which is known to the* LORD, *neither day nor night, but at evening time there shall be light.*
>
> *On that day living waters shall flow out from Jerusalem, half of them to the eastern sea and half of them to the western sea. It shall continue in summer as in winter.*
>
> *And the* LORD *will be king over all the earth. On that day the* LORD *will be one and his name one.*

Zechariah 14:6-9

Come, Lord Jesus! *Maranatha*.

Malachi

By the fifth century BC the temple in Jerusalem had been rebuilt and the priests were again sacrificing animals on its altar. Such sacrificial routines were intended to please the God of Judah. The prophet Malachi, in the last book of the Old Testament, says they do not!

> *Oh that there were one among you who would shut the doors, that you might not kindle fire on my altar in vain! I have no*

pleasure in you, says the LORD of hosts, and I will not accept an offering from your hand.

Malachi 1:10

Why would God not accept such offerings? Malachi makes it clear:

By offering polluted food upon my altar. But you say, 'How have we polluted you?' By saying that the LORD's table may be despised. When you offer blind animals in sacrifice, is that not evil? And when you offer those that are lame or sick, is that not evil? Present that to your governor; will he accept you or show you favor? says the LORD of hosts.

But you profane it when you say that the LORD's table is polluted, and its fruit, that is, its food may be despised. But you say, 'What a weariness this is,' and you snort at it, says the LORD of hosts. You bring what has been taken by violence or is lame or sick, and this you bring as your offering! Shall I accept that from your hand? says the LORD. Cursed be the cheat who has a male in his flock, and vows it, and yet sacrifices to the LORD what is blemished. For I am a great King, says the LORD of hosts, and my name will be feared among the nations.

Malachi 1:7-8, 12-14

The priests have failed terribly in their calling. They have no enthusiasm in their work. It matters little to them if the animal offered required real sacrifice on the part of the worshipper or if the offering happened to be a mere castaway of the flock or herd.

The priests had failed to teach the people the love of God (1:2-5). The men of Judah showed no reluctance to love foreign gods, introduced to them through the foreign women they had married. God hates the divorce which had given license to these men to leave their Israelite wives for idolatrous wives (2:11-16).

Will God then rescue His people or let them face stringent judgment? Malachi announces that the God of love has a plan. He will not immediately bring Judah into severe judgment. He will first send a messenger to prepare the way. His work will turn hearts to the LORD.

He will sit as a refiner and purifier of silver, and he will purify the sons of Levi and refine them like gold and silver, and they will bring offerings in righteousness to the LORD. Then the offering of Judah and Jerusalem will be pleasing to the LORD as in the days of old and as in former years.

Malachi 3:3-4

Then the LORD will draw near for judgment (3:5).

Who is this mysterious messenger? Malachi says that God will send the prophet Elijah before the great judgment day. This is not surprising since Elijah was understood to be "on call" by God, waiting in his chariot of fire to return to the earth (2 Kings 2:11).

In the first century AD, Elijah does indeed return to the earth, not in a chariot but in making an appearance with Jesus, along with Moses, in a dazzling spectacle before Peter, James, and John (Mark 9:4). But this transfiguration event according to the Gospels is not the completion of Malachi's prediction. Jesus explains to His disciples that John the Baptist played the role of Elijah (Matthew 17:11-13), even though John might not have understood this as his role (cf. John 1:21-27). Thus it would be 500 years before Malachi's messenger would actually be sent by God to prepare the way for King Jesus and His kingdom.

In Malachi's time, however, a response was demanded. The people of Judah were given the opportunity to return to the LORD, even as John the Baptist 500 years later would entreat the Jews to repent and be baptized. In Malachi's time, repentance meant keeping promises and pledges made to God, bringing the full tithes (3:8-12). Repentance involved a change of heart and mind, believing that God indeed blesses the righteous (3:10-15). The wicked may prosper, but only for a brief time. God knows those who speak respectfully to one another about His name (3:16-18).

Today, what pleases God first and foremost is knowing deeply His love for us, and in that knowledge turning to Him with respect for His name; offering the best fruits of our labor; employing the best speech; speaking truth to neighbor; caring for the orphan, widow, and aged; and acting with kindness and goodness to friend and foe alike. We begin by repenting of our sins and through trust in Jesus being immersed into His death that we might receive the comfort and strength of the Holy Spirit.

Matthew 1-4

Sometime during the last years of the reign of King Herod in the early first century AD, soldiers stormed into a small Judean village named Bethlehem and began killing every male child under the age of two. The wailing of Bethlehem's mothers filled the cold night air (2:16-18).

King Herod was known for similar atrocities, but what could have triggered such ruthlessness in the massacre of innocent children? The answer given in the opening chapters of Matthew's Gospel is unbelievable. Powerful King Herod was afraid of one little baby boy born in Bethlehem.

Religious astronomers from the East had traveled the distance to Jerusalem in pursuit of an irregular moving star. These interpreters of stars and of dreams had decided this star could only signify the birth of the king of the Jews. In consultation with the Jewish religious leaders in Jerusalem, Herod took these foreigners' perceptions with utmost seriousness (2:1-8). He decided to take no chances. When the intelligent men from the East failed to inform Herod about the exact location of this baby, he reacted by having all boys in Bethlehem under two years of age slain (2:16).

The baby Herod sought, however, had escaped.

The first Gospel in the New Testament begins its story by demonstrating how correct Herod was to perceive in this child a threat to the kingdoms of the world. This baby indeed was born to be King of kings, heir to the throne of David, a son of Abraham, a son of David (1:1). The religious astronomers had correctly read the significance of the star.

When Mary, the baby's unwed mother, was discovered to be pregnant, the baby forming in her womb appeared to be illegitimate. Joseph, Mary's fiancé, would have been expected to expose Mary to public shame for such indiscretion. Joseph, a righteous man, decided rather to end his engagement to Mary quietly (1:18-19).

While asleep, however, Joseph (as his namesake of old) in a dream was confronted by an angel. He learned that the baby Mary carried had not been conceived through any sexual relations with a man, but rather had been conceived by the Holy Spirit. A word of God spoken long ago through a prophet had come to fulfillment unexpectedly in Joseph's bride to be.

"Behold, the virgin shall conceive and bear a son,
and they shall call his name Immanuel"
(which means, God with us).

Matthew 1:23

Joseph took Mary as his wife but had no sexual relations with her until after the baby was born.

Joseph indeed adopted the boy as his son through the act of naming him. The boy Jesus thus acquired a legal lineage through Joseph all the way back to King David, and even further to father Abraham.

The genealogy Matthew reports is not, however, a straight line of descent from father to son. Four times women are mentioned who interrupt the sequence of genealogical recounting. The surprise naming of Tamar, Rahab, Ruth, and the wife of Uriah prepares one somewhat for the greatest surprise, God's presence in a baby born to a young virgin girl named Mary.

For all the joy and celebration we associate with Christmas, Jesus' birth was an occasion of great suffering for some: the mothers and fathers of Bethlehem who lost their precious sons as a result of Herod's fright and jealousy. Jesus has continued ever since to arouse the strongest reactions from those who truly understand the significance of His coming and His claims.

The great prophet John, who had come preaching a message of repentance in view of the kingdom's coming and a baptism in water for repentance, this John recognized Jesus' significance. He felt Jesus should baptize him. Nevertheless Jesus was baptized by John, not for repentance, but to manifest God's will. God acknowledged Jesus' righteous act:

> *And behold, a voice from heaven said, "This is my beloved Son, with whom I am well pleased"* (Matthew 3:17).

More than Joseph's son, Jesus was God's true Son, an obedient son. His obedience was tested in the wilderness. The sons of Israel had failed the test in the desert. Jesus, however, resists the devil's invitations to unfaithfulness in the wilderness.

> *Again, the devil took him to a very high mountain and showed him all the kingdoms of the world and their glory. And he said to him,*

> *"All these I will give you, if you will fall down and worship me."*
> *Then Jesus said to him, "Be gone, Satan! For it is written,*
> *"'You shall worship the Lord your God*
> *and him only shall you serve.'"*
> *Then the devil left him, and behold, angels came and were ministering to him.*
>
> Matthew 4:8-11

Angels who had come to Joseph in his dreams giving him direction, come also to Jesus in His needs, caring for Him, refreshing Him before he begins His own preaching.

Neither the wrath of King Herod nor the deception of the devil is able to alter the pleasure and plan of God in the life of Jesus. Jesus comes to earth not as a full grown man (like Adam) nor in some non-human form (like the living creatures in heaven). God comes, as we come into the world, as a baby. From the beginning the light enraged the darkness. But the darkness could not, and still cannot, overcome the light.

Matthew 5-7

No earthly nation can long exist without good citizens. If good citizenship and civility are not fostered at home and in school, a healthy society will not exist.

The prophet John appeared in the Judean wilderness to prepare the Jewish people for a coming heavenly kingdom. The reign of heaven was not intended as some safe harbor for the privileged elite. This kingdom made demands on lifestyle: repentance, baptism, confession of sins (3:1-12).

After John's arrest, Jesus continued the message of John. "From that time Jesus began to preach, saying, 'Repent, for the kingdom of heaven is at hand'" (4:17). Now, however, Jesus was demanding that a selected few not only obey His words but follow Him. To be Jesus' disciple meant both to hear His words and to follow His example (4:18-22).

It is in Matthew's Gospel that the most complete account of Jesus' teaching is recorded. It has become known as the "Sermon on the Mount" (chaps. 5-7). It is not merely an excellent moral lecture or simply the words of a profound sage. The words and commands are from the

Lord Emmanuel ("God with us"). This teaching describes and prescribes citizenship in the kingdom of heaven.

Jesus begins by describing what is health and normalcy under God's kingship:

> *"Blessed are the poor in spirit, for theirs is the kingdom of heaven.*
>
> *"Blessed are those who mourn, for they shall be comforted.*
>
> *"Blessed are the meek, for they shall inherit the earth.*
>
> *"Blessed are those who hunger and thirst for righteousness, for they shall be satisfied.*
>
> *"Blessed are the merciful, for they shall receive mercy.*
>
> *"Blessed are the pure in heart, for they shall see God.*
>
> *"Blessed are the peacemakers, for they shall be called sons of God.*
>
> *"Blessed are those who are persecuted for righteousness' sake, for theirs is the kingdom of heaven.*
>
> *"Blessed are you when others revile you and persecute you and utter all kinds of evil against you falsely on my account."*
>
> Matthew 5:3-11

In the culture of God's rule, wellbeing and happiness are redefined. Blessedness thrives among a people who are contrite in heart, who do not self promote, who strive to do the right thing, who show mercy, who seek peaceful solutions, who absorb abuse.

Such a people, citizens of the heavenly kingdom, are themselves light to their neighbors, a way out of darkness for both friends and enemies. The kingdom is thus meant to grow, though its increase cannot be humanly manufactured.

Such citizenship cannot be sustained by merely following endless rules. People of the kingdom are children of the King. Striving to put the kingdom first means nothing less than striving to be like the King, understanding God's ways in the world.

"You therefore must be perfect, as your heavenly Father is perfect" (5:48).

To be truly like the Father, the heart as well as the mind must be fully engaged. To love as God loves means more than keeping the Ten Commandments. Angry insults, selfish lust, careless swearing, and revengeful retaliation must cease.

Loving enemies begins by praying sincerely for them. Only prayer can enable bad habits to cease and loving actions to begin (5:17-48).The Father desires a righteousness from the deepest interior of the heart, where desire is born and ambition resides.

Such new responses to one's fellow man are a result of quiet secret activities before God. For Jews, three main acts of devotion were almsgiving, prayer, and fasting. When the devil had tested Jesus in the wilderness, he tested Him in these three very areas (4:1-11).

What Jesus reminds the child of the kingdom is that giving, praying, and fasting must be resolutely done without a thought to whether somebody might be watching and admiring such piety (6:1-18). At the heart of any activity, of life itself, is secret prayer to the Father.

> *"But when you pray, go into your room and shut the door and pray to your Father who is in secret. And your Father who sees in secret will reward you.*
>
> *"And when you pray, do not heap up empty phrases as the Gentiles do, for they think that they will be heard for their many words. Do not be like them, for your Father knows what you need before you ask him. Pray then like this:*
>
> *"Our Father in heaven,*
> *hallowed be your name.*
> *Your kingdom come,*
> *your will be done,*
> *on earth as it is in heaven.*
> *Give us this day our daily bread,*
> *and forgive us our debts,*
> *as we also have forgiven our debtors.*
> *And lead us not into temptation,*
> *but deliver us from evil."*

Matthew 6:6-13

Such daily prayer will lead inevitably to a realignment of priorities. It is to learn the path of righteousness. Worry about tomorrow's meal or tomorrow's apparel will be replaced with preoccupation about today's responsibilities to love God and neighbor (6:19-34). Judging and criticizing others will occupy less energy because recognitions of God's mercies and personal repentance will maintain humility of heart (7:1-12).

It's not easy to obey Jesus' words.

> *"Enter by the narrow gate. For the gate is wide and the way is easy that leads to destruction, and those who enter by it are many. For the gate is narrow and the way is hard that leads to life, and those who find it are few."*
>
> Matthew 7:13-14

Only the truly wise person will act upon these words (7:21-27). The One who makes such demands is no dictator. He is our Father in heaven who understands completely the needs and nature of His children. He has ears to hear the requests of His children. He speaks and commands only according to His loving care for His children. His children must ask. He has promised to listen and to respond in love.

Matthew 8-20

The first Gospel tells the story of the kingdom of heaven confronting the kingdoms of the earth. A customs collector named Matthew had left his allegiance to the kingdoms of earth to follow the man named Jesus, the One who had through His commanding presence taught with unsurpassed authority and wisdom about the kingdom of the Father on high.

This son of Mary not only taught, but cured diseases and cast out demons in ways never seen before in Israel (9:33)—cleansing lepers (8:1-4), healing the paralyzed (8:5-13; 9:6), reviving the unconscious, healing the bleeding (9:18-26), giving sight to the blind and voice to the mute (9:27-33).

Such healings attracted huge crowds.

Jesus, however, did not seek fame. He shied away from publicity (9:30). His healings and exorcisms were for a single purpose: to demonstrate that the kingdom of heaven was intruding forcefully on the earth (12:28);

that the Spirit had indeed anointed a special servant (12:18); that the anticipated son of David had come, exercising his authority, not over the rulers of earth but over the demonic spirits of the devil's domain!

Those disabled in senses called upon Jesus in their direst need as "son of David" (9:27; 12:23; 15:22; 20:29ff). The righteous Pharisees and other Jewish leaders attributed such power to the ruler of demons (12:24). The demons themselves, however, recognized Jesus as Son of God, not the son of Beelzebul (8:29).

The crowds were so large that Jesus could not physically touch or teach everyone (9:35-38). Jesus thus summoned twelve close students to His side and commissioned them to proclaim the presence of the kingdom, to heal and to exorcise (10:1-8). Jesus made it clear that they should expect suffering in their discipleship (10:9-39).

The twelve of course were not perfect. On one occasion they failed to cast out a demon because of their little faith (17:14-20). They continued to believe that following Jesus would lead to greatness on earth (18:1-5; 20:20-28). Jesus tried repeatedly to disabuse them of this by pointing to His own life—which would end in execution. Even Peter, whom Jesus first nicknamed "Rocky," was later called "Stumbling Block" because of his opposition to Jesus' suffering (16:18-28).

Jesus modeled for His closest disciples the kind of lifestyle appropriate to the kingdom of heaven. In feeding multitudes of eager followers, Jesus demonstrated both his compassion and his trust in God to provide the needed daily manna (chaps. 14-15). He also showed the worth of even the seemingly least of His followers:

> *"Truly, I say to you, unless you turn and become like children, you will never enter the kingdom of heaven. Whoever humbles himself like this child is the greatest in the kingdom of heaven.*
>
> *"Whoever receives one such child in my name receives me, but whoever causes one of these little ones who believe in me to sin, it would be better for him to have a great millstone fastened around his neck and to be drowned in the depth of the sea."*
>
> Matthew 18:3-6

Matthew himself had experienced firsthand God's mercy in Jesus' call to hated tax collectors. Like their Master, the disciples should forgive and show mercy (chaps. 18-20).

Jesus' healings and exorcisms were a signal of God's strong presence in the man Jesus. They reinforced his authority in teaching, not only in the Sermon on the Mount, but also in his more obscure—at least for some (13:11)—parables of the kingdom.

In these parables Jesus appeals to the imagination of His listeners as well as their thinking. He describes the unexpected, even unnoticed advance of the kingdom, the various places and reasons for its growth in the human heart, and its exclusive claim on the seeker (13:31-50).

Surprisingly, Jesus first announces the kingdom only to Israel. But Jesus does not turn away those non-Jews who display impressive faith: the military officer who cares for his servant (8:5-13) or the Canaanite woman who like a "dog" is willing to accept the "crumbs" of healing from Jesus' table for the sake of her sick daughter (15:21-28).

Opposition, however, mounts against this man. Jesus' continued message—that God wants mercy not sacrifice, that God loves the sinner as well as the righteous, that secrecy in doing good is preferable to publicity in doing good—this and Jesus' profound response to Pharisaic arguments began the momentum that would lead to the death of the Son of God (12:14). His transfiguration, in which God dismisses great Moses and great Elijah in favor of His beloved Son, disclosed for a fleeting moment the glory which was to be His (17:1-13). But first He must go to Jerusalem.

> *And as Jesus was going up to Jerusalem, he took the twelve disciples aside, and on the way he said to them, "See, we are going up to Jerusalem. And the Son of Man will be delivered over to the chief priests and scribes, and they will condemn him to death and deliver him over to the Gentiles to be mocked and flogged and crucified, and he will be raised on the third day."*
>
> Matthew 20:17-19

Matthew 21-28

Throughout the first Gospel, Matthew narrates that significant moments in Jesus' life "fulfill" sayings from the Old Testament prophets. These events are not outside God's governing control (26:54). This assurance is all the more important as the events of Jesus' suffering and death unfold and conclude Matthew's Gospel.

Jesus' entry into Jerusalem on a donkey, with the crowds hailing Him as the "son of David," is the beginning of the end, the fulfillment of divine prophecy (21:5-9). Jesus now opposes the Jewish identity associated with the temple. Dramatically, He disrupts commercial activity in the temple area claiming prayer as the true activity of the temple (21:13, 21). Prayer is, in fact, Jesus' refuge in Gethsemane in his darkest moment (26:36ff).

Jesus announces that the whole temple structure will be thrown down (24:2). The process commences when at his death the curtain in the temple veiling the holiest place is torn from top to bottom, from heaven to earth (27:51).

While Jesus' brief ministry had focused on announcing the coming kingdom to Israel, now near His death Jesus offers parables to inform and explain the enlargement of God's theocracy from Israel to encompass all nations. The wedding guests are no longer only Israel; now the invitees come from the streets. Henceforth there will be different tenants caring for God's vineyard (21:33-22:14). In the future, judgment will be favorable toward anyone who treats kindly the least member of God's church (25:31-46).

Near the end, Jesus dines not with the powerful or famous, but in the house of a leper. There a woman lavishly anoints Jesus with ointment, unwittingly perfuming His body in preparation for burial (26:12). From this dinner, Jesus invites the twelve to a final Passover meal (26:18).

The festive occasion is dampened by Jesus' announcement that one of the twelve would betray Him (26:21). Nevertheless, all—including the betrayer—are invited to eat a loaf of bread which Jesus surprisingly calls His "own body," and to drink from a cup which Jesus just as surprisingly calls His "blood of the covenant poured out for many for the forgiveness of sins" (26:26-29).

Perhaps most stunning to the twelve, Jesus says flatly that His "followers" will soon become his "deserters" (26:31, 56). This is realized most profoundly in the life of impulsive Peter, "Rocky," who progressively denies Jesus after his arrest: first a simple denial, then a denial with an oath, and a third, final denial with an oath and a curse! (26:69-75)

After the Last Supper and the singing of a Passover song (cf. Psalms 113–118), Jesus leads His followers to the Mount of Olives, just east of the temple, to the garden of Gethsemane. There He wrestles in prayer with God's will that He drink the cup of suffering death. The humanity of Jesus is clearly visible in the need for His three closest disciples to stay awake with Him during this agonizing struggle.

Through prayerful petition Jesus understands and yields to God's will (26:53).

The conspiracy to kill Jesus unfolds under the roof of the high priest Caiaphas. Jesus is handed over to the highest civil authority in Judea, Pontius Pilate. The Roman governor finds no guilt in Jesus, only jealous motivations among the Jewish leaders (27:18). Prompted by these leaders, Pilate permits the crowds to choose which prisoner to release, Jesus Barabbas or Jesus the Christ. The crowd chooses to crucify the Christ, whereupon Pilate assigns blood guilt to the people.

After abusive mocking, Jesus is offered a sedative of wine and gall which He refuses. He is taken to a somber place with the topography of a skull, and there He is executed on a Roman cross beside two criminals.

At His death there is darkness and an earthquake so intense that the soldiers confess Him as truly God's Son. None of Jesus' closest followers claim His corpse. It is a wealthy man named Joseph who takes the body and lays it in his own tomb.

But on the first day of the week, two women, both named Mary, are startled to meet an angel in brilliant light at the tomb. And most shocking, they encounter Jesus himself alive outside the tomb! Other dead people, now alive, are also encountered in the city (27:53).

At the close of Matthew's Gospel, Jesus is reunited with the remaining eleven disciples on a mountain in Galilee, some still skeptical at the sight.

> *And Jesus came and said to them, "All authority in heaven and on earth has been given to me. Go therefore and make disciples of all nations, baptizing them in the name of the Father and of the Son and of the Holy Spirit, teaching them to observe all that I have commanded you. And behold, I am with you always, to the end of the age."*
>
> Matthew 28:18-20

As Matthew had begun his Gospel with the announcement of the birth of a baby named Emmanuel, "God with us," so the Gospel closes with Jesus' promise, "I am with you always, to the end of the age."

The kingdom had come—and is still coming. Its presence was dramatically manifested in Jesus' ministry in the flesh, as even demons acknowledged him as the Son of God. The advance of the kingdom was yet more evident in the power unleashed in the resurrection of Jesus and the saints.

So the kingdom, God's reign, is also present today with power. The kingdom is present in the Spirit, dwelling in the human heart through faith and baptism. The kingdom is present in the lives of believers obeying Jesus' commands. And the kingdom is present through unfailing prayer to the Father above.

Mark 1-8

Even though the second Gospel is the shortest of the four, the stories it tells of Jesus' life offer more details than we find in the first. The author Mark was not an apostle, but he lived in a house where Jesus' closest disciples frequently met, talked, and prayed together (Acts 12:12). Mark labored with Paul in the mission to Gentiles (2 Timothy 4:11), and he was as close as a son to the apostle Peter (1 Peter 5:13). Mark's Gospel may in fact reflect the preaching of the fatherly apostle.

Mark begins the "message about Jesus Christ," not with Jesus' birth in Bethlehem, but with the appearance of a strange messenger in the wilderness:

> *As it is written in Isaiah the prophet,*
> *"Behold, I send my messenger before your face,*
> *who will prepare your way,*
> *the voice of one crying in the wilderness:*
> *'Prepare the way of the Lord,*
> *make his paths straight,'"*
> *John appeared, baptizing in the wilderness and proclaiming a baptism of repentance for the forgiveness of sins.*
>
> Mark 1:2-4

The Jewish people prepare for the coming kingdom of God by repenting, confessing their sins, and being immersed in the River Jordan. Only then does Jesus appear. He too is immersed by John, not for the forgiveness of sins, but rather as an occasion for the Holy Spirit to descend upon Him.

As with God's Spirit in the beginning hovering over the chaotic waters (Gen. 1), so God's Spirit hovers and descends as Jesus comes out of the water (Mark 1:9-11).

The Spirit's presence does not usher in peace and comfort, but immediately leads to testing, deep in the wilderness (1:12-13).

In Mark's Gospel, the power of the Spirit in Jesus is dramatic. When Jesus confronts the possessed, the "clean" Holy Spirit overwhelms the "unclean" spirits into an irrepressible acknowledgment of Jesus as the Son of God—a confession not yet made even by the disciples (3:11; 5:7). Jesus orders the demons not to speak in an effort to prevent misunderstanding of His identity as the Son (1:25, 34; 3:12).

Jesus' rebuke of the demons is matched by His rebuke of the threatening chaos of the windswept lake of Galilee (4:35-41). On one occasion, after Jesus had calmed an evening storm, He faced a wild Gerasene demoniac, naked in the tombs. His exorcism releases the unclean spirits into pigs who drown in a chaotic water grave in Lake Galilee (5:1-13).

Jesus' healings and exorcisms attract great crowds of people:

> *That evening at sundown they brought to him all who were sick or oppressed by demons. And the whole city was gathered together at the door. And he healed many who were sick with various diseases, and cast out many demons. And he would not permit the demons to speak, because they knew him.*
>
> *And rising very early in the morning, while it was still dark, he departed and went out to a desolate place, and there he prayed.*
>
> Mark 1:32-35

Sometimes whole villages gathered at the door of Jesus' residence (1:33; 2:2). His growing popularity frequently forced him to stay outside the city (1:45). Still the crowds pursued Him, and Jesus had to escape being crushed (3:9; 5:24). His apostles were also thronged by the people, and Jesus had to take them to deserted places for rest (6:31).

Popularity impeded privacy (7:24). Mark's Gospel emphasizes that Jesus' reputation created great hardships for His work. Jesus faced the danger of being perceived primarily as a great wonder worker. For this reason, He exited towns clamoring for more healings.

And Simon and those who were with him searched for him, and they found him and said to him, "Everyone is looking for you." And he said to them, "Let us go on to the next towns, that I may preach there also, for that is why I came out."

Mark 1:36-38

Jesus had come into the world to proclaim a message:

Now after John was arrested, Jesus came into Galilee, proclaiming the gospel of God, and saying, "The time is fulfilled, and the kingdom of God is at hand; repent and believe in the gospel."

Mark 1:14-15

Jesus healed with compassion. But His healings also validated His teaching and claim to forgive sins (2:10). If Jesus did not encounter faith, then He would not heal—as in His own hometown (6:5).

Partly for this reason, He ordered various people not to report His deeds of healing. After He had raised the daughter of a synagogue leader, he told Jairus not to tell anyone the circumstances (5:43). After Jesus cured a man of deafness, He ordered the man to tell no one about the private healing (7:36). Only to the cleansed Gerasene did Jesus permit grateful speech and proclamation of what mercy the Lord had shown (5:19).

Even though the second Gospel stresses Jesus' mission of coming into the world to preach, Mark includes very few of Jesus' public teachings contained in Matthew's Gospel. What we hear are Jesus' parables about the kingdom and its unexpected growth (chap. 4); His controversy with Jewish leaders about the requirements of God's law (chap. 7); His teaching on marriage and the dangers of wealth (chap. 10); His debates in the temple over the authority to teach and heal in God's name (chaps. 11–12); and His announcement of the coming judgment of God on Jerusalem (chap. 13).

The first half of Mark's Gospel is a rapid sequence of one event after another—until a decisive moment in Caesarea Philippi when Jesus begins to explain what it means, for one's very life, to confess Him as the Christ, the Messiah. Three times Jesus tells His disciples what will soon happen to Him. Their reaction is critical for the second half of Mark's story.

Mark 8-16

As one of the first men Jesus called, Simon Peter had stark recollections of following and deserting Jesus, of confessing and denying him. If Mark indeed was heavily influenced by Peter's memories, then it is not surprising to find in the Gospel according to Mark a strong concern for understanding Jesus' true identity and the nature of discipleship.

Peter's painful road to grasping discipleship began at Caesarea Philippi. It is a major turning point in Mark's Gospel. Until this moment, only unclean spirits had been making unsolicited confessions of Jesus as the Son of God—confessions Jesus had silenced. Now, halfway through Mark's story, Jesus finally seeks an answer from the disciples:

> *And Jesus went on with his disciples to the villages of Caesarea Philippi. And on the way he asked his disciples, "Who do people say that I am?" And they told him, "John the Baptist; and others say, Elijah; and others, one of the prophets." And he asked them, "But who do you say that I am?" Peter answered him, "You are the Christ." And he strictly charged them to tell no one about him.*
>
> Mark 8:27-29

Surprisingly, Jesus orders silence from His disciples. Then Jesus publicly began to explain, for the first time, that He would suffer, be rejected, be killed, and in three days rise again (8:31). Privately, Peter rebuked Jesus. Jesus responded:

> *But turning and seeing his disciples, he rebuked Peter and said, "Get behind me, Satan! For you are not setting your mind on the things of God, but on the things of man."*
>
> Mark 8:33

Jesus has to explain what it means to follow Him—intentional denial of what one might desire and a voluntary choice of the cross. "For whoever would save his life will lose it, but whoever loses his life for my sake and the gospel's will save it" (8:35).

Such strong conflict with Peter was necessary, not only to correct his misunderstanding of the Messiah's role, but for Peter's life as a disciple. What Peter thought about his teacher determined his self-understanding as a student! A victorious master meant glory for the servant; a suffering master meant something quite unattractive for the follower.

Two more times in Mark, Jesus tells the disciples that He will suffer and be killed (9:31f; 10:33f). Two more times the disciples fail to understand what following a crucified Messiah means (9:33ff; 10:36f). On both occasions the disciples are preoccupied with which one will be greatest in the kingdom—oblivious to the impending humiliation for them all in their Lord being publicly executed! Jesus again must explain the nature of following Him: they are to serve each other, not their own aspirations for honor and glory.

Knowing their confusion, Jesus charged them to tell no one of His coming suffering (8:30). The transfiguration, with God's command to listen to Jesus alone, was no doubt intended to reinforce in the disciples' hearts the difficult prospect of Jesus' suffering death.

Still, they could not fathom how He could suffer. They were afraid to ask (9:32). This misunderstanding of discipleship continued in their prohibitions of other exorcists:

> *John said to him, "Teacher, we saw someone casting out demons in your name, and we tried to stop him, because he was not following us." But Jesus said, "Do not stop him, for no one who does a mighty work in my name will be able soon afterward to speak evil of me. For the one who is not against us is for us. For truly, I say to you, whoever gives you a cup of water to drink because you belong to Christ will by no means lose his reward.*
> Mark 9:38-41

Jesus warns them not to cause other followers to stumble.

The hour, however, finally came. Jesus entered Jerusalem. One last time Jesus warned His disciples of tumultuous times for the city in the future. They were to be watchful, constantly alert (13:37). The disciple is not greater than the master.

Unique in Mark's Gospel is the somber recounting of Jesus' last week as well as the curious story of a youth who had been following Jesus. "And a young man followed him, with nothing but a linen cloth about his body. And they seized him, but he left the linen cloth and ran away naked" (14:51-52).

Is this Mark? Is he saying that even he abandoned Jesus in the end, as did Peter, his father in the faith? More than any other account of Jesus' death, the story in Mark's Gospel emphasizes the complete abandonment of Jesus by all.

In the end only Jesus confesses His identity in public. When the high priest asks, "Are you the Christ?" Jesus says, "I am." And when Pilate asks, "Are you king of the Jews?" Jesus answers, "You say so." So Jesus is crucified with this charge, "The King of the Jews."

As Mark ends his Gospel, the tomb is empty. Two Marys who visit the tomb find inside, not Jesus, but a young man dressed in a white robe! They are shocked. They are told to tell the news to the disciples and Peter. But in their fearful wonder, they are silent; they say nothing to anyone (16:1-8). Mark lingers with this irony. Time and again the disciples and others were told by Jesus to be silent lest they magnify misunderstanding by speaking. But now, with an empty tomb, the women are dumbfounded and find themselves unable to speak—at the very moment when speech should abound.

Mark understood failure and fear. He had himself abandoned Paul and Barnabas on a mission trip (Acts 13:13; 15:37-41). Mark could well grasp the fear and misunderstanding experienced by Jesus' first followers. Peter understood this well.

The Gospel of Mark will always remind the follower that the Christ suffered, and that the disciple is not greater than the master.

But cross bearing is not merely any unpleasant circumstance in which we find ourselves. Cross bearing is something intended, not merely circumstantial. It is seeking to serve others, knowing that such service may not be recognized or rewarded. It is knowing that service may bring the envy of others—or even suffering.

But suffering is not the meaning of life, nor is it the end of life. Jesus' suffering was unique and only His was ultimately for the life of the world. It is enough often to be silent and fearful of the mystery. To be alert for His will in this life.

Suffering preceded glory. Suffering was not the last chapter for the Messiah—or for us who believe today. He was raised. And so will we who believe that God raised Him from the dead.

Luke 1-3

Unlike the other three, Luke's Gospel begins with a dedication (1:1-4). The author, a medical doctor, dedicates his story of Jesus to a benefactor, Theophilus.

Luke intends for his account (compiled from eyewitnesses, Paul, and other co-workers) to reassure Theophilus of the credibility and meaning of recent extraordinary events, to verify how Jesus' life conformed to God's plan foretold long ago in Scripture. Jesus' life is no figment of a fertile imagination. It occurs in a defined place of time and space, in public view, with clear textual precedents. Luke will give precise historical dating to the events of Jesus' birth as well as the beginnings of John's ministry (2:1-2; 3:1-2).

The subsequent narrative in Luke's Gospel, however, does not begin as in Matthew's Gospel with the birth of Jesus or as in Mark's Gospel with John baptizing in the wilderness. It begins with the story of John the Baptizer's parents, Zechariah and Elizabeth, and their experience with the Holy Spirit.

For many years, Zechariah and his wife Elizabeth had prayed for a son. Though he was a priest, Zechariah did not believe it when the angel Gabriel appeared to him, announcing that a son would be born. God had again acted, giving a barren woman the child she had so longed for (1:5-25).

The same angel Gabriel appeared later to an engaged teenage girl named Mary. What the angel said to this virgin surely stunned her:

> *"The Holy Spirit will come upon you, and the power of the Most High will overshadow you; therefore the child to be born will be called holy—the Son of God. And behold, your relative Elizabeth in her old age has also conceived a son, and this is the sixth month with her who was called barren. For nothing will be impossible with God."*
>
> Luke 1:35-37

Mary visited Elizabeth. At her greeting, Elizabeth felt the baby somersault in her womb. During the aged woman's last trimester, the young pregnant Mary had time to absorb what was happening to her. She could remember Samuel's mother and reflect on Hannah's trust in God (1:26-56; cf. 1 Samuel 1-2).

The once-barren Elizabeth bears a son, John. Her husband Zechariah, filled with the Holy Spirit—as John also had been in the womb—glorifies God for his mercies:

> *"Blessed be the Lord God of Israel,*
> *for he has visited and redeemed his people*
> *and has raised up a horn of salvation for us*
> *in the house of his servant David,*
> *as he spoke by the mouth of his holy prophets from of old,*
> *that we should be saved from our enemies*
> *and from the hand of all who hate us."*
>
> Luke 1:68-71

When Mary's labor finally begins, she is not in the familiar surroundings of home and family. She is in the village of Bethlehem for a census registration. Her newborn baby is placed to sleep in a common feeding box for animals. The birth of the Savior of the world is announced to working shepherds, dirty and unclean—not simply spoken, but sung by a great heavenly chorus. The lowly shepherds feel at home seeing the baby where animals feed (2:1-19).

God sent his Son into the care of good parents, a righteous couple. Not surprisingly, they bring Jesus to Jerusalem for dedication as a first-born. There, an older man and woman, Simeon and Anna, both of them upright and prayerful, are blessed by God to see the child, a light to the Gentiles and glory to Israel (2:21-40).

The only recorded event from Jesus' adolescence comes at age 12 when He accompanied His parents to Jerusalem for the Passover festival. On the way home to Nazareth, his parents realized that he was not among their relatives and friends. After searching frantically for three days, they found Him still in the temple, listening to the teachers of the Law, asking astonishingly perceptive questions. For Mary, it was one of many memories she treasured as a mother (2:41-52).

Luke's story jumps from Jesus' precocious youth to the coming of the word of God in the wilderness to His cousin John. Not only does John preach a baptism for the forgiveness of sins, he challenges customs workers not to cheat and soldiers not to extort money by threats (3:1-20). Throughout his narrative, Luke will repeat stories which concern the use of possessions.

Following John's imprisonment by Herod and Jesus' baptism with the Holy Spirit descending upon Him, Luke turns to the narration proper of Jesus' ministry which begins at age 30. As in Matthew, Luke chronicles a lineage for Jesus. Unlike Matthew, he traces that heritage backward beyond David and Abraham, showing that Jesus is "son of Adam" and "son of God."

The beginning of Luke's story, its first three chapters, is unique among the four Gospels. His report of Jesus' infancy emphasizes the surprise and joy which surrounded the Savior's birth. Luke's account manifests what Mary had sung:

> *"And his mercy is for those who fear him*
> *from generation to generation.*
> *He has shown strength with his arm;*
> *he has scattered the proud in the thoughts of their hearts;*
> *he has brought down the mighty from their thrones*
> *and exalted those of humble estate;*
> *he has filled the hungry with good things,*
> *and the rich he has sent away empty.*
> *He has helped his servant Israel,*
> *in remembrance of his mercy,*
> *as he spoke to our fathers,*
> *to Abraham and to his offspring forever."*

Luke 1:50-55

Luke 4-19

Jesus' ministry begins in earnest one Sabbath day in His hometown, Nazareth of Galilee. He is asked to read Scripture in the synagogue.

> *And the scroll of the prophet Isaiah was given to him. He unrolled the scroll and found the place where it was written,*
>
> *"The Spirit of the Lord is upon me,*
> *because he has anointed me*
> *to proclaim good news to the poor.*
> *He has sent me to proclaim liberty to the captives*
> *and recovering of sight to the blind,*
> *to set at liberty those who are oppressed,*
> *to proclaim the year of the Lord's favor."*

And he rolled up the scroll and gave it back to the attendant and sat down. And the eyes of all in the synagogue were fixed on him. And he began to say to them, "Today this Scripture has been fulfilled in your hearing." And all spoke well of him and marveled at the gracious words that were coming from his mouth. And they said, "Is not this Joseph's son?" And he said to them, "Doubtless you will quote to me this proverb, '"Physician, heal yourself." What we have heard you did at Capernaum, do here in your hometown as well.'" And he said, "Truly, I say to you, no prophet is acceptable in his hometown."

Luke 4:17-24

When Jesus reminded them that God's prophets Elijah and Elisha had healed Gentiles rather than Israelites, their emotions turned from pleasure to rage. They tried unsuccessfully to throw Jesus off a cliff!

Jesus' words, however, were prophetic and true. He indeed had come to welcome the poor, the crippled, the lame, and the blind into the kingdom of God. He taught (14:14, 21) and lived this (18:35ff). Like Elisha and Elijah, Jesus touched the lives of non-Jews and the marginalized—the centurion soldier whose servant was ill, the woman in Nain whose only son had died. Jesus found great faith outside Israel and He was moved with compassion to heal (7:1-17).

The Spirit had anointed Jesus to bless the outcast. The stories Luke selected for inclusion in his Gospel give special attention to Jesus' ministry to the outcasts—the *unlovely*, the *unloved*, and the *unlovable*.

For Jesus' fellow Jews, the Samaritans were among the most *unlovable* of all—half-breed Jews, foreigners of questionable heritage. On one occasion, even Jesus' own disciples wanted to rain down fire on a Samaritan village and burn it up (9:54).

The Jews felt about the Samaritans the way some ethnic groups today feel about other ethnic groups. Jesus, however, found greatness even among the despised Samaritans. When Jesus healed ten lepers, only one turned back to thank him. The grateful recipient was a Samaritan (17:16). Most remarkable, though, was Jesus' response to a lawyer's question: Who is the neighbor I must love in order to keep God's commandments?

Jesus told the story of a traveling man beaten, robbed, and left to die on the road. A priest and Levite saw the half dead man and passed by. But another traveler not only stopped to help, he took the wounded man to a shelter and paid for his recovery! This rescuer was not a religious leader; the "neighbor" who helped was a Samaritan. Jesus refused to answer the lawyer's question the way he asked it: "Who is my neighbor? Whom do I have to love?" Jesus rather declared, "Be a neighbor to all."

Jesus taught the *unloved,* especially the greedy. He was not afraid to eat with despised tax collectors. One such officer named Zacchaeus responded with great interest and genuine repentance to Jesus' call:

> *And Zacchaeus stood and said to the Lord, "Behold, Lord, the half of my goods I give to the poor. And if I have defrauded anyone of anything, I restore it fourfold." And Jesus said to him, "Today salvation has come to this house, since he also is a son of Abraham."*
>
> Luke 19:8-9

Jesus did not neglect eating in the homes of religious leaders like the Pharisees (11:37; 14:1ff). He was not afraid to call even them to repentance from their love of money (16:14ff). He confronted them with the story of a rich man and a poor beggar whose positions were reversed after death in Hades. Jesus hoped that such stories would shock the hearers into trusting God, not money.

Jesus also pursued the *unlovely*, especially the lost. Jesus stressed the absolute resounding joy in heaven when God's lost ones are found. In three stories, unique to Luke's Gospel, Jesus depicts the joy of a shepherd finding a lost sheep, a woman finding a lost silver coin, and a father finding a lost son (15:1-32). The last story, a classic in Scripture, challenges the listener. One may feel a similar conviction to fall before God the Father confessing sin.

> *"And the son said to him, 'Father, I have sinned against heaven and before you. I am no longer worthy to be called your son.'"*
>
> Luke 15:21

The words of the elder brother reveal a pride which can only be broken in the face of a Father who welcomes the return of the unlovely.

Whether for the benefit of his benefactor Theophilus, a person of some wealth, or because of his own sensitivities, Luke highlights Jesus' call for single-minded allegiance to God the Father—an allegiance above any distraction in the world, whether money, pleasures, or cares.

And he said to his disciples, "Therefore I tell you, do not be anxious about your life, what you will eat, nor about your body, what you will put on. For life is more than food, and the body more than clothing.

Luke 12:22-23

Jesus knew that discipleship could mean broken relationships in families (12:49ff; 14:26; 18:29; 21:16). But He also promised abundant blessings for the one obedient to the Father's will.

Then his mother and his brothers came to him, but they could not reach him because of the crowd. And he was told, "Your mother and your brothers are standing outside, desiring to see you." But he answered them, "My mother and my brothers are those who hear the word of God and do it."

Luke 8:19-21

Luke 19-24

In Luke's Gospel, it is only near the end of His life that Jesus enters Jerusalem to teach. Until this time, the backdrop of Jesus' teaching has been outside the Jewish capital—in the country, on the road from Galilee to Jerusalem, in homes, in conversations at meal time.

But finally He enters the city of David. As He rides into Jerusalem, the crowds spread their coats on the road. The disciples praise God joyfully (19:28-40).

But Jesus weeps.

Jesus weeps because He sees the coming destruction of Jerusalem and the great suffering of its inhabitants. They will refuse to recognize God's visitation in the person of Jesus (19:41-44; 21:22). Indeed, within forty years of His lament, the temple and city will be laid waste by Rome.

Jesus calls the temple a house of prayer. But for the next few days He teaches, rather than prays, near God's house. In Luke, more than any other Gospel, Jesus' body is the house of prayer. Jesus prays before choosing the apostles (6:12). Jesus prays before His transfiguration (9:28). Jesus prays for Simon Peter (22:31f). And He admonishes the disciples to pray that they not come into difficult trials and temptations (22:40, 46). Jesus even compares the prayer life of a Pharisee and a tax collector!

But now Jesus must teach. He must teach the scribes, the chief priests, and Sadducees—no matter their motivations and pretensions (20:1-47). And He must teach His disciples to expect the destruction of the temple and the threat of persecution.

> *But before all this they will lay their hands on you and persecute you, delivering you up to the synagogues and prisons, and you will be brought before kings and governors for my name's sake. This will be your opportunity to bear witness. Settle it therefore in your minds not to meditate beforehand how to answer, for I will give you a mouth and wisdom, which none of your adversaries will be able to withstand or contradict.*
>
> Luke 21:12-15

Jesus Himself will soon exemplify controlled response under pressure.

Satan again enters the drama at an "opportune moment" (cf. 4:13). The Adversary enters the heart of the apostle named Judas, who has agreed to betray Jesus in private to the authorities (22:3-6). As it happens, the betrayal is neither private nor quiet (22:47-53).

Jesus' more immediate concern, however, is Satan's desire for Simon Peter:

> *"Simon, Simon, behold, Satan demanded to have you, that he might sift you like wheat, but I have prayed for you that your faith may not fail. And when you have turned again, strengthen your brothers." Peter said to him, "Lord, I am ready to go with you both to prison and to death." Jesus said, "I tell you, Peter, the rooster will not crow this day, until you deny three times that you know me."*
>
> Luke 22:31-34

When the cock crows, Jesus looks over and stares at Peter. It is Peter's turn to weep bitterly (22:61).

The charges brought against Jesus at His trial are clearly stated in Luke's account. There are three: (1) He prohibits the payment of taxes; (2) He claims to be king; and (3) He stirs up trouble among the people (23:1-5).

But Pilate acquits Him of all accusations. Even the centurion who watches the way Jesus dies will profess His innocence (23:47). Nevertheless (and Luke does not explain why), Pilate yields to the demands of the crowd to crucify Jesus (23:13-25).

The crucifixion is viewed in different ways by the four Gospels. Mark's Gospel records Jesus' utter abandonment. Luke, however, notes that one of the two criminals hanging next to Jesus in the end acknowledges His innocence and even requests mercy. The Lord grants a place for him in Paradise (23:40-43). Luke also records that the man Joseph, who took Jesus' body down for burial, had not agreed with the council's plot to kill Him (23:51).

Especially noteworthy, however, is Luke's appreciation for the role played by the women who supported Jesus and His disciples in their ministries. Indeed, a special group had provided all along from their own resources for His welfare (8:1ff). Such women grieved at His suffering. And Jesus grieved for them and the mothers who would soon encounter the horrors of armies invading Jerusalem (23:28-31). Such women, however, were privileged to experience the wonder of the empty tomb (24:1-12).

When Luke interviewed eyewitnesses before writing his Gospel, he must have heard many stories of Jesus' meal time conversations. But none could have been more memorable than the recollection of a certain disciple named Cleopas. After Jesus' death, Cleopas and another friend were talking on the way to the village of Emmaus. A stranger began walking with them. Cleopas lamented that they had hoped the prophet Jesus would free Israel from oppression. That evening, the stranger who stayed to eat with them, took bread, blessed and broke it. Suddenly, in the breaking of bread Cleopas' eyes were opened and he recognized the stranger as Jesus Himself (24:13-35).

As Luke's story began in the temple so there it ends, with the disciples rejoicing and praising God after Jesus' ascension. What endures, however, is not the temple at Jerusalem but Jesus' followers as living temples, His church, the body of Christ—meeting in each other's homes, cherishing His words, recognizing His continued presence in the breaking of bread.

John 1-7

In the first three Gospels, the power and presence of God's kingdom is dramatically displayed: The demons acknowledge Jesus' identity. Jesus exorcises unclean spirits. His healings manifest the final authority of the promised king, the son of David.

In the fourth Gospel, however, the viewpoint is different.

Here the story is told not so much from the context of Israel's expectations but more from a cosmological framework. Of importance here is Jesus' spatial identity "from above" and His temporal position "from before." Where Jesus is from and where Jesus is going are striking refrains in the Gospel according to John.

Jesus' life is interpreted from the perspective of His role "in the beginning" and His origin "with the Father." In John's Gospel, Jesus is not so much teacher of the kingdom as He is revealer of the Son and the Father. The faith of Jesus' followers here is more than believing the kingdom has come. Faith is seeing Jesus' signs of glory "from above" and "from before," and believing these signs.

This cosmic perspective is introduced in the lengthy prologue. Like the overture to a musical, John's beginning introduces the major themes which reoccur throughout his Gospel:

> *In the beginning was the Word, and the Word was with God, and the Word was God. He was in the beginning with God. All things were made through him, and without him was not any thing made that was made. In him was life, and the life was the light of men. The light shines in the darkness, and the darkness has not overcome it.*
>
> *There was a man sent from God, whose name was John. He came as a witness, to bear witness about the light, that all might believe through him. He was not the light, but came to bear witness about the light.*
>
> *The true light, which gives light to everyone, was coming into the world. He was in the world, and the world was made through him, yet the world did not know him. He came to his own, and his own people did not receive him. But to all who did receive him, who believed in his name, he gave the right to become*

children of God, who were born, not of blood nor of the will of the flesh nor of the will of man, but of God.

And the Word became flesh and dwelt among us, and we have seen his glory, glory as of the only Son from the Father, full of grace and truth.

John 1:1-14

John declares that God's creative power of life and light has come to dwell in flesh, though he makes no attempt to explain how. The irony characteristic of John's Gospel begins in the comment that the created world did not know its Creator when He entered the world! Irony and paradox abound throughout as Jesus' home "from above" and "from before" confronts and reinterprets the mundane realities of the world "present" and "below."

When at a wedding party Jesus' mother remarks that the wine has run out, His response seems out of touch with reality:

And Jesus said to her, "Woman, what does this have to do with me? My hour has not yet come."

John 2:4

In truth, Jesus' words on this occasion come "from above," for the hour to pour out His blood has not arrived. Nevertheless, Jesus acts as "from before," as Creator in the beginning, making wine out of water, revealing His glory (2:1-11).

When at night, a leader of the Pharisees named Nicodemus comes to Jesus (the one "from before" who created light), the Lord seems unresponsive:

Jesus answered him, "Truly, truly, I say to you, unless one is born again he cannot see the kingdom of God."

John 3:3

In truth, Jesus has spoken "from above" in challenging Nicodemus not merely to learn another doctrine about the kingdom but to be transformed completely through new birth "from above." Already, Jesus' disciples were immersing in water more followers than John the Immerser (3:22-4:3). To Nicodemus, Jesus announced the significance of baptism in water as the coming of the life-giving Spirit—a birth again, a birth from above (3:4-21).

When tired and thirsty in Samaria Jesus met a woman drawing water at Jacob's well, He seems presumptuous:

> *Jesus answered her, "If you knew the gift of God, and who it is that is saying to you, 'Give me a drink,' you would have asked him, and he would have given you living water."*
>
> John 4:10

In truth, Jesus has spoken "from above," offering a vitality from the Father's gift of the Spirit which physical water could only suggest:

> *Jesus said to her, "Everyone who drinks of this water will be thirsty again, but whoever drinks of the water that I will give him will never be thirsty again. The water that I will give him will become in him a spring of water welling up to eternal life."*
>
> John 4:13-14

When the crowds ask for the bread of God after hearing Jesus recall the Father's supply of manna in the wilderness, He seems sacrilegious.

> *Jesus said to them, "I am the bread of life; whoever comes to me shall not hunger, and whoever believes in me shall never thirst."*
>
> John 6:35

To speak in this way, as "I AM," was to speak as God. In truth, Jesus has spoken "from above," because the Father grants the Son authority to empower the children with eternal life.

> *All that the Father gives me will come to me, and whoever comes to me I will never cast out. For I have come down from heaven, not to do my own will but the will of him who sent me. And this is the will of him who sent me, that I should lose nothing of all that he has given me, but raise it up on the last day. For this is the will of my Father, that everyone who looks on the Son and believes in him should have eternal life, and I will raise him up on the last day."*
>
> John 6:37-40

As an apostle, John saw firsthand the signs of Jesus' glory—not merely at the transfiguration, but in the life and light revealed in the moments of His creating and healing. To this John testifies in his Gospel that faith in the Son may increase.

Jesus acts as He has seen the Father act.

Since the Father raises the dead, the Son also gives life. The Gospel of John stresses that the eternal life Jesus gives begins even in this life below. Eternal life does not begin after death; it begins now in the one who believes the testimony of the witnesses—those who came and saw Jesus, those who believed He was the bread of life and source of living waters.

John 8-13

It's normal to ask a stranger, "Where did you grow up?" or "What do you do?" We feel more comfortable if we know where the stranger is from and where he is going.

In the fourth Gospel, Jesus is the stranger.

People don't know where Jesus is from (9:29) or where He is going. Jesus' foes claim He comes from Samaria and is from the devil (8:48). Most, however, are simply puzzled by Him. He arouses suspicion and mistrust because He claims to be LIGHT and LIFE.

> *Again Jesus spoke to them, saying, "I am the light of the world. Whoever follows me will not walk in darkness, but will have the light of life." So the Pharisees said to him, "You are bearing witness about yourself; your testimony is not true." Jesus answered, "Even if I do bear witness about myself, my testimony is true, for I know where I came from and where I am going, but you do not know where I come from or where I am going."*
>
> John 8:12-14

Jesus comes *from above*. He has seen and heard God the Father. What He has seen is God the Father giving and yielding life, in the creation, in the beginning. He has seen the works of the Father, closely and directly. He has come to the world below from the realm of the Father above.

Not only does Jesus know where He came from, He knows where He is going. He is returning to the Father. Others, from the world below, cannot go where Jesus is going. Even Jesus' closest disciples cannot immediately go with Jesus, much less understand where He is going or what He must experience.

What proof is there that Jesus has come from the Father and is going back to Him? He makes the astonishing claim that He is LIGHT and LIFE, sharing the presence of the Father before and during creation. How can such testimony be believed?

Jesus sees a beggar born blind. The man does not ask to be healed. But in order to show the creative work of God, Jesus puts mud on the beggar's eyes. The man washes and he sees (9:1-34). Jesus is the LIGHT of the world. He can give the man light because He has seen the work of the Father in the beginning and as the only Son He too can give light. The Son's light shines in the darkness of human hearts, illuminating those who believe but blinding those who do not.

> *Jesus said, "For judgment I came into this world, that those who do not see may see, and those who see may become blind." Some of the Pharisees near him heard these things, and said to him, "Are we also blind?" Jesus said to them, "If you were blind, you would have no guilt; but now that you say, 'We see,' your guilt remains.*
>
> John 9:39-41

In John 11, Jesus hears that a dear friend named Lazarus is near death.

Surprisingly, He takes no immediate steps to heal Lazarus or console his sisters. Jesus lets Lazarus die and stay dead three days! When He beholds the family's grief, Jesus weeps. Then He calls into the tomb for Lazarus to come out. Alive once more, Lazarus emerges still wearing his burial clothes (11:1-44). Jesus is the Resurrection and the Life. He can restore life to Lazarus because He and the Father are one. As God's Son He has seen the transcendent life and work of the Father. The Son does the work of the Father in giving life and so glorifies God.

Through Jesus' imitation of the Father's work, in His healing the blind and raising the dead, testimony is given to the Son as LIFE and LIGHT.

Jesus' desire to give life and light also testifies to His relationship with the Father. Jesus demonstrates this intimate knowledge of God masterfully when He washes the feet of His disciples. Jesus does what He has seen in the Father. Now His followers are to do what they see in Jesus; they are to serve one another (13:1-16).

The disciples are to learn loving service from Jesus' love for them (13:34-35). Jesus the Son had experienced the love of God the Father. Jesus had seen the life-giving nature of God. Jesus reflected His own love for the Father supremely in His willingness to lay down His own life. He loved His own in the world as a good shepherd. He gave His life in order that others might have life abundantly, for the Father had given and shared His own life with the Son—in the beginning and in the resurrection (10:1-18).

The truth of where He came from and where He was going identifies this stranger named Jesus. Coming from God and returning to God He was truly LIGHT and LIFE. He was the Father's love—and the Father was the Son's love.

It was of the Son's very nature from His Father to give life—to inspire and finally to expire in the hour of His death.

And such He did, in the world below and present, because of the Father's love from above and before.

John 14-21

"Parting is such sweet sorrow."

Well-chosen words of good-bye linger long in separation—much more those thoughtful farewells of testament, those last summations of life and will from parent to child, those last expressions of care and love for those who remain.

Jesus faced separation from His friends, His disciples, His mother. He anticipated how they would feel and what they would face. Near the end of John's Gospel, Jesus delivers His last will and testament.

> *"Let not your hearts be troubled. Believe in God; believe also in me. In my Father's house are many rooms. If it were not so, would I have told you that I go to prepare a place for you? And if I go and prepare a place for you, I will come again and will take you to myself, that where I am you may be also."*
>
> John 14:1-3

"I will not leave you as orphans; I will come to you."

John 14:18

"Peace I leave with you; my peace I give to you. Not as the world gives do I give to you. Let not your hearts be troubled, neither let them be afraid."

John 14:27

"No longer do I call you servants, for the servant does not know what his master is doing; but I have called you friends, for all that I have heard from my Father I have made known to you."

John 15:15

"But because I have said these things to you, sorrow has filled your heart. Nevertheless, I tell you the truth: it is to your advantage that I go away, for if I do not go away, the Helper will not come to you. But if I go, I will send him to you."

John 16:6-7

"So also you have sorrow now, but I will see you again, and your hearts will rejoice, and no one will take your joy from you."

John 16:22

"I have said these things to you, that in me you may have peace. In the world you will have tribulation. But take heart; I have overcome the world."

John 16:33

Jesus prepares them for His absence by making two profound promises.

First, Jesus promises that He will hear and respond to their prayers when offered "in His name."

> *Whatever you ask in my name, this I will do, that the Father may be glorified in the Son. If you ask me anything in my name, I will do it.*
>
> John 14:13-14

> *If you abide in me, and my words abide in you, ask whatever you wish, and it will be done for you. By this my Father is glorified, that you bear much fruit and so prove to be my disciples.*
>
> John 15:7-8

In that day you will ask nothing of me. Truly, truly, I say to you, whatever you ask of the Father in my name, he will give it to you. Until now you have asked nothing in my name. Ask, and you will receive, that your joy may be full.

John 16:23-24

Jesus promises to do whatever His friends ask in prayer—not because He wants to please His friends, but because He wants to bring glory to the Father. Jesus expects the prayers "in His name" to reflect the concerns of the Father, to be prayed from hearts linked to Jesus' words. The disciples can pray in Jesus' name when as branches of the true Vine they bear fruit which glorifies God (15:1-16).

In His own petitions Jesus exemplifies what it means to pray "in His name."

In His farewell prayer (17:1-26), Jesus' central concern is that the Father be glorified. God has been glorified in Jesus' work. Jesus anticipates that God will now glorify the Son from His death to His life again in the oneness they had previously shared together in glory.

Jesus prays boldly that such glory now be given to the disciples in order that they might be united, to be one in love toward each other. Such glory is the life-giving presence of the Father Himself, a glory which radiates and infuses eternal life in the believer. Such glory unites. It appears and is sustained in the Father's love for the Son. Such love engulfs the believer. Such love overcomes separation.

Second, Jesus promises that He will ask the Father to send an Advocate to be present continually with His friends after He leaves (14:16).

Jesus understood the power of the Evil One, the Adversary whom Job had faced. Not only does Jesus pray for the Holy Father to protect them from the Evil One (17:15), He prays that this protection from the father of lies come through the abiding presence of the Holy Spirit, the Spirit of truth (14:25). By this Advocate the disciples will be guided into all truth, reminded of Jesus' words and their meaning (15:26; 16:13).

But for Jesus there remained one last arrangement to make before His departure.

Hanging on the cross, Jesus noticed His mother. Looking at His beloved friend John, He said poignantly to His mother, "Woman, here is your son" (19:26). John understood this trust as did Mary. In the next moment, as the sour wine touched His parched lips (19:29), Jesus must have remembered her plea, years earlier, for wedding wine at Cana.

> *When the wine ran out, the mother of Jesus said to him, "They have no wine." And Jesus said to her, "Woman, what does this have to do with me? My hour has not yet come."*
>
> John 2:3-4

Now on the cross His hour had come. He drinks the last wine, the bitter cup, to prepare the new wine.

As the first Adam began life in a garden, so the last Adam, Jesus, begins death in a garden tomb (19:41; cf. 1 Cor. 15:45-48).

But the Gardener, the one through whom the first garden was made, appears alive again to Mary Magdalene (John 20:15). And soon thereafter, Jesus begins keeping His promises, extending peace and the Holy Spirit to His disciples (20:19-22).

But there remains one last critical mission for Jesus before He ascends to the Father. He must restore Simon Peter, the man who had denied him three times.

And so, around a charcoal fire, with smells lingering from previous flames of denial (18:18; 21:9), Jesus asks Peter three times, "Do you love me, Simon, son of John?" For Peter's benefit and self-understanding, his lips must form words of admission, not denial. These words constitute his love again for Jesus. The Good Shepherd describes the fruit of such love: "Feed my sheep."

Peter will. Peter does.

The author of the fourth Gospel understood firsthand the transforming power of Jesus' love. John's thunderous, explosive temper—ready to kill Samaritans on one occasion—had been transformed by the stranger from above.

John had received the Son's gift of the Father's eternal life. And John knew that fresh blessings would also fall on future generations—on those who heard about this stranger's signs of glory and who believed He was indeed the Son of God (20:29-31)—blessings even upon us who hear and believe the Stranger from Above.

Acts 1-7

Written by Dr. Luke as a second volume dedicated to his benefactor Theophilus, the book of Acts relates the acts of influential first Christians under the power of the Holy Spirit. The book follows the Gospel according to John and narrates the continued ministry of Jesus in the church through the Spirit.

The story covers a period of some 30 years, beginning with the resurrected Jesus' 40-day teaching seminar with the disciples before His ascension (1:3) and ending with Paul's two-year teaching seminar in Rome while under house arrest (28:30f). The story traces the spread of the word of God westward toward Rome, primarily through the countries on the northern side of the Mediterranean Sea.

As the book opens, Jesus has ordered His disciples to remain in Jerusalem to wait for the promised baptism of the Holy Spirit (1:4-5). After Jesus' ascension, as the apostles are waiting in much prayer, they cast lots to select a witness to the resurrection who will replace the betrayer Judas. Through God's intervention a man named Matthias is chosen, and the complement of 12 apostles is restored.

Soon thereafter, as promised, the disciples experience the baptism of the Holy Spirit:

> *When the day of Pentecost arrived, they were all together in one place. And suddenly there came from heaven a sound like a mighty rushing wind, and it filled the entire house where they were sitting. And divided tongues as of fire appeared to them and rested on each one of them. And they were all filled with the Holy Spirit and began to speak in other tongues as the Spirit gave them utterance.*
>
> Acts 2:1-4

Filled with His Spirit, the Galilean disciples are enabled to speak of God's power in foreign languages they had not learned. Most striking is Peter's transformation and rehabilitation. Peter demonstrates his love for Jesus in feeding His sheep among the multicultural Jews staying in Jerusalem. Like Jesus' words to Peter (John 21:15-22), Peter's words to his fellow Jews are uncompromisingly direct:

> *"Men of Israel, hear these words: Jesus of Nazareth, a man attested to you by God with mighty works and wonders and signs that God did through him in your midst, as you yourselves know—this Jesus, delivered up according to the definite plan and foreknowledge of God, you crucified and killed by the hands of lawless men. God raised him up, loosing the pangs of death, because it was not possible for him to be held by it."*
>
> Acts 2:22-24

The response of the Jewish audience to Peter's preaching is exemplary for seekers of God's will even today.

> *Now when they heard this they were cut to the heart, and said to Peter and the rest of the apostles, "Brothers, what shall we do?" And Peter said to them, "Repent and be baptized every one of you in the name of Jesus Christ for the forgiveness of your sins, and you will receive the gift of the Holy Spirit. For the promise is for you and for your children and for all who are far off, everyone whom the Lord our God calls to himself." And with many other words he bore witness and continued to exhort them, saying, "Save yourselves from this crooked generation." So those who received his word were baptized, and there were added that day about three thousand souls.*
>
> *And they devoted themselves to the apostles' teaching and the fellowship, to the breaking of bread and the prayers.*
>
> Acts 2:37-42

The apostles perform many wonders and signs (2:43; 5:12)—greater works than Jesus even seemed to anticipate. Not simply garments, but the passing shadow of an apostle, is thought to effect healing (5:15).

The power of the Holy Spirit in the early part of Acts is not, however, in the healings. The power is first and foremost in the disciples, speaking with boldness about the resurrection of Jesus (4:8, 13, 31). Among the Sadducees and the temple priests, this message brings opposition and the arrest of Peter and John (4:3; 5:18). Among the disciples this Spirit-filled message inspires generosity.

Indeed, the significance and presence of the Holy Spirit in the early church are reflected in the believers' use of their possessions. For some, the gift of the Spirit stirred a willingness to give to the needy (2:44; 4:32-

35). One disciple was so generous that the apostles nicknamed him "Encourager" (4:36f). By contrast, one Christian couple pretended to be generous, but actually lied to the Holy Spirit about the sales price of their property. The young men who buried this couple would never forget their fatal perjury (5:1-11).

The early church was hardly perfect, but the Spirit within moved the believers to be more generous and seek solutions to their difficulties. When Greek-speaking Christians began complaining about the Aramaic-speaking Christians neglecting to give food to their widows, the dilemma with generosity became an opportunity for Spirit-filled leaders to emerge and address the difficulty (6:1-7).

One of the seven men chosen to help the apostles in solving the problem of distribution was a man named Stephen. As it happens, the Spirit soon inspired Stephen to speak boldly to immigrant Jews about Jesus. During one speech, when Stephen highlighted the pattern of the Jewish ancestors to reject God's prophets like Moses, and the tendency of some to confine God to the temple, his audience became so angry they dragged him outside the city and stoned him (7:1-58). But in death, the remarkable thing is Stephen's prayer:

> *And falling to his knees he cried out with a loud voice, "Lord, do not hold this sin against them." And when he had said this, he fell asleep.*
>
> Acts 7:60

From the beginning, the church devoted itself to prayer. On one occasion when the church had prayed, the house was shaken (4:23-31). Stephen's prayer is a defining moment in the story, for God indeed heard and answered Stephen's petition: The life of a young man named Saul, who held the garments of those who stoned Stephen, would never be the same.

Acts 8-15

The first disciples to see Jesus alive after His crucifixion stayed in Jerusalem, awaiting the promised gift of the Holy Spirit. After the baptism of the Spirit on Pentecost, the church devoted itself to prayer, teaching, and fellowship.

What was this church? Was it another Jewish sect like the Pharisees and Sadducees? Or was it a kind of philosophical association or school or get-together of friends?

The membership and identity of this small band that followed Jesus' "way" would be forever forged through the violent death of Stephen, the first martyr. Stephen's death led to Gentiles becoming believers and occasioned the choice of Paul as missionary to the Gentiles (7:60-8:3).

Stephen's death was the beginning of great persecution against Jesus' disciples, forcing many to leave Jerusalem. Wherever they went, they proclaimed His resurrection from the dead. One associate of Stephen's, Philip by name, took the gospel to the Samaritans, a people one step removed from traditional Judaism. The defeat of magic and superstition by the gospel was signified in Samaria by the conversion of one Simon the magician. After his baptism, however, Simon tried to buy the ability to transfer God's Spirit into people and was sharply rebuked by Peter.

> *But Peter said to him, "May your silver perish with you, because you thought you could obtain the gift of God with money! You have neither part nor lot in this matter, for your heart is not right before God. Repent, therefore, of this wickedness of yours, and pray to the Lord that, if possible, the intent of your heart may be forgiven you. For I see that you are in the gall of bitterness and in the bond of iniquity." And Simon answered, "Pray for me to the Lord, that nothing of what you have said may come upon me."*
>
> Acts 8:20-24

Philip was also given opportunity to extend the reach of the Word through his encounter with the finance minister of the queen of Ethiopia. He met this official reading a passage out loud from Isaiah in his chariot. When Philip explained the references to Jesus, the Ethiopian eunuch insisted on being immersed in a pool of nearby water (8:26-40).

The baptisms of the Samaritans and this Southerner by Philip were preludes to the conversion of a consequential figure in Acts and the signifying drama of the momentous second baptism of God's Spirit.

This second outpouring of the Holy Spirit occurred in the house of a Gentile military officer. The man Cornelius was beloved by many Jews for his generosity. He was also a man of prayer (10:1-43). While Peter was preaching to Cornelius' household, the gift of the Spirit was unexpectedly poured out on the Gentiles in the room. God's holy presence was a clear indication that the Gentiles had received the repentance which brought eternal life (10:44-11:18).

More Gentiles would soon believe as Christians forced to leave Jerusalem preached in Syrian Antioch to the north, the third largest city in the world.

But another drama in the heavenlies had occurred at Stephen's death with crucial ramifications for the church. While Jesus was standing in heaven at the spectacle, Stephen prayed that God would forgive his executioners. God answered this prayer by calling a zealous Pharisee standing nearby at the stoning.

This aggressive Pharisee named Saul acted on what he believed. And he believed the followers of Jesus were dangerous. On his way to capture more disciples, Saul himself was captured by Jesus.

> *Now as he went on his way, he approached Damascus, and suddenly a light from heaven shone around him. And falling to the ground, he heard a voice saying to him, "Saul, Saul, why are you persecuting me?" And he said, "Who are you, Lord?" And he said, "I am Jesus, whom you are persecuting. But rise and enter the city, and you will be told what you are to do."*
>
> Acts 9:3-6

In Damascus, a follower named Ananias was instructed to lay hands on Saul that he might regain his sight. He does somewhat reluctantly and Saul is baptized (9:10-19).

So begins the career of the greatest missionary of the first century—the apostle Paul—who will bring the name of Jesus to Jews, Gentiles, and kings, as well as suffer much for that name (9:15-16). But for now, Saul-Paul has much to learn. After having escaped embarrassingly from Damascus in a basket let down the city wall, Saul goes home to Tarsus. Encourager Barnabas soon brings Saul to the disciples in the great city of Antioch where he learns more about faith in Christ and love for His church (11:19-30).

The church is saddened by the news of the violent death of another Christian: James, the brother of the beloved John, is killed on the orders of King Herod. But the opposition and arrests which ensue are but the occasion for God to rescue His servants. The word of God advances as more and more believe (12:1-25).

The church in Antioch recognizes the gifts of Barnabas and Saul and the Holy Spirit commissions them to leave the city and travel north and west proclaiming the word of God. On this trip, Saul emerges as a powerful spokesman and people begin calling him Paul. Paul is more ready than Barnabas to debate and oppose evil (13:1-14:7). In one rural town, the people believe Paul to be Hermes, the glib speaker, and Barnabas to be Zeus in human form. Both men quickly run from such descriptions. Still, fiery Paul attracts opposition; he is stoned and dragged out of one city for dead (14:8-20).

The trip of Paul and Barnabas demonstrated that indeed God had opened the doors of faith to Gentiles. Many were entering the kingdom of God through persecutions. God was doing a marvelous work (14:21-28).

Acts 15-17

For Jewish males in the first century, circumcision was a proud mark of membership as God's people. When non-Jews became Christians, Jewish disciples were forced to address the issue: "Must Gentiles be circumcised before they can be part of God's people?"

Midway through the story of Acts, the apostles and elders in Jerusalem, under pressure from Christian Pharisees, met with a delegation of believers from Antioch to debate the necessity of circumcision. Their decision—under the influence of the Holy Spirit and the wisdom of Peter and James, the half-brother of Jesus—was not to require circumcision of Gentiles, but rather to ask them to observe the prohibitions already stated in the law for strangers (cf. Leviticus 17:8-13; 18:26).

> *"For it has seemed good to the Holy Spirit and to us to lay on you no greater burden than these requirements: that you abstain from what has been sacrificed to idols, and from blood, and from what has been strangled, and from sexual immorality. If you keep yourselves from these, you will do well. Farewell."*
>
> Acts 15:28-29

The strain this decision relieves is only temporary, however. A new tension surfaces between two dear friends, Paul and his mentor Barnabas. Strong persons of faith can disagree, and disagree Paul and Barnabas did—over whether to have Mark (the eventual author of the second

Gospel) accompany them on their next journey. As it happens, they part company. Barnabas takes Mark while Paul takes Silas (Acts 15:36-41). Later, Paul will write appreciatively of Mark's work, and he no doubt has Barnabas to thank for manifesting his characteristic patience with the young in faith (2 Timothy 4:11).

As the story continues in Acts, the evangelistic work of Barnabas and other Christians who travel to the east and south of Jerusalem is not recounted. The author, Dr. Luke, focuses rather on Paul's ventures into Greece—on which trips Luke accompanies him.

Paul had wanted to travel into Asia, but his plans were often hindered by the Spirit of God (16:6-10). Consequently, Paul is called to Macedonia in Greece and significant events occur in three towns there: Philippi, Thessalonica, and Beroea.

Philippi was a Roman colony with a large contingent of retired military personnel. Apparently there was no synagogue there, so on the Sabbath Paul went to a river outside town where women were praying. A business woman named Lydia heard Paul. She, her household, and other associates were immersed in the nearby river (16:11-15).

On another day in Philippi, Paul was confronted by a poor slave girl who made money for her owners as a fortune-teller. When Paul cast the oracular spirit from the girl, her owners, deprived of their income, were furious and had Paul beaten and imprisoned in chains—actions quite illegal against uncondemned Roman citizens (16:16-24, 37).

After midnight, Paul and Silas were singing and praying in prison. An earthquake awakened the jailer, who was dismayed to see the prison doors wide open! No prisoner, however, had tried to escape. The jailer asked Paul how he might be saved. Soon, the jailer was cleansing Paul's wounds. And soon, the jailer himself was cleansed—in baptism—along with his household. The jailer demonstrated his faith by showing hospitality to Paul with joy (16:25-34).

From his experiences in the Gentile city of Philippi, Paul traveled to Thessalonica where there was a synagogue. Some Jews believed his message of a suffering Messiah, but others pursued him from town to town (17:1-9). In the nearby city of Beroea, the Jews were more receptive, taking time to examine the Scriptures. Many believed, including Greek women and prominent men.

The call to enter Macedonia resulted in many conversions in Philippi, Thessalonica, and Beroea. But Paul was eager to go to the intellectual capital of the world, Athens.

On arrival, however, Paul was shocked. The city was filled with idols. Paul argued with various philosophers. Some despised him as a dilettante, a mere bird collecting random seeds of thought. Others heard Paul as a preacher of foreign gods.

At the Areopagus, Athens' forum for ideas, Paul brought to his polytheistic audience a classic theology of the one God who is Creator and Parent.

> *So Paul, standing in the midst of the Areopagus, said: "Men of Athens, I perceive that in every way you are very religious. For as I passed along and observed the objects of your worship, I found also an altar with this inscription: 'To the unknown god.' What therefore you worship as unknown, this I proclaim to you. The God who made the world and everything in it, being Lord of heaven and earth, does not live in temples made by man, nor is he served by human hands, as though he needed anything, since he himself gives to all mankind life and breath and everything. And he made from one man every nation of mankind to live on all the face of the earth, having determined allotted periods and the boundaries of their dwelling place, that they should seek God, and perhaps feel their way toward him and find him. Yet he is actually not far from each one of us, for*
>
> *"'In him we live and move and have our being';*
>
> *as even some of your own poets have said,*
>
> *"'For we are indeed his offspring.'*
>
> *Being then God's offspring, we ought not to think that the divine being is like gold or silver or stone, an image formed by the art and imagination of man. The times of ignorance God overlooked, but now he commands all people everywhere to repent, because he has fixed a day on which he will judge the world in righteousness by a man whom he has appointed; and of this he has given assurance to all by raising him from the dead."*
>
> Acts 17:22-31

Thinking people often think more than they act. In Athens, the active response to Paul's message amounts to little. A few believe, but most of the intellectuals find the message merely interesting, leaving the forum simply to return to their routines—leaving behind the greatest news and the greatest discovery they could ever conceive or would ever find.

Acts 18-21

The great apostle-missionary Paul was also the artisan-businessman Paul. We learn in Acts that Paul was by trade a leather worker. His closest friends in the great seaport city of Corinth were also leather workers—a Jewish Christian married couple named Aquila and Priscilla (18:1-4, 18).

As he worked with leather, cutting and sewing, Paul no doubt carried on many a conversation with customers and fellow artisans, discussing the Way of Christ. Paul's teaching certainly matured Priscilla and Aquila, for later in Ephesus they were able to correct a talented preacher named Apollos, who had an inadequate understanding of baptism (18:24-28). Paul also later met and taught disciples in Ephesus who had to be baptized again, their second immersion in the name of Jesus (19:1-7).

In his workshop at Corinth, Paul was able to persuade many Gentile God-fearers to believe in Jesus and be immersed in water. Apparently, the conversion of these Gentiles led some Jews, as in the case of a local synagogue leader named Crispus, to also become believers (18:7-11; cf. Romans 11:11-15). Other Jews, however, tried to persuade local officials that Paul was upsetting the peace (*Pax Romana*) Rome had brought. Time and again, proconsuls and city officials dismissed such accusations against Paul (18:12-17).

How Christianity can impact the business and economics of a city is profiled dramatically in Paul's three-year stay at Ephesus. Ephesus, with its inviolable temple of Artemis, was the great banking capital of Asia. Many a businessman and artisan made their living in connection with the goddess and her temple. One silversmith who made shrines of Artemis quickly realized that Paul's preaching of one God could mean economic collapse for any business associated with Artemis. The attempt by Demetrius the silversmith to stir up a riot against Paul was thwarted by a sensible town clerk who warned the crowd to follow legal rather than vigilante remedies of resolution (19:23-41).

Those who believed in Ephesus understood that the Way of Christ meant repentance—changing their ways of thinking and living. When they saw how God did extraordinary things through Paul, even by the sweat bands he wore in his work (19:11-16), many abandoned their old superstitions and reliance on magic.

> *And a number of those who had practiced magic arts brought their books together and burned them in the sight of all. And they counted the value of them and found it came to fifty thousand pieces of silver. So the word of the Lord continued to increase and prevail mightily.*
>
> Acts 19:19-20

Paul, of course, did not always hold everyone in rapt attention, even during his sermons. At one late-night Sunday gathering of Christians in a third floor apartment at Troas, a stuffy room and a long-winded Paul led to an incident which thankfully had a happy ending.

> *And a young man named Eutychus, sitting at the window, sank into a deep sleep as Paul talked still longer. And being overcome by sleep, he fell down from the third story and was taken up dead. But Paul went down and bent over him, and taking him in his arms, said, "Do not be alarmed, for his life is in him." And when Paul had gone up and had broken bread and eaten, he conversed with them a long while, until daybreak, and so departed. And they took the youth away alive, and were not a little comforted.*
>
> Acts 20:9-12

As Acts moves toward its conclusion, Paul also moves ever closer to his final showdown in Jerusalem and a final voyage west to Rome. But as he first travels toward Jerusalem for Pentecost, Paul calls the elders of the church in Ephesus to meet him one last time, in Miletus (20:13-27). There Paul delivers the only sermon to church members recorded in Acts.

> *Pay careful attention to yourselves and to all the flock, in which the Holy Spirit has made you overseers, to care for the church of God, which he obtained with his own blood. I know that after my departure fierce wolves will come in among you, not sparing the flock; and from among your own selves will arise men speaking twisted things, to draw away the disciples after them. Therefore be alert, remembering that for three years I did not cease night or day to admonish every one with tears. And now I commend you to God and to the word of his grace, which is able to build*

you up and to give you the inheritance among all those who are sanctified. I coveted no one's silver or gold or apparel. You yourselves know that these hands ministered to my necessities and to those who were with me. In all things I have shown you that by working hard in this way we must help the weak and remember the words of the Lord Jesus, how he himself said, 'It is more blessed to give than to receive.'"

Acts 20:28-35

Paul then journeys on to Jerusalem via Tyre, Ptolemais, and Caesarea. In the latter city he stays with the evangelist Philip, one of the seven Spirit-filled men who had been chosen much earlier to assist the apostles in Jerusalem. Philip has four daughters, all unmarried, all prophets. More significantly, another prophet, Agabus, comes to Paul and announces:

"Thus says the Holy Spirit, 'This is how the Jews at Jerusalem will bind the man who owns this belt and deliver him into the hands of the Gentiles.'" When we heard this, we and the people there urged him not to go up to Jerusalem. Then Paul answered, "What are you doing, weeping and breaking my heart? For I am ready not only to be imprisoned but even to die in Jerusalem for the name of the Lord Jesus." And since he would not be persuaded, we ceased and said, "Let the will of the Lord be done."

Acts 21:11b-14

So Paul travels on to Jerusalem, knowing the Lord's will would be done, that he would declare the message about the Nazarene finally in the imperial capital city—Rome itself.

Acts 22-28

The book of Acts recounts what happened when the hope of the Jewish faith also became the hope of the Gentile world.

In retelling this story, Acts records how Jewish Christians cautiously came to accept in fellowship Gentile believers. The transformations which occurred in churches of mixed ethnicity eventually brought to the surface a defining question: Is this new Way (this sect of the Nazarenes) opposed to everything Jewish—the people, the law, the temple (21:21, 28)? The last part of Acts, through the person of Paul, deals with this question.

At the end of Acts, Paul is making his final journey to Jerusalem. He is warned through church and prophetic word that he will become a prisoner. He does and will remain one till the end of Acts—in Rome.

Paul does not deny or abandon his Jewish heritage and traditions. In Jerusalem he pays the expenses of others who are completing vows. Nevertheless, Paul faces accusations against himself and the Way.

> *When the seven days were almost completed, the Jews from Asia, seeing him in the temple, stirred up the whole crowd and laid hands on him, crying out, "Men of Israel, help! This is the man who is teaching everyone everywhere against the people and the law and this place. Moreover, he even brought Greeks into the temple and has defiled this holy place."*
>
> Acts 21:27-28

Paul's defense is to emphasize his connection to Jerusalem and his identity as a Pharisee (21:37-22:5). Paul had taken his religion so seriously that he had been willing not only to argue but to apprehend and abuse the Jews who had become the first followers of Jesus (26:9-11). Jesus, however, had appeared to Paul and spoken to him (22:6-13). Paul heard the commission.

> *"And he said, 'The God of our fathers appointed you to know his will, to see the Righteous One and to hear a voice from his mouth; for you will be a witness for him to everyone of what you have seen and heard. And now why do you wait? Rise and be baptized and wash away your sins, calling on his name.'"*
>
> Acts 22:14-16

In spite of his honest recollections, Paul faces assassination plots by groups of zealous Jews. He is only rescued by his nephew who informs the Roman authorities of the conspiracy to kill him (23:12-35).

After Paul is whisked away at night to Caesarea, the seat of Roman government in Palestine, never again to see Jerusalem, he is able to offer his defense successively to three different officials—two governors, Felix and Festus, and the king, Agrippa II. In these defenses, Paul does not retreat from remonstrating that he is a faithful Jew.

> *But this I confess to you, that according to the Way, which they call a sect, I worship the God of our fathers, believing everything*

laid down by the Law and written in the Prophets, having a hope in God, which these men themselves accept, that there will be a resurrection of both the just and the unjust. So I always take pains to have a clear conscience toward both God and man.

Acts 24:14-16

Paul argued in his defense, "Neither against the law of the Jews, nor against the temple, nor against Caesar have I committed any offense."

Acts 25:8

Paul reiterates his message:

To this day I have had the help that comes from God, and so I stand here testifying both to small and great, saying nothing but what the prophets and Moses said would come to pass: that the Christ must suffer and that, by being the first to rise from the dead, he would proclaim light both to our people and to the Gentiles."

Acts 26:22-23

No Roman authority finds that Paul has done anything to deserve either death or imprisonment (26:31). Nevertheless, he is assigned captive-passage to Rome since he has exercised his privilege of Roman citizenship in appealing to the emperor himself for a hearing of innocence. So begins in the last two chapters of Acts Paul's perilous sea journey to Rome.

Eventually after storm and shipwreck, being marooned on Malta, and finally embarking to Rome, Paul arrives for the first time of his life in Italy, at the port of Puteoli (27:1-28:13). There he meets with believers in churches he did not establish, still under house arrest (28:14-16).

In Rome, he invites Jewish leaders to meet him and tells them, "Brothers, though I had done nothing against our people or the customs of our fathers, yet I was delivered as a prisoner from Jerusalem into the hands of the Romans" (28:17b).

As Acts closes, Paul has been in Rome two years. Some Jews become believers but most do not, leading Paul to recall the passage from Isaiah:

"'Go to this people, and say,
"You will indeed hear but never understand,

and you will indeed see but never perceive."
For this people's heart has grown dull,
and with their ears they can barely hear,
and their eyes they have closed;
lest they should see with their eyes
and hear with their ears
and understand with their heart
and turn, and I would heal them.'"

Acts 28:26-27

Is the way of Jesus then a hostile, aggressive rejection of the law of Moses and the Jewish people? Through the words of the Pharisee Paul, Acts answers a resounding "no!"

Paul speaks on behalf of the hope springing from the Jewish Scriptures, the hope dear to Pharisees, the hope of resurrection from the dead (23:6). Rather than a rejection, Paul understands the way of Jesus as completing the prophetic words of Scripture. Just as Paul the Jew had to repent and be baptized to wash away his sins (22:16), so he expects his fellow Jews, as well as Gentiles, to repent and be baptized (26:20). The book of Acts preserves the hope that the Jews may see in Jesus the fulfillment of hope predicted by their own prophets.

Romans 1-6

Paul's first letter in the New Testament is addressed to "God's beloved in Rome, called to be saints" (1:7). In Scripture, Paul's letters are arranged not by their chronology, but by their length. Though the letter to the Romans comes first, it is not Paul's earliest. It is, however, the longest, dictated to his secretary Tertius, while Paul was living in Corinth (16:22-23).

By his own standards, Paul bordered on contradicting himself in even writing the Christians there. Paul had not founded the church in Rome, and he had made it a practice of not intruding in churches he had not begun. However, Paul wanted to travel to Spain, and Rome was a convenient place to stop on the way (15:14-24). A letter would introduce him and the gospel he preached to the many Christians he had not met and the many who had never prayed for him (15:30-32).

But Paul also wrote from a profound sense of personal obligation, as the apostle called by Jesus to the Gentiles, to preach and bring the obedience of faith in the very capital of the Gentile world, Rome.

> *I do not want you to be unaware, brothers, that I have often intended to come to you (but thus far have been prevented), in order that I may reap some harvest among you as well as among the rest of the Gentiles. I am under obligation both to Greeks and to barbarians, both to the wise and to the foolish. So I am eager to preach the gospel to you also who are in Rome.*
>
> *For I am not ashamed of the gospel, for it is the power of God for salvation to everyone who believes, to the Jew first and also to the Greek. For in it the righteousness of God is revealed from faith for faith, as it is written, "The righteous shall live by faith."*
>
> *For the wrath of God is revealed from heaven against all ungodliness and unrighteousness of men, who by their unrighteousness suppress the truth.*
>
> Romans 1:13-18

The reason for God's wrath, Paul says, is not atheism. Most people in history have known there is a God because of the power and design evident in the ordered world. God's wrath is revealed from heaven, not because of ignorance but because of ingratitude. Ingratitude and thanklessness have combined with human pride, and such arrogance has led to idolatry, the exchanging of the glory of God for idols (1:19-23).

As humans have worshipped each other rather than the Creator, God has progressively allowed the restraints to human behavior to erode. Desire has grown in the playground of darkened thinking (1:24-25). Homosexuality appeared (1:26-27). Wickedness of all sorts has expanded. Idolatry is at the root of dark thinking and wicked lives (1:28-32).

Of course it is easier to see the wickedness in others than in oneself. Paul sternly warns against so easily judging others when one's own life may be selfish and self-seeking. Paul as a Jew had had to reckon with good moral Gentiles who had often been more obedient to the law of Moses than many Jews. Paul makes a shocking statement:

> *For no one is a Jew who is merely one outwardly, nor is circumcision outward and physical. But a Jew is one inwardly,*

and circumcision is a matter of the heart, by the Spirit, not by the letter. His praise is not from man but from God.

Romans 2:28-29

This raised the question whether there had been any advantage in being a Jew. Paul says "absolutely." It was a unique blessing to have been entrusted with the oracles of God (3:1-8). Yet no Jew could come to a right relationship with God through attempts to keep the law, no matter the zeal and conscientiousness. Sin has exercised controlling power in every human's life, Jew and Gentile (3:1-20).

In such a bleak, hopeless situation Paul declares that God took decisive action in putting forward Jesus Christ to set us free from the inescapable control of Sin. It was God's gracious decision, not motivated by human attractiveness or obedience (3:21-31).

Surprisingly, Paul found a precedent for God's action toward Gentiles (and Jews) in God's relation with Abraham, the father of Israel. Actually, Abraham is father of us all. As one "ungodly," Abraham believed God could raise the dead, and God was pleased with Abraham before he was circumcised. We are challenged to believe that God raised Jesus from the dead and to understand why (4:1-25).

More than that, we are challenged to grasp how and why Christ would die for weak, sinful enemies of God. Paul's only explanation is love: God loves us. And God wants us to share in His coming glory, a glory we had earlier exchanged for idols (5:1-11). God's grace has abounded (5:12-21).

But grace abounding doesn't mean sin can abound as well! The gospel means that Christ's death was a "death to sin" (6:10). In baptism the believer is plunged into Christ's death—united with Christ in His death (6:3-5). The believer exits the time and space of normal life to enter into the death of Jesus and so participate in death to Sin. There is a change of worlds. No longer does Sin have to be obeyed. No more fatalism.

The believer can, of course, choose Sin as master again (6:12ff). Habits die hard. Memories linger. But the stranglehold of Sin is no more. In Christ, in His death, the relation to Sin has changed.

It is truly difficult, however, to focus attention on the new condition "in Christ" (6:11). Nevertheless, it is necessary to view oneself as "dead to Sin, alive to God, in Christ." It takes concentration and reminders to do this. Sin is a power. Death is a power. The gospel means that "in Christ" such powers are finally harmless. Suffering still exists, yes, and temptations arise. But "in Christ," destiny is no longer on the side of wickedness.

But Paul as a Jew could not be satisfied until he had grappled with the place of the law of Moses in this picture of the human situation. How could Sin find opportunity in the holy law?

Romans 7-11

As Paul dictated his letter to the Christians at Rome, he had much on his mind. He was preparing to leave for Jerusalem and he knew that he might face a disheartening rejection of his relief efforts (15:25-27, 30-32). He was also thinking beyond Jerusalem to a much-desired trip to Rome, and then to Spain (15:28-29).

Paul thus writes to Christians he knows in Rome, hoping they will commend his work to those whom he has not yet met (16:3-16). He feels obliged to share the gospel he has lived and preached. In his letter he does so, with great vigor and intense engagement.

For Paul, Christ's death was the decisive finish to any Jewish confidence that keeping the law made things right with God (10:3-4). The law in weakened flesh could not bring freedom (8:3). On the contrary, matters only became worse.

> *Yet if it had not been for the law, I would not have known sin. For I would not have known what it is to covet if the law had not said, "You shall not covet." But sin, seizing an opportunity through the commandment, produced in me all kinds of covetousness. For apart from the law, sin lies dead. I was once alive apart from the law, but when the commandment came, sin came alive and I died. The very commandment that promised life proved to be death to me. For sin, seizing an opportunity through the commandment, deceived me and through it killed me.*
>
> Romans 7:7b-11

Paul rejects any suggestion thereby that the law was sin and caused death. No! The law is holy, just, and good; the law is spiritual (7:12-14). The law dwells in my mind and inner self. I understand through the law what is good and right to do. Sin, however, dwells in my members in the flesh, and I wind up doing what I don't want to do (7:16-20). I am a walking battlefield of opposing forces. And in all of this, Sin tragically exploits the law!

Paul says that such self-condemnation has come to an end with the new existence in Christ (7:24-25; 8:1). In sending His Son in flesh, God condemned not me, but sin (8:3-4). God's love is poured out through the Holy Spirit (5:5). The Spirit now dwells in me, not sin. Now the Spirit can put to death the deeds of evil in the body (8:9-13) as the wait continues for the redemption of the body in the resurrection.

For the moment, however, we continue to suffer, even as Christ suffered. Paul says that suffering must happen before we can be glorified one day with Christ. The creation shares this predicament as it too decays. The Spirit within the believer communicates the condition and heart of the believer to God (8:15-27). The Spirit is shared by God's love.

Life is sustained only by the love of God. Paul asserts that nothing can separate us from this love:

> *For I am sure that neither death nor life, nor angels nor rulers, nor things present nor things to come, nor powers, nor height nor depth, nor anything else in all creation, will be able to separate us from the love of God in Christ Jesus our Lord.*
>
> Romans 8:38-39

Shockingly, however, Paul says in the very next sentence that he wishes he could be separated from God's love—if it would mean the immediate salvation of his kinsmen, his fellow Jews!

> *I am speaking the truth in Christ—I am not lying; my conscience bears me witness in the Holy Spirit—that I have great sorrow and unceasing anguish in my heart. For I could wish that I myself were accursed and cut off from Christ for the sake of my brothers, my kinsmen according to the flesh.*
>
> Romans 9:1-3

As Paul labors through his thinking and feelings and emotions, he recalls the independence of God's actions in Israel and the utter, constant dependence of humans upon God's tender mercy (9:6-27).

Like Stephen's prayer for Saul, Paul too can only pray for Israel (10:1). Paul, however, cannot help but think of his own responsibilities and his apostleship. And the Romans overhear Paul reasserting that everyone needs to hear the word of Christ; and that hearing means someone is proclaiming; and the someone who proclaims must be sent (10:5-17). Paul is preparing the Christians at Rome for his time among them before he goes to Spain.

But the Roman Christians become privy to much more, for Paul reveals what he thinks is really happening in his own ministry as regards his fellow Jews. Paul does not, cannot, accept the idea that God has rejected His chosen people (11:1, 29). On one level, God clearly has not rejected them. Look at Paul—God has accepted Paul, and Paul is an Israelite, a member of the tribe of Benjamin. Certainly there is a part of Israel, a remnant, who believes the word of Christ (11:2-6).

But the problem is with the rest, the majority. What about them? Remarkably, Paul says that they were hardened; God made them slow and dull. As a result, they have stumbled. But it is not the end; they are not out of the race:

> *So I ask, did they stumble in order that they might fall? By no means! Rather, through their trespass salvation has come to the Gentiles, so as to make Israel jealous. Now if their trespass means riches for the world, and if their failure means riches for the Gentiles, how much more will their full inclusion mean!*
>
> *Now I am speaking to you Gentiles. Inasmuch then as I am an apostle to the Gentiles, I magnify my ministry in order somehow to make my fellow Jews jealous, and thus save some of them. For if their rejection means the reconciliation of the world, what will their acceptance mean but life from the dead?*
>
> Romans 11:11-15

During this hardening of Israel, Gentiles have heard the gospel. But Paul understands a hidden purpose in this for the Jews. As more Gentiles have become believers, Paul has seen the zealous character of his kinsmen turn to jealousy at God's acceptance of the Gentiles. As a result, some have been saved. But there is another secret:

> *Lest you be wise in your own sight, I do not want you to be unaware of this mystery, brothers: a partial hardening has come*

upon Israel, until the fullness of the Gentiles has come in. And in this way all Israel will be saved, as it is written,

"The Deliverer will come from Zion,
he will banish ungodliness from Jacob."

Romans 11:25-26

It is easier then to understand Paul's ambition and relentless drive. He understood his mission to the Gentiles as a mission to the Jews as well. He also thought their disobedience was necessary before God could extend them the mercy they needed. Paul doesn't pretend to understand it all. He can only trust God's purposes to be good and right and true.

Oh, the depth of the riches and wisdom and knowledge of God! How unsearchable are his judgments and how inscrutable his ways!

Romans 11:33

Romans 12-16

How could a good Pharisee ever consider his lifework to be persuading non-Jews to obey the God of Jesus? The Pharisee Saul didn't have this in mind; he was busy persecuting Jesus' followers. Saul was convinced he had things right with God. But one day on a dusty road to Damascus, his world was turned upside down. Jesus dramatically appeared to him. No man could have been more surprised!

From that day forward, Paul understood mercy. No one had to explain it. God had mercifully called a violent man to reality. It is not surprising that in his letter to the Christians in Rome Paul feels so strongly, and utters so clearly, God's tender mercies—mercies, not only for Gentiles, but for all Israel, even in her disobedience. Mercy, not law, was now making its appeal.

I appeal to you therefore, brothers, by the mercies of God, to present your bodies as a living sacrifice, holy and acceptable to God, which is your spiritual worship. Do not be conformed to this world, but be transformed by the renewal of your mind, that by testing you may discern what is the will of God, what is good and acceptable and perfect.

Romans 12:1-2

Not dead animal sacrifices. God desires a living sacrifice—one's entire body! The Christian sacrifices himself when he exercises his gifts for the health of the church, the body of Christ (12:3-7). Such sacrifice should be genuine, with developing feelings of real care.

> *Let love be genuine. Abhor what is evil; hold fast to what is good. Love one another with brotherly affection. Outdo one another in showing honor. Do not be slothful in zeal, be fervent in spirit, serve the Lord.*
>
> Romans 12:9-11

It is a difficult sacrifice, for example, not to return evil for evil. It is a most difficult sacrifice to bless those who do evil, only possible with renewed thinking "in Christ," only possible within modest self-appraisal.

> *Beloved, never avenge yourselves, but leave it to the wrath of God, for it is written, "Vengeance is mine, I will repay, says the Lord." To the contrary, "if your enemy is hungry, feed him; if he is thirsty, give him something to drink; for by so doing you will heap burning coals on his head." Do not be overcome by evil, but overcome evil with good.*
>
> Romans 12:19-21

Human governments are intended by God to commend the good and punish the wrongdoer (13:1-5). The church in Rome had memories of government action, when Emperor Claudius had expelled all Jews from Rome (Acts 18:2). Paul himself had experienced imprisonments and beatings. Paul writes Romans in the early reign of Nero. If tradition is correct, Paul will later die in Rome under Nero. Governments legislate and enforce laws for civility. Sometimes, however, the good and the best of us fall victim to governments blind to the will of the Creator.

Christ, of course, had submitted to Roman execution. Paul recognized in this Jesus' willingness to please God, not to please Himself.

> *We who are strong have an obligation to bear with the failings of the weak, and not to please ourselves. Let each of us please his neighbor for his good, to build him up. For Christ did not please himself, but as it is written, "The reproaches of those who reproached you fell on me."*
>
> Romans 15:1-3

Paul saw a direct application of Jesus' example to a perennial situation in the church between Christians whose consciences were overly scrupulous and Christians who had a clearer understanding of God's directives (14:1-15:6). Concretely, Paul knew of Christians who abstained from meat and wine. Unhappily, some of them were critical of others who ate meat and drank wine. Paul says flatly that nothing is inherently unclean. These Christians "weak in faith" should not judge the Christians who have no problem with diet.

But Paul knows that this does not solve the problem. The reality is that it is difficult for the weak to become strong. The burden is really on the strong. First, the strong should not despise or make fun of the abstainers. Secondly, the strong must be careful not to encourage the weak, through any blatant action, to eat or drink what they believe is wrong to eat or drink.

> *Do not, for the sake of food, destroy the work of God. Everything is indeed clean, but it is wrong for anyone to make another stumble by what he eats. It is good not to eat meat or drink wine or do anything that causes your brother to stumble.*
>
> Romans 14:20-21

Interestingly, Paul does not define the weak as the Jewish Christian and the strong as the Gentile Christian. Perhaps most of the Christians at Rome were Gentiles. Certainly Paul wants all the Gentile Christians to live at peace with each other, seeking ways to love each other, for Paul wants the sacrifice of their lives to be acceptable to God (15:16, 9-13; 12:1-2).

As he closes his letter to the house churches in Rome, Paul draws attention to many friends and co-workers who are now living there; twenty seven names are mentioned! (16:3-15) Such people can provide living testimonials of Paul to others who did not know him. Paul strongly desired that all would be able to thoughtfully pray for him (15:30-32) even as he closes his letter in prayer:

> *Now to him who is able to strengthen you according to my gospel and the preaching of Jesus Christ, according to the revelation of the mystery that was kept secret for long ages but has now been disclosed and through the prophetic writings has been made known to all nations, according to the command of the eternal God, to bring about the obedience of faith—to the only wise God be glory forevermore through Jesus Christ! Amen.*
>
> Romans 16:25-27

1 Corinthians 1-6

"It's whom you know that really counts"—so thought the Christians in Corinth. Such thinking, however, had led to feuding. The converts had taken excessive pride in their favorite teacher or in the person who had baptized them.

> *For it has been reported to me by Chloe's people that there is quarreling among you, my brothers. What I mean is that each one of you says, "I follow Paul," or "I follow Apollos," or "I follow Cephas," or "I follow Christ." Is Christ divided? Was Paul crucified for you? Or were you baptized in the name of Paul?*
>
> 1 Corinthians 1:11-13

What could Paul say to stop such quarreling?

Paul had written a letter earlier (now lost) reminding the Corinthians not to associate with immoral people (1 Cor. 5:9). After receiving a letter from them with many questions (7:1) and after talking with traveling Corinthians (16:17; 1:11), Paul was thankful (1:4) but also anxious (4:21). He decided to write a second letter to Corinth which we call "First Corinthians."

Paul chides them for having forgotten the message that had formed them as the church of God. The message had for Jews been a stone to stumble on; for Gentiles, foolishness (1:18-25)—the message about a young Jew, executed in a backwater eastern province, who was now proclaimed Lord and Christ.

And what of the credentials and resumes of these Corinthians who had believed such a message? Paul says God had chosen them—foolish, weak, low, even despised—to confound the wise and strong just as the message about a crucified Messiah had been an object of scorn to many.

Had the Corinthians forgotten their humble roots (1:26-31)? Or perhaps they had forgotten Paul's personal preaching style. Paul had not displayed great oratory skills, at least not like other preachers and teachers such as Apollos.

> *And I was with you in weakness and in fear and much trembling, and my speech and my message were not in plausible words of*

wisdom, but in demonstration of the Spirit and of power, so that your faith might not rest in the wisdom of men but in the power of God.

1 Corinthians 2:3-5

Indeed, misplaced security had led to a partisan spirit among the believers. Elevating one teacher above another was not the way to security and assurance.

What then is Apollos? What is Paul? Servants through whom you believed, as the Lord assigned to each. I planted, Apollos watered, but God gave the growth. So neither he who plants nor he who waters is anything, but only God who gives the growth.

1 Corinthians 3:5-7

The Corinthians had actually been too parochial, too narrow in their thinking, for in fact all things belonged to them. They need not fight for their own turf to achieve security.

So let no one boast in men. For all things are yours, whether Paul or Apollos or Cephas or the world or life or death or the present or the future—all are yours, and you are Christ's, and Christ is God's.

1 Corinthians 3:21-23

Again, Paul did not want the Corinthians to forget the status of the teachers they so much admired and desired to imitate:

To the present hour we hunger and thirst, we are poorly dressed and buffeted and homeless, and we labor, working with our own hands. When reviled, we bless; when persecuted, we endure; when slandered, we entreat. We have become, and are still, like the scum of the world, the refuse of all things.

1 Corinthians 4:11-13

Had they really wanted to imitate the apostles—men sentenced to death?

Already you have all you want! Already you have become rich! Without us you have become kings! And would that you did reign, so that we might share the rule with you! For I think that God has exhibited us apostles as last of all, like men sentenced to death, because we have become a spectacle to the world, to angels, and to men.

1 Corinthians 4:8-9

In their attitudes toward their teachers, Paul diagnoses a pervasive arrogance of heart. He sees evidence of this in their toleration of one Christian who is living with his stepmother. Paul pronounces judgment:

> *When you are assembled in the name of the Lord Jesus and my spirit is present, with the power of our Lord Jesus, you are to deliver this man to Satan for the destruction of the flesh, so that his spirit may be saved in the day of the Lord.*
>
> 1 Corinthians 5:4-5

Paul is also disturbed that they are going to the Roman courtroom to decide issues between brothers. Better to accept being defrauded and wronged than to be involved in asserting rights in the world (6:1-11).

"Rights" as well as all possessions are in fact the Lord's—including the body. The believers in Corinth were wrestling with how to understand the body and all its desires. When among them Paul had preached that a Christian was free, that in baptism a person received the Spirit. But how to understand the implications of this for one's body? Is everything permissible?

Paul explains that freedom in Christ does not mean freedom to do anything one likes. Not every action benefits. Besides, the desires of the body are not of equal weight. And too, desires are not necessarily needs. The sexual drive is not the same as the hunger for food (6:12-14). It is unthinkable that a man should unite his body—a member of Christ—into a prostitute.

> *Flee from sexual immorality. Every other sin a person commits is outside the body, but the sexually immoral person sins against his own body. Or do you not know that your body is a temple of the Holy Spirit within you, whom you have from God? You are not your own, for you were bought with a price. So glorify God in your body.*
>
> 1 Corinthians 6:18-20

Not all of the Corinthians were so liberal in thinking about their bodies. Some were much more conservative, trying to understand Paul's choice to be celibate. Paul addresses some of their questions in chapter 7.

1 Corinthians 7-10

In a letter written to the apostle from Corinth, Paul was asked whether a man should have sexual contact with a woman (7:1). The question sounds strange because Paul knew that some there were not at all disapproving of a member who was sexually active with his stepmother (5:1). Paul had criticized those who believed Christians were free in the body to be joined with prostitutes (6:12-20).

In the letter from Corinth to Paul, there are no questions from the sexually permissive members. The questions apparently come from the more ascetic, modest Corinthians. Or perhaps from those who thought they were repeating what he had told them when he was there—for they remembered Paul was celibate and that he wished others might, during difficult times, remain unmarried as he (7:7, 26).

Whatever the circumstances, Paul responds that the only celibacy he sees justifiable between married Christians who desire each other is abstinence for a predetermined period for prayer. At the same time, Paul reassures the Christians married to non-Christians that sexual contact with their unbelieving spouse is permitted.

> *If any woman has a husband who is an unbeliever, and he consents to live with her, she should not divorce him. For the unbelieving husband is made holy because of his wife, and the unbelieving wife is made holy because of her husband. Otherwise your children would be unclean, but as it is, they are holy. But if the unbelieving partner separates, let it be so. In such cases the brother or sister is not enslaved. God has called you to peace.*
>
> 1 Corinthians 7:13-15

Paul's comments here require cautious interpretation because we do not have the Corinthians' letter to Paul. We do know that Paul writes as a spiritual father who wants to help his children avoid all unnecessary anxieties (7:32-35). This is his primary motivation.

In their letter, the Corinthians had apparently asked Paul about eating meat which had come from animals slaughtered for pagan sacrifices. Paul agreed with those who understood such meat was not contaminated because the sacrifices were indeed to non-gods (8:4-6).

But for Paul, that was not the critical issue. What about that brother who grew up believing in idols and for whom strong associations with the power of idols still linger in his heart?

> *For if anyone sees you who have knowledge eating in an idol's temple, will he not be encouraged, if his conscience is weak, to eat food offered to idols? And so by your knowledge this weak person is destroyed, the brother for whom Christ died. Thus, sinning against your brothers and wounding their conscience when it is weak, you sin against Christ. Therefore, if food makes my brother stumble, I will never eat meat, lest I make my brother stumble.*
>
> 1 Corinthians 8:10-12

Paul understands that we may have primitive, subconscious associations which may make us vulnerable to idolatry. The stronger brother must be sensitive to the biography of the weak. Is this too much for Paul to ask of the strong, to give up their legitimate rights to eat in pagan temples? Paul thinks not. He appeals to his own example.

Paul had every "right" to expect money from those whom he had taught. Paul, however, had consciously, deliberately chosen not to make use of this right to reap material benefit from his preaching. He made the gospel free of charge (9:6-18). He gave up his "rights" on behalf of the weak so that there would be no obstacle in the way of the gospel.

> *To the weak I became weak, that I might win the weak. I have become all things to all people, that by all means I might save some. I do it all for the sake of the gospel, that I may share with them in its blessings.*
>
> 1 Corinthians 9:22-23

Paul is also concerned about the faithfulness of the so-called "strong." If they frequent temple banquets, do they think themselves so strong as to be invincible to idol worship? Paul remembers God's people in the wilderness who experienced His protection. Yet many of them became idolaters and immoral.

> *No, I imply that what pagans sacrifice they offer to demons and not to God. I do not want you to be participants with demons. You cannot drink the cup of the Lord and the cup of demons. You cannot partake of the table of the Lord and the table of demons.*
>
> 1 Corinthians 10:20-21

Paul concludes his thoughts by recommending one eat without question what is purchased at the meat market and what is placed on the table by the host. However, if a weak brother is there and identifies the meat as "sacred food," then one is not to eat.

> *So, whether you eat or drink, or whatever you do, do all to the glory of God. Give no offense to Jews or to Greeks or to the church of God, just as I try to please everyone in everything I do, not seeking my own advantage, but that of many, that they may be saved. Be imitators of me, as I am of Christ.*
>
> 1 Corinthians 10:31-11:1

1 Corinthians 11-16

Paul heard that all was not well in the church's assemblies on Sunday. The meal they were eating together to honor Jesus was not at all honoring the Lord. Members were not waiting for the latecomers. Some were going ahead to eat and finishing the food before others arrived. Paul has to remind them that the bread in their meal together is Jesus' body. They are failing to discern the church as Jesus' body when they disrespect the latecomers at their common meal by not leaving anything to eat (11:17-34). For Paul this is symptomatic of an uncaring individualism in the church.

Paul had begun his letter to Corinth shaming them for their petty favoritism toward individual teachers. It had caused quarrels in church. In Paul's thinking, the Corinthians had failed to understand the church as a body and to realize the interdependence of the members on one another.

> *For just as the body is one and has many members, and all the members of the body, though many, are one body, so it is with Christ. For in one Spirit we were all baptized into one body—Jews or Greeks, slaves or free—and all were made to drink of one Spirit.*
>
> 1 Corinthians 12:12-13

By the Spirit, God had activated a variety of gifts in the members of the body to be used for the common good. The Corinthians, however, were thinking of individual spiritual gifts as reassurances of their spirituality rather than as occasions for loving others.

If I speak in the tongues of men and of angels, but have not love, I am a noisy gong or a clanging cymbal. And if I have prophetic powers, and understand all mysteries and all knowledge, and if I have all faith, so as to remove mountains, but have not love, I am nothing. If I give away all I have, and if I deliver up my body to be burned, but have not love, I gain nothing.

1 Corinthians 13:1-3

The Corinthians' spirituality had become a particular problem in the matter of tongues. The tongues in Corinth were human words not intelligible to other humans, unless someone interpreted. Paul doesn't prohibit tongue speaking, but wisely promotes another gift, hoping they will become preoccupied with gifts more profitable for the entire church.

Pursue love, and earnestly desire the spiritual gifts, especially that you may prophesy. For one who speaks in a tongue speaks not to men but to God; for no one understands him, but he utters mysteries in the Spirit. On the other hand, the one who prophesies speaks to people for their upbuilding and encouragement and consolation. The one who speaks in a tongue builds up himself, but the one who prophesies builds up the church. Now I want you all to speak in tongues, but even more to prophesy. The one who prophesies is greater than the one who speaks in tongues, unless someone interprets, so that the church may be built up.

1 Corinthians 14:1-5

The face of the assembly should reflect the character of God. Since God is a God of peace and not disorder, so the assembly should be conducted with order and decorum (14:33, 40).

Paul reminds them of the basic message of the gospel because their behavior was reflecting a loss of memory.

For I delivered to you as of first importance what I also received: that Christ died for our sins in accordance with the Scriptures, that he was buried, that he was raised on the third day in accordance with the Scriptures.

1 Corinthians 15:3-4

Had the Christians forgotten that Christ died for their sins? Who were they to have any pride or self-importance or partisanship? The Lord had died! The meal they ate in the bread and cup proclaimed His death.

Some in Corinth did not believe their own bodies would be raised after being dead. Paul is shocked by this, for it made a sham of Christ's resurrection.

> *But if there is no resurrection of the dead, then not even Christ has been raised. And if Christ has not been raised, then our preaching is in vain and your faith is in vain.*
>
> 1 Corinthians 15:13-14

Others in Corinth may have continued to believe, as many of their pagan neighbors, that the body was bad or at best irrelevant. Paul, however, insists that we will be raised as bodies—not as souls or spirits. The body will be raised to life again. And how?

> *And what you sow is not the body that is to be, but a bare kernel, perhaps of wheat or of some other grain.*
>
> *It is sown a natural body; it is raised a spiritual body. If there is a natural body, there is also a spiritual body.*
>
> *Just as we have borne the image of the man of dust, we shall also bear the image of the man of heaven.*
>
> *I tell you this, brothers: flesh and blood cannot inherit the kingdom of God, nor does the perishable inherit the imperishable. Behold! I tell you a mystery. We shall not all sleep, but we shall all be changed, in a moment, in the twinkling of an eye, at the last trumpet. For the trumpet will sound, and the dead will be raised imperishable, and we shall be changed. For this perishable body must put on the imperishable, and this mortal body must put on immortality. When the perishable puts on the imperishable, and the mortal puts on immortality, then shall come to pass the saying that is written:*
>
> *"Death is swallowed up in victory."*
> *"O death, where is your victory?*
> *O death, where is your sting?"*
>
> *The sting of death is sin, and the power of sin is the law. But thanks be to God, who gives us the victory through our Lord Jesus Christ.*
>
> 1 Corinthians 15:37, 44, 49-57

As he concludes, Paul reminds the Corinthians what love for each other means—concretely. Love means responding to those in need, even if far away. The Corinthians had agreed to give money to the "saints" in Jerusalem suffering from famine (16:1-4).

Love means honoring those who have worked tirelessly in service to the church as Paul's assistant Timothy, as even their own special servant Stephanas had done (16:16, 18). Love means being genuinely kind and warm toward each other, in speech and deed.

> *The grace of the Lord Jesus be with you. My love be with you all in Christ Jesus. Amen.*
>
> 1 Corinthians 16:23-24

2 Corinthians 1-7

During the mid-50s AD, the apostle Paul wrote at least four letters to the church of God in Corinth (cf. 1 Cor. 5:9; 2 Cor. 7:8). Two of these letters are in the New Testament. Before he wrote the last letter (which we call 2 Corinthians), Paul had made a visit to Corinth which was very upsetting. The apostle does not relate any details but his visit was very painful (2:1). Apparently one of the Christians had wronged Paul. Instead of returning immediately to Corinth, Paul decided to send a letter.

> *And I wrote as I did, so that when I came I might not suffer pain from those who should have made me rejoice, for I felt sure of all of you, that my joy would be the joy of you all. For I wrote to you out of much affliction and anguish of heart and with many tears, not to cause you pain but to let you know the abundant love that I have for you.*
>
> 2 Corinthians 2:3-4

Some interpreted Paul's decision to delay as vacillation and duplicity (1:15-2:2). To make matters worse, other missionaries had come to Corinth criticizing his work and sincerity. Paul's heart was lifted, however, when his assistant Titus returned from Corinth reporting that the church had responded favorably to Paul's painful third letter.

> *For even if I made you grieve with my letter, I do not regret it—though I did regret it, for I see that that letter grieved you, though only for a while. As it is, I rejoice, not because you were grieved, but because you were grieved into repenting. For you felt a godly grief, so that you suffered no loss through us.*

For godly grief produces a repentance that leads to salvation without regret, whereas worldly grief produces death.
2 Corinthians 7:8-10

Paul thus begins to write 2 Corinthians with a great measure of relief:

Blessed be the God and Father of our Lord Jesus Christ, the Father of mercies and God of all comfort, who comforts us in all our affliction, so that we may be able to comfort those who are in any affliction, with the comfort with which we ourselves are comforted by God. For as we share abundantly in Christ's sufferings, so through Christ we share abundantly in comfort too.
2 Corinthians 1:3-5

He is very concerned, however, that the one who had wronged him now be forgiven and that the church be deliberate in reaffirming its love for this brother (2:5-11). Paul again gives no details about what happened, for he in fact has forgiven the brother of the offense.

Anyone whom you forgive, I also forgive. Indeed, what I have forgiven, if I have forgiven anything, has been for your sake in the presence of Christ, so that we would not be outwitted by Satan; for we are not ignorant of his designs.
2 Corinthians 2:10-11

But damage remained in Corinth. Paul's ministry had come under attack. Paul devotes much of 2 Corinthians to describing the nature of true ministry. This is Paul's most emotional letter as he reveals his own heart through his self-descriptions and warmth for the church.

Paul doesn't doubt that some will be offended by his ministry. He is like a prisoner of war marching in procession. The odor emitted is for those being saved like a fragrant perfume, but for those perishing a stench of death (2:14-17).

Paul has not qualified himself to be a minister. God alone had made Paul competent to minister and the Corinthians' own conversion was testimony to Paul's credibility (3:1-6). His sincerity in proclaiming the death and life of Jesus could be readily seen in the sufferings of his own body.

But we have this treasure in jars of clay, to show that the surpassing power belongs to God and not to us. We are afflicted in every way, but not crushed; perplexed, but not driven to despair; persecuted, but not forsaken; struck down, but not destroyed; always carrying in the body the death of Jesus, so that the life of Jesus may also be manifested in our bodies.

2 Corinthians 4:7-10

Paul could see such affliction actually preparing him for "an eternal weight of glory" (4:17).

Paul really had no other option than to see everything anew "in Christ." God had made him an ambassador. As such Paul was charged to bring a message of reconciliation from God to the world (5:16-21).

For the love of Christ controls us, because we have concluded this: that one has died for all, therefore all have died; and he died for all, that those who live might no longer live for themselves but for him who for their sake died and was raised.

2 Corinthians 5:14-15

Whether his detractors liked it or not, whether some of the Corinthians liked it or not, Paul's life was not one of ease. His ambassadorship had brought him mistreatment.

We put no obstacle in anyone's way, so that no fault may be found with our ministry, but as servants of God we commend ourselves in every way: by great endurance, in afflictions, hardships, calamities, beatings, imprisonments, riots, labors, sleepless nights, hunger.

2 Corinthians 6:3-5

Paul's emotions and affections had been exercised and stretched in ministry. He is no Stoic; he is rough on the edges. He hopes the Corinthians will continue to open their hearts to him in the manner reported by Titus.

Make room in your hearts for us. We have wronged no one, we have corrupted no one, we have taken advantage of no one. I do not say this to condemn you, for I said before that you are in our hearts, to die together and to live together. I am acting with great boldness toward you; I have great pride in you; I am filled with comfort. In all our affliction, I am overflowing with joy.

2 Corinthians 7:2-4

Paul's intensity in describing and defending his ministry is important because the Corinthians must continue to trust Paul's good faith efforts in raising and coordinating a large collection of funds for the poor in Judea. Paul's heart was committed to this relief effort.

2 Corinthians 8-13

Should teachers of the gospel be paid? The apostle Paul thought so, "while they long for you and pray for you, because of the surpassing grace of God upon you" (9:14). Indeed, after Paul had left Corinth, the Christians there paid certain teachers who had recently arrived. In spite of approving the principle, Paul had for himself firmly decided not to receive any support from the church:

> *Or did I commit a sin in humbling myself so that you might be exalted, because I preached God's gospel to you free of charge? I robbed other churches by accepting support from them in order to serve you. And when I was with you and was in need, I did not burden anyone, for the brothers who came from Macedonia supplied my need. So I refrained and will refrain from burdening you in any way.*
>
> *Here for the third time I am ready to come to you. And I will not be a burden, for I seek not what is yours but you. For children are not obligated to save up for their parents, but parents for their children.*
>
> 2 Corinthians 11:7-9; 12:14

Because of this, some had accused Paul of deceit! (12:16) His critics apparently insinuated that in the collection for the poor in Jerusalem Paul was keeping part of the money for himself (12:14-18; cf. 8:20-21). He didn't need to take money for teaching, the critics said, because he was fraudulently taking money from the fund-raising efforts.

In responding to this slander, Paul was faced with two dilemmas. On the one hand, his work with the Corinthians was in jeopardy if these "superior" apostles, these false apostles, were to be believed. Paul must defend himself. On the other hand, his relief effort for the poor was jeopardized if the Corinthians did not complete their pledges. Paul devotes the last half of 2 Corinthians to addressing these twin concerns.

To prompt them to keep their pledge, Paul plays on the Corinthians' pride (8:7). Paul had already boasted to others of their eagerness to contribute (9:1-4). Their zeal had encouraged Macedonian Christians, who were in extreme poverty, to overflow in rich generosity. Paul had already made careful plans to ensure trustworthy administration of the collection.

The Macedonians had enjoyed the grace of God. The Corinthians must now understand fully the grace of Jesus, who being rich had become poor in order to make others rich. Paul wanted them to understand that in keeping their pledge they were actually sowing seed which would bear a bountiful harvest of righteousness.

> *You will be enriched in every way to be generous in every way, which through us will produce thanksgiving to God. For the ministry of this service is not only supplying the needs of the saints but is also overflowing in many thanksgivings to God. By their approval of this service, they will glorify God because of your submission that comes from your confession of the gospel of Christ, and the generosity of your contribution for them and for all others, while they long for you and pray for you, because of the surpassing grace of God upon you. Thanks be to God for his inexpressible gift!*
>
> 2 Corinthians 9:11-15

But would they believe his words? Paul, the critics say, can write a tough letter, but in person he is weak and his speech unimpressive (10:10). To these opponents Paul responds:

> *Indeed, I consider that I am not in the least inferior to these super-apostles. Even if I am unskilled in speaking, I am not so in knowledge; indeed, in every way we have made this plain to you in all things.*
>
> *And what I am doing I will continue to do, in order to undermine the claim of those who would like to claim that in their boasted mission they work on the same terms as we do. For such men are false apostles, deceitful workmen, disguising themselves as apostles of Christ. And no wonder, for even Satan disguises himself as an angel of light.*
>
> 2 Corinthians 11:5-6, 12-14

Paul feels uncomfortable having to defend himself among Christians who themselves should have been the first to defend him. Paul admits he is speaking like a fool in entering a boasting competition with these false apostles. But he will, if only to boast about those things which show his weaknesses, not his strengths—unlike the super apostles:

> *Are they servants of Christ? I am a better one—I am talking like a madman—with far greater labors, far more imprisonments, with countless beatings, and often near death. Five times I received at the hands of the Jews the forty lashes less one. Three times I was beaten with rods. Once I was stoned. Three times I was shipwrecked; a night and a day I was adrift at sea; on frequent journeys, in danger from rivers, danger from robbers, danger from my own people, danger from Gentiles, danger in the city, danger in the wilderness, danger at sea, danger from false brothers; in toil and hardship, through many a sleepless night, in hunger and thirst, often without food, in cold and exposure.*
>
> 2 Corinthians 11:23-27

Paul faced hardships in the normal course of proclaiming the gospel and nurturing the churches. He could have bragged about being caught up 14 years earlier into the third heaven, into Paradise, but he cannot and will not. In fact, a thorn in the flesh (not explained), a messenger of Satan, had been given to torment Paul and keep him from pride (12:1-10).

Paul had done signs and wonders when first with the Corinthians (12:12). But the real character of his ministry, of all Christian service, was serving through weakness—a weakness which gave opportunity for Christ to display his wondrous power.

> *But he said to me, "My grace is sufficient for you, for my power is made perfect in weakness." Therefore I will boast all the more gladly of my weaknesses, so that the power of Christ may rest upon me. For the sake of Christ, then, I am content with weaknesses, insults, hardships, persecutions, and calamities. For when I am weak, then I am strong.*
>
> 2 Corinthians 12:9-10

Galatians

Wherever he traveled Paul proclaimed a simple message: Jesus has died for our sins according to the will of God to free us from the present evil age (1:4). This message, simple yet breathtaking, was for some too good to be true. Something "more" surely needed to be done to merit such freedom.

For certain first-century Christians that "more" which could assure such freedom was circumcision. Paul's letter to the churches in Galatia is a strong reaction to rival missionaries who had come to Asia insisting that Christians must be circumcised:

> *I am astonished that you are so quickly deserting him who called you in the grace of Christ and are turning to a different gospel—not that there is another one, but there are some who trouble you and want to distort the gospel of Christ.*
>
> *Look: I, Paul, say to you that if you accept circumcision, Christ will be of no advantage to you. I testify again to every man who accepts circumcision that he is obligated to keep the whole law.*
>
> *I wish those who unsettle you would emasculate themselves!*
>
> Galatians 1:6-7; 5:2-3, 12

Paul understood clearly that the gospel he preached, which the Galatians had believed, was irreconcilable with a message that demanded circumcision. Paul reminded the Galatians that Titus, a Greek, had not been compelled to be circumcised by leaders in Jerusalem—leaders apparently respected by the circumcising missionaries! (2:1-10) Paul is perplexed and dismayed by the Galatians' willingness to retreat from the grace of God in the faithfulness of Christ:

> *O foolish Galatians! Who has bewitched you? It was before your eyes that Jesus Christ was publicly portrayed as crucified. Let me ask you only this: Did you receive the Spirit by works of the law or by hearing with faith? Are you so foolish? Having begun by the Spirit, are you now being perfected by the flesh?*
>
> Galatians 3:1-3

The uncircumcised Galatians had indeed experienced the Spirit—not by personal achievements, but by believing what they heard. In Christ Jesus, the Gentiles were experiencing the blessing of Abraham.

For as many of you as were baptized into Christ have put on Christ. There is neither Jew nor Greek, there is neither slave nor free, there is no male and female, for you are all one in Christ Jesus. And if you are Christ's, then you are Abraham's offspring, heirs according to promise.

Galatians 3:27-29

The Galatians were now "in Christ," children of God, legitimate heirs in the present to God's Spirit. Paul saw clearly that relying on works of the law (including circumcision) was giving up one's freedom as an heir and going back to the legal status of "minor," not able to enjoy the inheritance.

I mean that the heir, as long as he is a child, is no different from a slave, though he is the owner of everything, but he is under guardians and managers until the date set by his father. In the same way we also, when we were children, were enslaved to the elementary principles of the world. But when the fullness of time had come, God sent forth his Son, born of woman, born under the law, to redeem those who were under the law, so that we might receive adoption as sons.

Galatians 4:1-5

The missionaries who had come insisting on circumcision were not as interested in the Galatians' welfare as they were in their own strategies for achieving security (4:17; 6:12-13). Paul is wary that this "yeast" for fleshly concerns might "leaven" the lump of the church (5:9). Paul warns the church that freedom is not freedom from caring about each other:

For you were called to freedom, brothers. Only do not use your freedom as an opportunity for the flesh, but through love serve one another. For the whole law is fulfilled in one word: "You shall love your neighbor as yourself." But if you bite and devour one another, watch out that you are not consumed by one another.

Galatians 5:13-15

Instead of preoccupation with circumcision, the Galatians should be concerned with living by the Spirit rather than by works of the flesh.

But the fruit of the Spirit is love, joy, peace, patience, kindness, goodness, faithfulness, gentleness, self-control; against such things there is no law. And those who belong to Christ Jesus have crucified the flesh with its passions and desires.

If we live by the Spirit, let us also keep in step with the Spirit. Let us not become conceited, provoking one another, envying one another.

Galatians 5:22-26

Paul finally reminds the Galatians that it is not the marks of circumcision which identify one as a child of God and a member of the Israel of God. What really matters is whether one bears the marks of Jesus—not the marks of circumcision.

But far be it from me to boast except in the cross of our Lord Jesus Christ, by which the world has been crucified to me, and I to the world. For neither circumcision counts for anything, nor uncircumcision, but a new creation. And as for all who walk by this rule, peace and mercy be upon them, and upon the Israel of God.

From now on let no one cause me trouble, for I bear on my body the marks of Jesus.

The grace of our Lord Jesus Christ be with your spirit, brothers. Amen.

Galatians 6:14-18

Ephesians

As a servant of Christ, the apostle Paul spent many days in Roman prisons. It was a time for him of singing, praying, teaching and letter writing. During one imprisonment, Paul composed a letter which was circulated among various churches in Asia. As it has happened, the letter which was saved by the church in Ephesus has become a part of our New Testament and is known among Paul's letters as "Ephesians" (1:1)

In this letter, Paul describes himself paradoxically as "an ambassador in chains" (6:20). His prison is God's embassy. He has been charged to boldly proclaim a peace plan to people who have been at war with each another (2:13-17). The plan has not resulted from negotiations between the warring parties. It has been formulated and inaugurated outside their initiatives and agenda.

Paul reveals the peace plan for the first time in human history. God had been keeping it secret. Before He created the universe, God had devised the plan as a way to reunite all the brokenness and discord in heaven and on earth (1:4-11). God had not made the plan in anger or dismay. The plan gave God pleasure in its design to bring Him glory.

The plan was this: God would create a new humanity, uniting the two great divisions of humankind, Jew and Gentile, into one new body—Christ's body—through the cross (2:14-16). Peace would result.

Paul understood that the separations between people were not caused simply by bad families or bad teachers or bad countries or bad environments. The solution was not better education or better politics or better economics. No, there were spiritual forces in the heavenlies which excited conflicts between people.

> *For we do not wrestle against flesh and blood, but against the rulers, against the authorities, against the cosmic powers over this present darkness, against the spiritual forces of evil in the heavenly places.*
>
> *And you were dead in the trespasses and sins in which you once walked, following the course of this world, following the prince of the power of the air, the spirit that is now at work in the sons of disobedience—among whom we all once lived in the passions of our flesh, carrying out the desires of the body and the mind, and were by nature children of wrath, like the rest of mankind.*
>
> Ephesians 6:12; 2:1-3

Only one thing could effectively deal with such disasters from malevolent forces above:

> *But God, being rich in mercy, because of the great love with which he loved us, even when we were dead in our trespasses, made us alive together with Christ—by grace you have been saved—and raised us up with him and seated us with him in the heavenly places in Christ Jesus, so that in the coming ages he might show the immeasurable riches of his grace in kindness toward us in Christ Jesus.*
>
> Ephesians 2:4-7

Remarkably, in seating Jesus at His right hand in the heavenlies, God also seated at His right hand all those included in the body of Jesus.

Present with Christ—far above all rule, authority, power, and dominion—believers could receive protection (1:19-23). The perspective of looking down from the heavenlies rather than looking up into the ominous cosmic forces is more than imaginary fiction. It is reality for Paul and it leads him to express thanksgiving:

> *Blessed be the God and Father of our Lord Jesus Christ, who has blessed us in Christ with every spiritual blessing in the heavenly places, even as he chose us in him before the foundation of the world, that we should be holy and blameless before him.*
>
> Ephesians 1:3-4

Paul is not so naive as to think that all is now well, that people in Christ, seated in the heavenlies, will no longer face hostilities and pain. No. Christians must remember that Jesus absorbed hostility in His own body on the cross. He became peace through absorbing hostility and not returning evil for evil. Believers must time and again meditate on such love which transcends scientific and social explanations.

> *... having the eyes of your hearts enlightened, that you may know what is the hope to which he has called you, what are the riches of his glorious inheritance in the saints, and what is the immeasurable greatness of his power toward us who believe, according to the working of his great might.*
>
> Ephesians 1:18-19

Paul doesn't hesitate in appealing to Christians to work on maintaining such unity of the Spirit in the bond of peace (4:1-6). Paul admonishes them to avoid actions which invariably lead to disunity.

> *Therefore, having put away falsehood, let each one of you speak the truth with his neighbor, for we are members one of another. Be angry and do not sin; do not let the sun go down on your anger, and give no opportunity to the devil. Let the thief no longer steal, but rather let him labor, doing honest work with his own hands, so that he may have something to share with anyone in need. Let no corrupting talk come out of your mouths, but only such as is good for building up, as fits the occasion, that it may give grace to those who hear.*
>
> Ephesians 4:25-29

The only antidote for harmful speech is grateful speech. The church is built up in peace when it sings gratefully in the Spirit—Psalms, hymns and spiritual songs (5:3-20). The admiration for Christ expressed in singing reminds Paul of the imprint of Christ's love for the church on the relationships in the household: wives, husbands; children, fathers; slaves, masters; each must learn from Christ's love for the church (5:20-6:9).

Each must also, however, put on God's armor, for the hostilities in the household are not merely of human origin; they are battles against heavenly forces and require the protection of God's armor.

> *Therefore take up the whole armor of God, that you may be able to withstand in the evil day, and having done all, to stand firm. Stand therefore, having fastened on the belt of truth, and having put on the breastplate of righteousness, and, as shoes for your feet, having put on the readiness given by the gospel of peace. In all circumstances take up the shield of faith, with which you can extinguish all the flaming darts of the evil one; and take the helmet of salvation, and the sword of the Spirit, which is the word of God.*
>
> Ephesians 6:13-17

Though sufferings still exist for the believer, Paul is confident that God's power can enable us to endure—to endure in prospect of the glorious inheritance awaiting those who now by the Spirit share in Christ His dominion above the cosmic forces.

In the meantime, God's wisdom in beginning His grand reunification through peaceful relationships in the church will produce a marvelous spectacle above, to the surprise of all the powers in the heavenlies.

Philippians

What does a church do when two strong-willed, opinionated Christian women are at each other's throat? While in prison, Paul heard about two such women in Philippi. The conflict was apparently open and serious enough that Paul in his letter to Philippi can mention them by name, Euodia and Syntyche, while acknowledging their valuable service for the gospel (4:2-3).

Paul, of course, was no stranger to personal conflict. On one occasion he had disagreed so strongly with his mentor Barnabas that they parted company (Acts 15:39). Paul knew well how quickly disagreements between a few could escalate to conflict among the many as people took sides. Paul wrote to the saints in Philippi to prevent the flame from becoming a fire.

At the first and last of the letter, Paul thanks the Philippians for the gifts they had sent him in his imprisonment (Phil. 1:5; 4:18). The Philippian Christians were by no means wealthy (cf. 2 Cor. 8:2). Paul was thus all the more touched by their generosity in caring for him in his distress (Phil. 4:14-17). Paul hoped their generous hearts would lead to the healing of any disputes simmering in the church.

Paul reminded them that even in apparently discouraging situations there were unexpected occasions for rejoicing. His imprisonment, for example, had already become the occasion for members of the emperor's household to become Christians (4:22; 1:13). Others had been prompted to proclaim Christ. Through it all Paul had learned to rejoice (1:15-18). The Philippians could learn a lesson from this.

Whether he had seen it in himself or simply understood human behavior, Paul knew that conceit and selfish ambition could destroy churches—and entrench the positions of strong-willed, disagreeing members. Paul frequently offered the advice that each person should look not to his own interests, but to the interests of others (2:4). In Philippians it occurred to Paul brilliantly to quote a hymn which they may have sung in church that proclaimed powerfully the reason for selflessly yielding to one another:

> *Have this mind among yourselves, which is yours in Christ Jesus, who, though he was in the form of God, did not count equality with God a thing to be grasped, but emptied himself, by taking the form of a servant, being born in the likeness of men. And being found in human form, he humbled himself by becoming obedient to the point of death, even death on a cross. Therefore God has highly exalted him and bestowed on him the name that is above every name, so that at the name of Jesus every knee should bow, in heaven and on earth and under the earth, and every tongue confess that Jesus Christ is Lord, to the glory of God the Father.*
>
> Philippians 2:5-11

This mind of Christ, which he hoped the two women would learn to reflect, had its concrete manifestation in the life of Timothy—who had been genuinely concerned for the Philippians' welfare (2:20). One of their own members, Epaphroditus, had also set an example in his willingness to risk his own life for the work of Christ in representing them before Paul (2:25-30).

Paul himself had had to give up his own pride and achievements before the overpowering mercy of Christ:

> *But whatever gain I had, I counted as loss for the sake of Christ. Indeed, I count everything as loss because of the surpassing worth of knowing Christ Jesus my Lord. For his sake I have suffered the loss of all things and count them as rubbish, in order that I may gain Christ and be found in him, not having a righteousness of my own that comes from the law, but that which comes through faith in Christ, the righteousness from God that depends on faith—that I may know him and the power of his resurrection, and may share his sufferings, becoming like him in his death, that by any means possible I may attain the resurrection from the dead.*
>
> Philippians 3:7-11

Paul had learned to forget the past—its hurts and its achievements—and strain forward toward the future and the promise of resurrection (3:12-16). Paul called upon the Philippians to join in imitating him, to forget past hurts, to lay aside conceit, to look to the citizenship in heaven (3:17-4:1)

Paul may have heard that arguments and murmuring were occupying way too much time in the Philippian church (2:14). As a way to arrest such preoccupations, Paul recommends other concentrations:

> *Finally, brothers, whatever is true, whatever is honorable, whatever is just, whatever is pure, whatever is lovely, whatever is commendable, if there is any excellence, if there is anything worthy of praise, think about these things. What you have learned and received and heard and seen in me—practice these things, and the God of peace will be with you.*
>
> Philippians 4:8-9

The time had come for the church to quit moaning and groaning and to see once again the greatest cause for wonder and rejoicing. It was time for thanksgiving. They could be assured of God's peace in their midst.

Rejoice in the Lord always; again I will say, rejoice. Let your reasonableness be known to everyone. The Lord is at hand; do not be anxious about anything, but in everything by prayer and supplication with thanksgiving let your requests be made known to God. And the peace of God, which surpasses all understanding, will guard your hearts and your minds in Christ Jesus.

Philippians 4:4-7

Perhaps Euodia and Syntyche found themselves able again to pray together, as sisters whose names each were in the book of life (4:2-3).

Colossians

What is a spiritual person? Some identify spirituality with intense abuse of the body; others, with seeing visions. The question of spirituality and wisdom puzzled Christians in the first century. In his letter to the saints in Colossae (a town in southwestern Asia Minor), the apostle Paul, writing from prison, addressed this burning topic of who are "spiritual" Christians.

The founder of the church in Colossae, Epaphras, had shared with Paul his own deep struggles in prayer over the maturity and growth of its members (4:12; 1:7). Apparently, their maturing had been threatened by some in town who insisted on their maintaining certain ascetic guidelines and regulations for the body.

See to it that no one takes you captive by philosophy and empty deceit, according to human tradition, according to the elemental spirits of the world, and not according to Christ.

Therefore let no one pass judgment on you in questions of food and drink, or with regard to a festival or a new moon or a Sabbath. These are a shadow of the things to come, but the substance belongs to Christ. Let no one disqualify you, insisting on asceticism and worship of angels, going on in detail about visions, puffed up without reason by his sensuous mind, and not holding fast to the Head, from whom the whole body, nourished and knit together through its joints and ligaments, grows with a growth that is from God.

If with Christ you died to the elemental spirits of the world, why, as if you were still alive in the world, do you submit to regulations—"Do not handle, Do not taste, Do not touch" (referring to things that all perish as they are used)—according to human precepts and teachings? These have indeed an appearance of wisdom in promoting self-made religion and asceticism and severity to the body, but they are of no value in stopping the indulgence of the flesh.

Colossians 2:8, 16-23

Paul knew well it was very tempting for Christians to elevate asceticism and quasi-mystical experiences and speculations on the angelic realm as the highest goal of the Christian life. For Paul such pursuits were wrong-headed.

Paul himself had actually experienced, at least on one occasion, some kind of transport into a third heaven. Paul had learned, however, that such experiences can easily become occasions for pride (2 Cor. 12:6-7). Paul tells the Colossians that ascetic practices do indeed have the glowing appearance of wisdom. But in reality such experiences don't and can't control one's lust! They do not prevent self-indulgence.

At root, Paul sees such extra-curricular disciplines as symptomatic of an incomplete understanding of the sufficiency and completeness of the work of Christ. Paul paraphrases a hymn they may have sung in church:

He is the image of the invisible God, the firstborn of all creation. For by him all things were created, in heaven and on earth, visible and invisible, whether thrones or dominions or rulers or authorities—all things were created through him and for him. And he is before all things, and in him all things hold together. And he is the head of the body, the church. He is the beginning, the firstborn from the dead, that in everything he might be preeminent. For in him all the fullness of God was pleased to dwell, and through him to reconcile to himself all things, whether on earth or in heaven, making peace by the blood of his cross.

Colossians 1:15-20

The emphasis in this hymn is on Christ's relationship to creation. All things have been created through Christ and for Christ. Any abuse or disregard of the body through asceticism must be avoided because Christ came to the earth in a physical body, and through Him all things, including bodies, were created.

The Colossian Christians had begun their lives of faith on the right track, the non-ascetic track, by bearing fruit in every good work (1:3-13). Paul insists they stay on this path:

> *Walk in wisdom toward outsiders, making the best use of the time. Let your speech always be gracious, seasoned with salt, so that you may know how you ought to answer each person.*
>
> Colossians 4:5-6

Rather than being so concerned about visionary experiences in the heavens, Paul thinks they have a lot to do on earth. In baptism they had taken off and put on clothes in being submerged in water and in leaving the water. They should follow through in life in taking off all their malicious clothing and putting on the fresh clothes of love:

> *But now you must put them all away: anger, wrath, malice, slander, and obscene talk from your mouth. Do not lie to one another, seeing that you have put off the old self with its practices and have put on the new self, which is being renewed in knowledge after the image of its creator.*
>
> *Put on then, as God's chosen ones, holy and beloved, compassionate hearts, kindness, humility, meekness, and patience, bearing with one another and, if one has a complaint against another, forgiving each other; as the Lord has forgiven you, so you also must forgive. And above all these put on love, which binds everything together in perfect harmony.*
>
> Colossians 3:8-10, 12-14

The Colossian Christians wanted to be wise. Paul insisted that in Christ they have all the treasures of God's wisdom. No personal strivings could achieve such wisdom. God had already raised the Colossians with Christ. They should now be thankful—in word, in deed, in song—with love characterizing all their household relationships (3:16-4:1).

The faithful minister Epaphras had struggled in prayer over the Colossians. Paul too was praying that they might be filled with the knowledge of God's will, in all spiritual wisdom and understanding.

> *... being strengthened with all power, according to his glorious might, for all endurance and patience with joy; giving thanks to the Father, who has qualified you to share in the inheritance of*

the saints in light. He has delivered us from the domain of darkness and transferred us to the kingdom of his beloved Son, in whom we have redemption, the forgiveness of sins.

Colossians 1:11-14

We do not know if the Colossians finally learned that spirituality is not in the extraordinary experiences of life but rather in the ordinary—in the mundane routines of avoiding evil and being kind and forgiving. In truth, it has been a difficult lesson for Christians to learn in any age, including our own.

1 Thessalonians

In the first century AD, most people believed in many gods. When the gospel about Jesus, the Anointed One, entered the polytheistic world, people were challenged to believe in one God—not multiple gods.

Paul faced this challenge when he wrote to the church in Thessalonica, a prominent city in northern Greece. In his first letter to them (Paul's earliest letter in the New Testament), the apostle selected two critical issues to discuss: brotherly love and holiness. Not surprisingly, these two subjects occupied Paul's prayers.

And may the Lord make you increase and abound in love for one another and for all, as we do for you, so that he may establish your hearts blameless in holiness before our God and Father, at the coming of our Lord Jesus with all his saints.

1 Thessalonians 3:12-13

Not many months before he wrote his letter, many of these Christians had worshipped idols. Only recently had they repented and turned from idols to serve the true God (1:9). The various deities they had previously worshipped had not demanded much of their personal behavior. It would be different now with God the Father.

God's will for them was "sanctification" (4:3)—that they be holy and dedicated to God with their bodies. Since they had received the Holy Spirit, Christians were now to avoid casual sexual relations. Since men would routinely be together with other men's wives in church, Paul warns them about taking advantage of a brother's wife (4:6). Paul prayed earnestly about their sanctification:

Now may the God of peace himself sanctify you completely, and may your whole spirit and soul and body be kept blameless at the coming of our Lord Jesus Christ.

1 Thessalonians 5:23

Paul also stressed their need to love each other:

Now concerning brotherly love you have no need for anyone to write to you, for you yourselves have been taught by God to love one another, for that indeed is what you are doing to all the brothers throughout Macedonia. But we urge you, brothers, to do this more and more, and to aspire to live quietly, and to mind your own affairs, and to work with your hands, as we instructed you, so that you may walk properly before outsiders and be dependent on no one.

1 Thessalonians 4:9-12

Love did not mean simply providing food for those who could work, but did not. Paul knew that some lazy people would try to take advantage of "brotherly love." Paul says that such idlers must be admonished (5:14). Paul had been careful when he was in Thessalonica not to depend on the believers for food and money. He wanted them to remember his example.

For you remember, brothers, our labor and toil: we worked night and day, that we might not be a burden to any of you, while we proclaimed to you the gospel of God. You are witnesses, and God also, how holy and righteous and blameless was our conduct toward you believers.

1 Thessalonians 2:9-10

What is remarkable about Paul's first letter to the Thessalonians is how much space he devotes to his feelings for them—in fact, half the letter (chapters 1-3)!

Clearly, Paul hopes that they see in him an example of what brotherly love concretely means in action. They had already begun to love one another and they were growing in love for their leaders (1:3-8; 5:13, 26). Paul's example as their father was impressive; but he had also acted as a nursing mother:

But we were gentle among you, like a nursing mother taking care of her own children. So, being affectionately desirous of you, we were ready to share with you not only the gospel of God but also our own selves, because you had become very dear to us.

1 Thessalonians 2:7-8

Paul compares his feelings for them to a mother who is gently caring for her unweaned children.

Paul had no interest in gaining their approval or their money:

For we never came with words of flattery, as you know, nor with a pretext for greed—God is witness. Nor did we seek glory from people, whether from you or from others, though we could have made demands as apostles of Christ.

1 Thessalonians 2:5-6

He hoped their love for one another would exhibit the same purity of motive.

Paul goes into some detail about his failure to quickly return and see them, when he had sent Timothy instead to encourage them. Paul reveals his own anxiety that the "tempter" might have enticed the Thessalonians into falling away. Paul had himself experienced the work of Satan in being blocked from seeing the young church. Paul could only describe the experience of being separated from the Thessalonians as that of an orphan—bereft and longing to see family. Paul, however, was relieved to hear from Timothy about their mutual love for him.

But now that Timothy has come to us from you, and has brought us the good news of your faith and love and reported that you always remember us kindly and long to see us, as we long to see you—for this reason, brothers, in all our distress and affliction we have been comforted about you through your faith. For now we live, if you are standing fast in the Lord. For what thanksgiving can we return to God for you, for all the joy that we feel for your sake before our God, as we pray most earnestly night and day that we may see you face to face and supply what is lacking in your faith?

1 Thessalonians 3:6-10

Paul recalls his recent experiences with them in order to exhibit before them brotherly love. They would have opportunity enough for such love to come under fire. They were to remember, however, love's response:

> *See that no one repays anyone evil for evil, but always seek to do good to one another and to everyone. Rejoice always, pray without ceasing, give thanks in all circumstances; for this is the will of God in Christ Jesus for you.*
>
> 1 Thessalonians 5:15-18

Finally, the Thessalonian Christians were not to grieve as others who have no hope. In fact, the dead in Christ, Paul says, will be raised first; then the living will join them in the clouds to meet Christ together. When the Lord will return no one knows (4:13-5:3). Paul exhorts the believers to live as children of the day, awake and sober, ready to meet Him:

> *But since we belong to the day, let us be sober, having put on the breastplate of faith and love, and for a helmet the hope of salvation. For God has not destined us for wrath, but to obtain salvation through our Lord Jesus Christ, who died for us so that whether we are awake or asleep we might live with him.*
>
> 1 Thessalonians 5:8-10

Paul expected a lot of his children. He prayed constantly for them. His next letter will indicate if they were in fact able to grow and mature.

2 Thessalonians

Without hope it is impossible to endure suffering. Hope sustains. Hope understands. Hope endures.

Soon after they had become Christians, Paul's converts in Thessalonica encountered suffering (1 Thess. 2:14; 2 Thess. 1:4). The nature and extent of their distress is not clear, but they were experiencing mistreatment. They had little teaching to remember and few heroes of faith to give counsel on enduring such abuse. They needed explanations. "Why should I be suffering for doing what pleases God?" They needed understanding. They needed hope.

Paul had told them when he was first with them that a period of calamity and lawlessness would precede Jesus' coming (2:3-5). Some had concluded from this that their present sufferings were indeed the signal of the Lord's imminent coming, a return at any moment. They were enduring with this hope (1:4). Paul, however, says their thinking is wrong.

Now concerning the coming of our Lord Jesus Christ and our being gathered together to him, we ask you, brothers, not to be quickly shaken in mind or alarmed, either by a spirit or a spoken word, or a letter seeming to be from us, to the effect that the day of the Lord has come.

2 Thessalonians 2:1-2

Paul explains that their sufferings are not the climax of the rebellion and suffering which is to precede Jesus' return. Yes, there will be a period of lawlessness before Jesus comes, but it will be clear to all when Jesus actually returns.

And then the lawless one will be revealed, whom the Lord Jesus will kill with the breath of his mouth and bring to nothing by the appearance of his coming.

2 Thessalonians 2:8

In the meantime, Christians are not to harbor feelings of revenge, much less take revenge against those who have afflicted them. Paul reminds them that it is God's work, and not man's, to finally address evil:

Since indeed God considers it just to repay with affliction those who afflict you, and to grant relief to you who are afflicted as well as to us, when the Lord Jesus is revealed from heaven with his mighty angels in flaming fire, inflicting vengeance on those who do not know God and on those who do not obey the gospel of our Lord Jesus. They will suffer the punishment of eternal destruction, away from the presence of the Lord and from the glory of his might, when he comes on that day to be glorified in his saints, and to be marveled at among all who have believed, because our testimony to you was believed.

2 Thessalonians 1:6-10

But why then did they have to suffer? Paul does not explain why except to say, "This is evidence of the righteous judgment of God, that you may be considered worthy of the kingdom of God, for which you are also suffering" (1:5). Paul prays that the Lord might direct their hearts to the love of God and the endurance of Christ (3:5). The love of God rescues through suffering—through the suffering of the faithful and innocent. Paul wants the Thessalonians to remember this profound truth.

Now may our Lord Jesus Christ himself, and God our Father, who loved us and gave us eternal comfort and good hope through grace, comfort your hearts and establish them in every good work and word.

2 Thessalonians 2:16-17

In the meantime, in the midst of affliction, the Thessalonians are to be God's instruments completing every good intention and good work of faith:

To this end we always pray for you, that our God may make you worthy of his calling and may fulfill every resolve for good and every work of faith by his power, so that the name of our Lord Jesus may be glorified in you, and you in him, according to the grace of our God and the Lord Jesus Christ.

2 Thessalonians 1:11-12

They can trust that God will not overlook their travail. He can and will rescue them from the evil one. Paul covets their prayers even on his own behalf. The apostle needs their prayers!

Finally, brothers, pray for us, that the word of the Lord may speed ahead and be honored, as happened among you, and that we may be delivered from wicked and evil men. For not all have faith. But the Lord is faithful. He will establish you and guard you against the evil one.

2 Thessalonians 3:1-3

As he had said in his first letter, so now in his second letter, Paul believes the church's identity is bound up in Jesus' command to love one another.

We ought always to give thanks to God for you, brothers, as is right, because your faith is growing abundantly, and the love of every one of you for one another is increasing.

2 Thessalonians 1:3

Unhappily in Thessalonica there remained a few Christians who saw in the love command an opportunity to take advantage of the kindness of others. Paul's words about those members who could work but do not are direct and unambiguous:

Now we command you, brothers, in the name of our Lord Jesus Christ, that you keep away from any brother who is walking in idleness and not in accord with the tradition that you received from us. For you yourselves know how you ought to imitate us, because we were not idle when we were with you, nor did we eat anyone's bread without paying for it, but with toil and labor we worked night and day, that we might not be a burden to any of you. It was not because we do not have that right, but to give you in ourselves an example to imitate. For even when we were with you, we would give you this command: If anyone is not willing to work, let him not eat. For we hear that some among you walk in idleness, not busy at work, but busybodies. Now such persons we command and encourage in the Lord Jesus Christ to do their work quietly and to earn their own living.

As for you, brothers, do not grow weary in doing good. If anyone does not obey what we say in this letter, take note of that person, and have nothing to do with him, that he may be ashamed. Do not regard him as an enemy, but warn him as a brother.

2 Corinthians 3:6-15

Paul's two letters to the new converts in Thessalonica reveal the crucial importance of faith, love, and hope for the vitality and life of the church. They also indicate the truly wondrous power and love of God to transform humans from idolaters to people dedicated to God—people willing to suffer for the name of Jesus, people who put aside impulses for vengeance, people who progress in loving others, people who await the return of Christ in glory.

1 Timothy

In addition to Paul's letters to seven churches, the New Testament also contains letters he wrote to three individuals—Timothy, Titus, and Philemon.

Timothy had been identified early in the churches of his region as a capable young man. The son of a Greek father and a Jewish mother, Timothy developed great respect for Paul. Soon after their first meeting, Timothy had yielded to Paul's request that he be circumcised so that the work among his hometown Jewish population would not be hindered (Acts 16:3).

Paul had deep affection for Timothy; he was his son (Phil. 2:20-22), his beloved child (1 Cor 4:17), his fellow worker (1 Thess. 3:2). Paul trusted

Timothy as his delegate in visiting various churches which Paul was unable to see. In six of Paul's letter to churches, Timothy is mentioned in the opening as one of the senders of the letter.

After his three-year stay in Ephesus (Acts 20:31), Paul wrote Timothy a letter.

> *As I urged you when I was going to Macedonia, remain at Ephesus so that you may charge certain persons not to teach any different doctrine, nor to devote themselves to myths and endless genealogies, which promote speculations rather than the stewardship from God that is by faith.*
>
> 1 Timothy 1:3-4

Ephesus was the center of magic and the occult in the Roman world. During Paul's work there, many believers had confessed their practices while others had burned their magic books (Acts 19:19-20). But there remained among a few in Ephesus a love for speculation and controversy about the unseen.

> *O Timothy, guard the deposit entrusted to you. Avoid the irreverent babble and contradictions of what is falsely called "knowledge," for by professing it some have swerved from the faith.*
>
> 1 Timothy 6:20-21

Interpretations of certain portions of the law of Moses by teachers in the church had fueled esoteric speculations.

> *Certain persons, by swerving from these, have wandered away into vain discussion, desiring to be teachers of the law, without understanding either what they are saying or the things about which they make confident assertions.*
>
> 1 Timothy 1:6-7

Some had even interpreted the Scripture as forbidding marriage and outlawing certain foods (4:3).

In the face of such unhealthy interpretations, Paul asked Timothy to call the church to prayer and thanksgiving (2:1-6), giving special prominence again to the public reading of Scripture, while avoiding controversial speculations on the law (4:13). Marriage and procreation were upheld in the story of Adam and Eve—not degraded (2:13-15). Younger widows were to be encouraged to marry and bear children (5:14). Paul warned Timothy not to get trapped by the attractiveness of any ascetic disciplines.

> *Have nothing to do with irreverent, silly myths. Rather train yourself for godliness; for while bodily training is of some value, godliness is of value in every way, as it holds promise for the present life and also for the life to come.*
>
> 1 Timothy 4:7-8

Timothy himself was not to avoid wine, as some ascetics apparently urged, but rather to rely on its medicinal value (5:23). In general, Timothy was to remind the church that God had declared in the beginning that the creation was "good," not "bad" as the ascetics implied:

> *[They] forbid marriage and require abstinence from foods that God created to be received with thanksgiving by those who believe and know the truth. For everything created by God is good, and nothing is to be rejected if it is received with thanksgiving, for it is made holy by the word of God and prayer.*
>
> 1 Timothy 4:3-5

To help Timothy keep his equilibrium in the controversies, Paul offered two fundamental pieces of advice: remember the mercy of God and rely on the relationships in the household of God.

First, Timothy is to remember the reason for the church's very existence—the overflowing grace of God:

> *The saying is trustworthy and deserving of full acceptance, that Christ Jesus came into the world to save sinners, of whom I am the foremost. But I received mercy for this reason, that in me, as the foremost, Jesus Christ might display his perfect patience as an example to those who were to believe in him for eternal life.*
>
> 1 Timothy 1:15-16

The church will know it has kept its identity if it can, by the mercy of God, care for the real widow in its midst (5:3-16).

Second, Timothy is to rely on the work of overseers (3:1-7) and their assistants, the deacons (3:8-13), to take care of God's church (3:5; 5:17). It is not all on Timothy's shoulders. Timothy must, however, be exemplary in his behavior.

> *Let no one despise you for your youth, but set the believers an example in speech, in conduct, in love, in faith, in purity.*
>
> *Practice these things, immerse yourself in them, so that all may see your progress. Keep a close watch on yourself and on the teaching. Persist in this, for by so doing you will save both yourself and your hearers.*
>
> 1 Timothy 4:12, 15-16

Finally, Paul alerts Timothy to the special dangers for wealthy believers. Ephesus was the economic center of Asia with the great marble temple of Artemis, one of the seven wonders of the world (cf. Acts 19:23-41). More importantly, the temple was a great bank vault for the region's wealth. Paul knew that wealth could be immodestly displayed in church by the women (1 Tim 2:9). More importantly, Paul understood there were serious traps awaiting the wealthy:

> *But those who desire to be rich fall into temptation, into a snare, into many senseless and harmful desires that plunge people into ruin and destruction. For the love of money is a root of all kinds of evils. It is through this craving that some have wandered away from the faith and pierced themselves with many pangs.*
>
> 1 Timothy 6:9-10

Paul doesn't advise the wealthy to become paupers. Rather,

> *As for the rich in this present age, charge them not to be haughty, nor to set their hopes on the uncertainty of riches, but on God, who richly provides us with everything to enjoy. They are to do good, to be rich in good works, to be generous and ready to share, thus storing up treasure for themselves as a good foundation for the future, so that they may take hold of that which is truly life.*
>
> 1 Timothy 6:17-19

Paul has confidence in Timothy to instruct with a firm but gentle hand in Ephesus:

> *But as for you, O man of God, flee these things. Pursue righteousness, godliness, faith, love, steadfastness, gentleness. Fight the good fight of the faith. Take hold of the eternal life to which you were called and about which you made the good confession in the presence of many witnesses.*
>
> 1 Timothy 6:11-12

2 Timothy

What child can forget the final words of a parent near death? Every word becomes etched in the memory. So must have been the experience of Timothy when he read Paul's last letter to him.

Paul wrote this letter, his last will and testament, from prison in Rome (1:8; 2:9). Paul sensed his life was near an end.

> *For I am already being poured out as a drink offering, and the time of my departure has come. I have fought the good fight, I have finished the race, I have kept the faith. Henceforth there is laid up for me the crown of righteousness, which the Lord, the righteous judge, will award to me on that day, and not only to me but also to all who have loved his appearing.*
>
> 2 Timothy 4:6-8

He hoped Timothy could come to him before winter, bringing the warm coat and books to read which he had left in Troas (4:9, 13, 21). But there was no guarantee Timothy could come, and we do not know if he did.

More than in any of his other letters, Paul laments that some of his associates have abandoned him.

> *You are aware that all who are in Asia turned away from me, among whom are Phygelus and Hermogenes.*
>
> *Do your best to come to me soon. For Demas, in love with this present world, has deserted me and gone to Thessalonica. Crescens has gone to Galatia, Titus to Dalmatia.*
>
> *Alexander the coppersmith did me great harm; the Lord will repay him according to his deeds.*
>
> 2 Timothy 1:15; 4:9-10, 14

Paul is not bitter, but rather in the tradition of Stephen who had prayed for Paul (Saul) at his death (Acts 7:58-59), he now prays for those who have deserted him: "May it not be counted against them" (4:16).

Paul recounts his own reaction to persecution and loneliness because he foresees suffering ahead for his beloved child Timothy.

> *Share in suffering as a good soldier of Christ Jesus.*

> *Indeed, all who desire to live a godly life in Christ Jesus will be persecuted,*
>
> *As for you, always be sober-minded, endure suffering, do the work of an evangelist, fulfill your ministry.*
>
> 2 Timothy 2:3; 3:12; 4:5

Timothy should be reassured through Paul's own experience of being rescued and strengthened for service by the Lord (4:17-18). Paul could also mention by name a few brothers who had provided refreshment at an opportune moment (1:16-17; 4:11, 21).

Timothy can also be reassured in the midst of difficult times by remaining focused on the grace of Christ Jesus. Paul's experience of grace had, of course, been unique—having been dramatically called by Jesus on the road to Damascus. But Timothy could also look to grace in his own life in the form of his grandmother and mother who had taught him the faith (1:5, 3:14) and at his ordination when Paul and others had laid hands on Timothy (1:6).

Paul wants Timothy's eyes to be wide open to what he is facing in his preaching. He will encounter Christians whose unhealthy teaching can spread like gangrene through the body—such as those who were asserting the resurrection had already occurred (2:17-18). Timothy should correct such teachers, explaining the word of truth (2:14-16). He should be aware, however, that it is all too easy to get involved in controversies over words and forget Jesus Christ, "raised from the dead, descended from David" (2:8). Timothy's patience will be tested.

> *And the Lord's servant must not be quarrelsome but kind to everyone, able to teach, patiently enduring evil, correcting his opponents with gentleness. God may perhaps grant them repentance leading to a knowledge of the truth.*
>
> 2 Timothy 2:24-25

More difficult, however, are the counterfeit teachers who parade a godliness with their lips but actually are a sea of corruption:

> *For people will be lovers of self, lovers of money, proud, arrogant, abusive, disobedient to their parents, ungrateful, unholy, heartless, unappeasable, slanderous, without self-control, brutal, not loving good, treacherous, reckless, swollen with conceit, lovers*

of pleasure rather than lovers of God, having the appearance of godliness, but denying its power. Avoid such people.

2 Timothy 3:2-5

Timothy should not take time to teach them; they should be avoided. Such impostors are so sinister that they even prey on vulnerable women.

For among them are those who creep into households and capture weak women, burdened with sins and led astray by various passions, always learning and never able to arrive at a knowledge of the truth.

2 Timothy 3:6-7

Timothy should not wait, however, until everything is perfect in order to teach. He must instruct patiently whether the time is favorable or not. Such effort, of course, will find its opposition. Worse, some Christians will seek out their own teachers to convey only what they want to hear. They will surely wander into all sorts of myths (4:1-4).

Timothy's governor and compass in the pressure of it all is Scripture:

All Scripture is breathed out by God and profitable for teaching, for reproof, for correction, and for training in righteousness, that the man of God may be complete, equipped for every good work.

2 Timothy 3:16-17

Timothy need not look to visions or special revelations, to tongues or esoteric, ascetic sayings. He knows from childhood lives lived in faith, and he knows from childhood the stories in Scripture which shape a healthy imagination.

Above all, Timothy should never forget his father, Paul. His love, his conduct, his faith, his teaching, his life—a legacy forever etched in his heart (3:10). From that, he could well understand life's pursuit of righteousness, faith, love, and peace (2:22).

Titus

Can the gospel penetrate the hearts of people who are lawless and uncivilized? What should a Christian say to people who are filled with hate, malice, and envy?

In the first century AD, Crete had the reputation of a difficult, uncivilized place to live. A famous proverb said, "Cretans are always liars, evil beasts, lazy gluttons" (Titus 1:12). Crete was not the most inviting place for a Christian teacher!

Paul, however, knew of one young Christian who could survive in Crete, a young Greek named Titus. Paul had relied on Titus as an intermediary with the Christians in Corinth during a particularly tense time in their relations with the apostle. He had been impressed with Titus' maturity in handling the situation.

Paul now writes Titus, calling upon him to stay in "wild" Crete until others arrive and he could be reunited with Paul during the winter in Nicopolis (1:5; 3:12). What good could young Titus do in Crete?

Paul assures him first of all that he does not bear the sole responsibility for teaching. Titus should appoint overseers in every town on the island who can preach healthy teaching and refute those who oppose it (1:5, 9). Paul insists that such men be blameless:

> *... above reproach, the husband of one wife, and his children are believers and not open to the charge of debauchery or insubordination. For an overseer, as God's steward, must be above reproach. He must not be arrogant or quick-tempered or a drunkard or violent or greedy for gain, but hospitable, a lover of good, self-controlled, upright, holy, and disciplined.*
>
> Titus 1:6-8

Paul knew of Jewish-Christian missionaries in Crete who were upsetting entire households. Paul doesn't want to provide a soapbox for their unhealthy teaching by repeating any details, so he counsels Titus simply to avoid such teaching: "But avoid foolish controversies, genealogies, dissensions, and quarrels about the law, for they are unprofitable and worthless" (3:9).

Paul sensed that the missionaries' motives were mainly monetary and greedy.

> *For there are many who are insubordinate, empty talkers and deceivers, especially those of the circumcision party. They must be silenced, since they are upsetting whole families by teaching for shameful gain what they ought not to teach.*

They profess to know God, but they deny him by their works. They are detestable, disobedient, unfit for any good work.

Titus 1:10-11, 16

Paul advises Titus (along with the elders) to rebuke such teachers (1:13). If they persist after two admonitions, then they are to be avoided (3:10-11).

But what about the Cretan Christians themselves? How can courtesy and kindness arise in such a culture? Paul's strategy with Titus is that he should first call the older Christians to mature, temperate behavior. They should sense that such is the right thing to do.

Older men are to be sober-minded, dignified, self-controlled, sound in faith, in love, and in steadfastness. Older women likewise are to be reverent in behavior, not slanderers or slaves to much wine. They are to teach what is good.

Titus 2:2-3

Next, the older women should teach the younger women to love their families (2:4-5). Titus should set the example for the younger men in good works (2:6-8). Paul doesn't want the slaves being disrespectful to their masters (2:9-10), much less the Christians in general exhibiting any civil disobedience (3:1-2).

Above all, what Titus must remember is that God's grace has appeared even in Crete. Certainly the Cretans hadn't earned salvation! They, more than some, could appreciate God's absolute goodness and love in reaching even to them. Such grace had appeared to transform their lives, not merely to further tolerate their behavior.

For the grace of God has appeared, bringing salvation for all people, training us to renounce ungodliness and worldly passions, and to live self-controlled, upright, and godly lives in the present age.

Titus 2:11-12

Through their rebirth at baptism and their renewal by the Holy Spirit, they were now to be a people devoted to good works (3:8). And that is Paul's major advice to Titus.

You cannot change feelings, emotions, or attitudes overnight. What Christians can change, however, is what they do and how they act. They may still feel a certain way, but they can decide to act differently.

Paul stresses many times in this that the Cretans must concentrate on good works. They think of themselves too much as lazy and unchangeable. Wrong! The kindness of God, despite man's unkindness, teaches and empowers His children to acts of kindness and goodness. Over time, the Cretans' acts of goodness would lead to changed emotions, feelings, and attitudes. There was indeed power through redemption. Our God and Savior Jesus Christ

> *gave himself for us to redeem us from all lawlessness and to purify for himself a people for his own possession who are zealous for good works.*
>
> *Declare these things; exhort and rebuke with all authority. Let no one disregard you.*
>
> Titus 2:14-15

Philemon

Forgiving is difficult.

Forgiving is one of the most difficult of all human acts. We forgive others only with the greatest reluctance. Jesus' words from the Sermon on the Mount remain a challenge to daily pray: "Forgive us our debts *as we also* have forgiven our debtors" (Matt. 6:12).

On one occasion, Paul faced the serious challenge of persuading one dear brother to forgive another dear brother. As it happened, the brother who needed to forgive was master-owner of a slave. Writing from prison to this slave owner named Philemon, Paul illustrates in Christ the very real difference forgiveness can make in human relationships—even delicate business relationships.

This slave owner Philemon, his wife, and son had evidently become Christians through the teaching of Paul. Not all of Philemon's household, however, had become Christians. One member, a slave named Onesimus, had later appeared in Rome and visited Paul in prison. It is there and then that Philemon's slave became a Christian and began rendering valuable service to Paul during his imprisonment. Why and how Onesimus came to Rome is not clear, but apparently he had either run away from his master or extended a stay in Rome beyond Philemon's instructions.

This leaves Paul in a predicament. Onesimus could stay with Paul and be very "useful" (as Onesimus' very name implied), but he was a slave and had a societal-legal obligation to Philemon. If Onesimus stayed, Paul could be accused of harboring a runaway slave. Paul, however, did not want to presume upon or force any unwilling generosity from Philemon.

In his letters, Paul had never told any slave owner to release his servants, much less slaves to revolt against an owner. To the contrary, he advised masters to remember that they too had a Master in heaven, and He counseled slaves to work with integrity for their earthly masters, knowing their real service was to their Lord in heaven (Col. 3:22-4:1). Paul could not and would not ask Philemon directly to free Onesimus or send him back to Paul.

As much as he needed Onesimus, Paul saw a much larger issue at stake: the reconciliation between two brothers in Christ—a master and his servant. Paul believed that the very event of Christians forgiving each other revealed wondrously to all the powers in the heavenlies God's plan for reunifying the brokenness of the world and the universe (Eph. 3:10).

In his appeal, Paul in effect interchanges himself for Onesimus to enable Philemon to receive and forgive his new brother. Paul's letter is a wonderful example of how peacemaking and forgiveness can take place, prompted according to the example of Christ.

> *I appeal to you for my child, Onesimus, whose father I became in my imprisonment. (Formerly he was useless to you, but now he is indeed useful to you and to me.) I am sending him back to you, sending my very heart. I would have been glad to keep him with me, in order that he might serve me on your behalf during my imprisonment for the gospel, but I preferred to do nothing without your consent in order that your goodness might not be by compulsion but of your own accord. For this perhaps is why he was parted from you for a while, that you might have him back forever, 16 no longer as a bondservant but more than a bondservant, as a beloved brother—especially to me, but how much more to you, both in the flesh and in the Lord.*
>
> *So if you consider me your partner, receive him as you would receive me. If he has wronged you at all, or owes you anything, charge that to my account. I, Paul, write this with my own hand: I will repay it—to say nothing of your owing me even your own*

self. Yes, brother, I want some benefit from you in the Lord. Refresh my heart in Christ.

Confident of your obedience, I write to you, knowing that you will do even more than I say.

Philemon 10-21

Philemon hosted the church at his house in Colossae. He was a man of hospitality. He was entertainment and refreshment to so many (vss. 7, 20). Paul knew he could stay with him anytime (vs. 22).

Paul fully expected Philemon to welcome Onesimus back to his household with open arms, as if he were welcoming Paul, as if he were handling Paul's heart, as if he were receiving Christ himself—for indeed Philemon was. Onesimus was now, as was Philemon, a new man in Christ—two brothers, both dependent on the one Lord, serving the same Master, awaiting the Lord's return.

"Forgive us our sins as we have forgiven those who have sinned against us." Forgiveness is not so difficult for the person who understands God's forgiveness. Forgiving eyes see in the one being forgiven the eyes of Christ. Who can remember the wrongs of the one for whom Christ has died?

Hebrews 1-7

The road of life is long and hard. It's easy to grow weary. When discouraged and fatigued, Christians have sometimes responded by neglecting prayer and by leaving the church.

A heartening New Testament letter was written to just such Christians who were neglecting prayer and avoiding church (cf. 10:22-25). The title attached years later calls it a letter written to Hebrews. It may just as likely have been written to Gentile Christians who had at one time believed in many gods (cf. 6:1). More importantly, it was written to Christians who had recently endured considerable suffering.

But recall the former days when, after you were enlightened, you endured a hard struggle with sufferings, sometimes being publicly exposed to reproach and affliction, and sometimes being partners with those so treated. For you had compassion on those in prison, and you joyfully accepted the plundering of your property, since you knew that you yourselves had a better possession and an abiding one.

Hebrews 10:32-34

Now these same Christians have begun to feel the pinch from the loss of their possessions. Some have retreated within themselves, failing to grow.

About this we have much to say, and it is hard to explain, since you have become dull of hearing. For though by this time you ought to be teachers, you need someone to teach you again the basic principles of the oracles of God. You need milk, not solid food, for everyone who lives on milk is unskilled in the word of righteousness, since he is a child.

Hebrews 5:11-13

The unknown author writes his letter to arouse these weary Christians to prayer and to action. The way he goes about reviving their confidence is quite remarkable and unique in the New Testament. He reminds them that they have a great high priest. He begins by telling them that the one in whose name they had prayed was the very Son of God. Had they forgotten their prayers were in the keeping of the one through whom the worlds were created? (1:1-4)

They had been privileged to pray not through a created being, like an angel, but through the Father's Son. No angel had ever been called God's Son, the King. The angels were heavenly beings obligated to worship the Son and to serve those who would inherit the promises of God (1:5-14).

Yet, remarkably, though greater than the angels, the Son willingly became lower than the angels in order to help those who would pray in His name (2:5-13). The Son's "lowering" entailed suffering, for no angel suffers.

Since therefore the children share in flesh and blood, he himself likewise partook of the same things, that through death he might destroy the one who has the power of death, that is, the devil, and deliver all those who through fear of death were subject to lifelong slavery. For surely it is not angels that he helps, but he helps the offspring of Abraham. Therefore he had to be made like his brothers in every respect, so that he might become a merciful and faithful high priest in the service of God, to make propitiation for the sins of the people. For because he himself has suffered when tempted, he is able to help those who are being tempted.

Hebrews 2:14-18

The Christians, weary and tired, need rest. They are in danger of missing rest, however, by their failure to endure through prayer. Though they are tested in life, like the children of Israel in the wilderness, they must believe that God will answer prayer and give the rest He has promised (3:7-4:13). The author reassures them:

Since then we have a great high priest who has passed through the heavens, Jesus, the Son of God, let us hold fast our confession. For we do not have a high priest who is unable to sympathize with our weaknesses, but one who in every respect has been tempted as we are, yet without sin. Let us then with confidence draw near to the throne of grace, that we may receive mercy and find grace to help in time of need.

Hebrews 4:14-16

In the days of His flesh Jesus also had prayed routinely, often with loud cries and tears. Jesus understood that sometimes we pray in the darkest moments when God's promises seem the most threatened—as had Jesus when the prospect of being dead seemed to threaten God's promise to Him of an eternal priesthood (5:1-10). Jesus was heard—and so are we, even in, and because of, suffering.

As high priest therefore on our behalf, Jesus, understanding our human predicament, gives us access to approach the very throne of God! Who would want to throw away this privilege?

Perhaps, however, God might change his mind tomorrow and decide to bar access to His presence because of our sin. Might this happen?

In possibly the most humbling accommodation of God as God to human frailties anywhere in Scripture, the author says that God decided to reassure us that He would always recognize Jesus' high priesthood by swearing an oath to Jesus:

And it was not without an oath. For those who formerly became priests were made such without an oath, but this one was made a priest with an oath by the one who said to him:

"The Lord has sworn
and will not change his mind,
'You are a priest forever.'"

This makes Jesus the guarantor of a better covenant.

For the law appoints men in their weakness as high priests, but the word of the oath, which came later than the law, appoints a Son who has been made perfect forever.

Hebrews 7:20-22, 28

It would be enough to believe God at His word. But God goes further: He acts the double. He both swears an oath and at the same moment witnesses the oath.

So when God desired to show more convincingly to the heirs of the promise the unchangeable character of his purpose, he guaranteed it with an oath, so that by two unchangeable things, in which it is impossible for God to lie, we who have fled for refuge might have strong encouragement to hold fast to the hope set before us. We have this as a sure and steadfast anchor of the soul, a hope that enters into the inner place behind the curtain, where Jesus has gone as a forerunner on our behalf, having become a high priest forever after the order of Melchizedek.

Hebrews 6:17-20

The letter of Hebrews is written to arouse and embolden weary Christians to endure in prayer and in church by remembering the promises of God, and above all the blessing of having a great high priest like Jesus. The author explains to them what it really means to end their prayers by saying "in Jesus' name." If they neglect this great blessing, where can they turn for help and renewal?

Hebrews 8-10

For Christians, there are few gifts greater than prayer. Yet sometimes we forsake the habit of prayer. Prayers unanswered, distractions of circumstance, failed commitments, weariness—all of these and more contribute to the neglect.

Christians addressed by the author of Hebrews were not praying, as well as not meeting with other believers in the assembly. These Christians had lost their confidence to pray; their hopes were faltering.

The author attempts to revitalize his readers' dispositions to prayer in a striking way—by concentrating their attention on the high priesthood of Jesus. As strange as it may sound, he sees the remedy to this neglect in a deeper, richer understanding of the incomparable benefits of Jesus' ministry as high priest and sacrifice.

Indeed, Jesus' priesthood could sound like a thing too good to be true:

> *But when Christ appeared as a high priest of the good things that have come, then through the greater and more perfect tent (not made with hands, that is, not of this creation) he entered once for all into the holy places, not by means of the blood of goats and calves but by means of his own blood, thus securing an eternal redemption. For if the blood of goats and bulls, and the sprinkling of defiled persons with the ashes of a heifer, sanctify for the purification of the flesh, how much more will the blood of Christ, who through the eternal Spirit offered himself without blemish to God, purify our conscience from dead works to serve the living God.*
>
> Hebrews 9:11-14

When we do not pray, we may either attempt to just try harder to forget our sins, or worse, try to fill our emptiness with busyness. No amount of human effort, however, can create cleansing inside or help us escape a persistent threat of punishment. A clear conscience can only come through relying on Jesus' priesthood and sacrifice of blood.

> *For since the law has but a shadow of the good things to come instead of the true form of these realities, it can never, by the same sacrifices that are continually offered every year, make perfect those who draw near. Otherwise, would they not have ceased to be offered, since the worshipers, having once been cleansed, would no longer have any consciousness of sins? But in these sacrifices there is a reminder of sins every year. For it is impossible for the blood of bulls and goats to take away sins.*
>
> *And every priest stands daily at his service, offering repeatedly the same sacrifices, which can never take away sins. But when Christ had offered for all time a single sacrifice for sins, he sat down at the right hand of God, waiting from that time until his enemies should be made a footstool for his feet. For by a single*

offering he has perfected for all time those who are being sanctified.

Hebrews 10:1-4, 11-14

By His own blood, with the sacrifice of His own body, Jesus entered the temple in heaven where God is enthroned:

> *For Christ has entered, not into holy places made with hands, which are copies of the true things, but into heaven itself, now to appear in the presence of God on our behalf. Nor was it to offer himself repeatedly, as the high priest enters the holy places every year with blood not his own, for then he would have had to suffer repeatedly since the foundation of the world. But as it is, he has appeared once for all at the end of the ages to put away sin by the sacrifice of himself.*

Hebrews 9:24-26

What Jesus did He did once for all humanity. No priests on earth can effect what Jesus accomplished uniquely. Jesus' high priesthood enables every Christian to become a priest and so enter the holiest of holies in heaven—to approach God in prayer. No special priest on earth is necessary to achieve such intercession. All that is required is Jesus' service as high priest and our having been sprinkled clean through baptism, immersion in water.

> *Therefore, brothers, since we have confidence to enter the holy places by the blood of Jesus, by the new and living way that he opened for us through the curtain, that is, through his flesh, and since we have a great priest over the house of God, let us draw near with a true heart in full assurance of faith, with our hearts sprinkled clean from an evil conscience and our bodies washed with pure water. Let us hold fast the confession of our hope without wavering, for he who promised is faithful.*

Hebrews 10:19-23

The Christians addressed in Hebrews had forgotten the power of Jesus' priesthood.

Unlike the blood of bulls and goats, Jesus' blood has the power to penetrate to the very heart of human memory where reside all the habits which bring death. Jesus' blood, and His alone, cleanses the memory from its consciousness of sins and dead works.

The Christians in Hebrews had failed to pray and meet together, in part because they had failed to remember how great was their high priest. Sin had darkened their understanding. They were living by sight rather than by faith. The author of Hebrews tries to arouse them, and us, to see again by faith the invisible sanctuary in heaven whose entrance has been opened up to us by the blood of Jesus so that we might have full confidence to pray to God on His throne, the One who cares about our sorrows and rewards our faithful endurance.

Hebrews 11-13

Where precepts fail, examples succeed.

The Christians to whom Hebrews was written needed endurance (10:36). The author attempts to arouse them to endurance not only by precepts but also with examples—heroes in Scripture who embodied faithful endurance (11:1-2).

There were few greater examples of faith than Abraham:

> *By faith Abraham obeyed when he was called to go out to a place that he was to receive as an inheritance. And he went out, not knowing where he was going. By faith he went to live in the land of promise, as in a foreign land, living in tents with Isaac and Jacob, heirs with him of the same promise. For he was looking forward to the city that has foundations, whose designer and builder is God. By faith Sarah herself received power to conceive, even when she was past the age, since she considered him faithful who had promised. Therefore from one man, and him as good as dead, were born descendants as many as the stars of heaven and as many as the innumerable grains of sand by the seashore.*
>
> *These all died in faith, not having received the things promised, but having seen them and greeted them from afar, and having acknowledged that they were strangers and exiles on the earth. For people who speak thus make it clear that they are seeking a homeland. If they had been thinking of that land from which they had gone out, they would have had opportunity to return.*
>
> Hebrews 11:8-15

The Christians could see themselves in Abraham, because they like Abraham had received promises from God—promises of rest and a permanent city. Through Abraham they could also see that God's promises often encounter the most severe threats. Such dangers are to be expected. In the face of such trials, Abraham was firm in hope, no matter the most severe test:

> *By faith Abraham, when he was tested, offered up Isaac, and he who had received the promises was in the act of offering up his only son, of whom it was said, "Through Isaac shall your offspring be named." He considered that God was able even to raise him from the dead, from which, figuratively speaking, he did receive him back.*
>
> Hebrews 11:17-19

Times were also difficult for the believers whose property the government had confiscated. The author of Hebrews assures his readers that they will inherit property far greater than that which they had lost. In Abraham, the readers had the example of one who had lived relentlessly in hope for a permanent city. He had even died waiting for it.

The Christians were in a far better position than Abraham. Jesus had come and had already begun to bring them into God's permanent city through His priesthood, opening a way into the inner presence of God through prayer in His name.

> *But you have come to Mount Zion and to the city of the living God, the heavenly Jerusalem, and to innumerable angels in festal gathering, and to the assembly of the firstborn who are enrolled in heaven, and to God, the judge of all, and to the spirits of the righteous made perfect, and to Jesus, the mediator of a new covenant, and to the sprinkled blood that speaks a better word than the blood of Abel.*
>
> Hebrews 12:22-24

Believers could also take strength through the example of Moses who chose to live not by sight but by faith:

> *By faith Moses, when he was grown up, refused to be called the son of Pharaoh's daughter, choosing rather to be mistreated with the people of God than to enjoy the fleeting pleasures of sin. He*

considered the reproach of Christ greater wealth than the treasures of Egypt, for he was looking to the reward.

Hebrews 11:24-26

The Christian life is a marathon race as in the Olympics. In the stadium around are all the heroes of Scripture who lived by faith and died in faith, cheering the faithful on to victory. One alone sets the pace—Jesus, who disregarded in His own race the threats to God's promises, enduring until the very end and finally receiving the promise of eternal priesthood at God's right hand.

Therefore, since we are surrounded by so great a cloud of witnesses, let us also lay aside every weight, and sin which clings so closely, and let us run with endurance the race that is set before us, looking to Jesus, the founder and perfecter of our faith, who for the joy that was set before him endured the cross, despising the shame, and is seated at the right hand of the throne of God.

Hebrews 12:1-2

Why all the discipline for the race? Why all the rigors? Why the long distance? Why the threats to God's promises and such discouragements on the way? An answer is suggested in a quotation from Proverbs 3:

And have you forgotten the exhortation that addresses you as sons?

"My son, do not regard lightly the discipline of the Lord,
nor be weary when reproved by him.
For the Lord disciplines the one he loves,
and chastises every son whom he receives."

Hebrews 12:5-6

Indeed, God wants us to be holy—as He is holy. Significantly, our holiness is not through some kind of extraordinary ascetic exercise. It is not in seeing some vision in the night. No. Rather, holiness comes through God's disciplining us through the sufferings we experience as we faithfully await, in the daily routines of our life, for God's promises to ripen. In such hope there is power to endure.

Therefore lift your drooping hands and strengthen your weak knees, and make straight paths for your feet, so that what is lame may not be put out of joint but rather be healed. Strive for peace with everyone, and for the holiness without which no one will see the Lord.

Hebrews 12:12-14

James

The Gospels indicate that Jesus had brothers and sisters. Two of his half-brothers, James and Jude, wrote letters which have been preserved in the New Testament.

From the story in Acts, we learn that one of these brothers, James, was a very influential leader in the Jerusalem church. In fact, when the acceptance of Gentiles was so hotly debated, it was James who formulated an approach which influenced Pharisaic Christians to fellowship non-circumcised Gentile Christians.

James' wisdom is clearly displayed in his New Testament letter. As Matthew functions among the Gospels as a clear manual for church life, so James functions among the letters as a clear, direct exhortation to prudent church behavior. Both writings are also deeply indebted to Jesus' teachings in the Sermon on the Mount.

In his letter, James stresses humility as the precondition for God's work in the human heart:

> *Let the lowly brother boast in his exaltation, and the rich in his humiliation, because like a flower of the grass he will pass away.*
>
> *But he gives more grace. Therefore it says, "God opposes the proud but gives grace to the humble." Submit yourselves therefore to God. Resist the devil, and he will flee from you.*
>
> *Humble yourselves before the Lord, and he will exalt you.*
>
> James 1:9-10; 4:6-7, 10

One can imagine that James was influenced by his mother Mary, who in her own life had been touched by Hannah's devotion and song. No doubt Mary had reminded James often through her own experiences that God "brought down the powerful and lifted up the lowly" (Luke 1:52).

In humility, James had learned to speak of himself as a "slave of the Lord Jesus Christ" (1:1)—a slave to his own half-brother whom he had at one time thought crazy. No more. James now confessed his half-brother as Lord who would return one day as Judge (5:7-9).

James encountered arrogance inside and outside the church. After the shock of Stephen's death, he must have been dismayed by divisive conflicts among Christians. James saw how bitter envy, selfish ambition, and the craving to possess and control could grip human lives.

> *What causes quarrels and what causes fights among you? Is it not this, that your passions are at war within you? You desire and do not have, so you murder. You covet and cannot obtain, so you fight and quarrel. You do not have, because you do not ask. You ask and do not receive, because you ask wrongly, to spend it on your passions.*
>
> James 4:1-3

From the beginning of his letter, James advises his fellow believers to ask God for wisdom (1:5-8). Only wisdom from God could begin to neutralize and redirect the selfish desires of the heart to possess and control.

> *But the wisdom from above is first pure, then peaceable, gentle, open to reason, full of mercy and good fruits, impartial and sincere.*
>
> James 3:17

Such wisdom only comes through careful listening:

> *Know this, my beloved brothers: let every person be quick to hear, slow to speak, slow to anger.*
>
> James 1:19

The tongue must be controlled long enough to hear the word, even if the message hurts and irritates. God, the generous Father, will not fail to give truthful words of wisdom.

Such listening must be accompanied with acting upon what is heard:

> *But be doers of the word, and not hearers only, deceiving yourselves. For if anyone is a hearer of the word and not a doer, he is like a man who looks intently at his natural face in a mirror. For he looks at himself and goes away and at once forgets what he was like. But the one who looks into the perfect law, the law of liberty, and perseveres, being no hearer who forgets but a doer who acts, he will be blessed in his doing.*
>
> James 1:22-25

For James the word to be obeyed is clear. One must keep the royal law, the law to love neighbor (2:8)—concretely to love and care for orphans and widows in distress (1:27) and to supply the physical needs of brethren in need (2:16). Such acts of kindness are both the completion of faith (2:22) as well as the result of God's wisdom (3:13).

Controlling the tongue permits God's wisdom to enter the human heart. Controlling the tongue also preempts slander against neighbor (4:11-14) and swearing foolishly (5:12). Admittedly, however, the tongue is a fire which can quickly start other fires, even infernos in the human heart.

> *For every kind of beast and bird, of reptile and sea creature, can be tamed and has been tamed by mankind, but no human being can tame the tongue. It is a restless evil, full of deadly poison. With it we bless our Lord and Father, and with it we curse people who are made in the likeness of God. From the same mouth come blessing and cursing. My brothers, these things ought not to be so.*
>
> James 3:7-10

James had seen firsthand the destructive effect of the tongue in the church. When fires begin, sins must be confessed:

> *Therefore, confess your sins to one another and pray for one another, that you may be healed. The prayer of a righteous person has great power as it is working.*
>
> James 5:16

James strongly urges a mutual alertness to those who wander from the truth. It is the responsibility of a leader as well as each individual member to bring back sinners from paths of destruction (5:19-20).

James asked God for wisdom even as Solomon had long ago. James understood that God's wisdom was the true power for enacting deeds of kindness and words of blessing.

1 Peter

Before His ascension, Jesus commissioned Peter to feed His sheep. Peter did. In Jerusalem on Pentecost, Peter fed the sheep of the house of Israel with the message of Jesus' resurrection.

But this was not the end. Peter found himself soon, unexpectedly, dramatically, feeding Jesus' sheep again—Jesus' other sheep, the Gentiles—through the centurion Cornelius. Peter continued feeding many Gentile sheep, especially through his letters.

The sheep Peter addresses in his first letter are facing opposition because they wear the name of Christ:

> *Beloved, do not be surprised at the fiery trial when it comes upon you to test you, as though something strange were happening to you. But rejoice insofar as you share Christ's sufferings, that you may also rejoice and be glad when his glory is revealed. If you are insulted for the name of Christ, you are blessed, because the Spirit of glory and of God rests upon you.*
>
> 1 Peter 4:12-14

Peter's letter is written to encourage them to understand their suffering as evidence of the true grace of God.

> *In this you rejoice, though now for a little while, if necessary, you have been grieved by various trials, so that the tested genuineness of your faith—more precious than gold that perishes though it is tested by fire—may be found to result in praise and glory and honor at the revelation of Jesus Christ.*
>
> 1 Peter 1:6-7

Peter encourages his fellow shepherds to set an example to the flock (5:1-4).

There is no indication that any of the Christians addressed had faced the death of fellow believers. Their refusals to join neighbors in carousing, drunkenness, and idolatry had evidently generated animosities and insults.

> *With respect to this they are surprised when you do not join them in the same flood of debauchery, and they malign you.*
>
> 1 Peter 4:4

Believers had become the brunt of jokes; they were being maligned and slandered. It was an unpleasant environment. In his letter, Peter's clear strategy is to lead his readers to think of themselves as being in captivity. He begins by addressing them as exiles in the Diaspora (1:1, 17; 2:11)—as if it is the exile of the sixth century BC. They like Judah are in a kind of Babylonia. Peter like Ezekiel is writing about a future/present when dry bones come to life and a new temple exists (Ezekiel 35ff).

And it has happened: The exiles Peter addresses have experienced a new birth into a living hope through Jesus' resurrection:

> *since you have been born again, not of perishable seed but of imperishable, through the living and abiding word of God.*
>
> 1 Peter 1:23

The bones have life; the Christians have become living stones in a new temple. As the spiritual house they are a holy priesthood offering spiritual sacrifices to God through Jesus (2:5). The Christians are equipped in their exile to approach God by the blood of Jesus (1:19).

Not only are they protected by the power of God, they are also given encouragement by the example of Jesus who endured hardship.

> *But rejoice insofar as you share Christ's sufferings, that you may also rejoice and be glad when his glory is revealed. If you are insulted for the name of Christ, you are blessed, because the Spirit of glory and of God rests upon you.*
>
> 1 Peter 4:13-14

Peter, of course, had witnessed firsthand the sufferings of Christ (5:1). He had been the one who had strongly objected to Jesus' suffering. But Peter had learned painfully about the necessity of suffering, as well as the subsequent glory to follow. He had learned through Jesus' rebuke as well as through Jesus' interpretation of Scripture (1:10-12).

As exiles, Christians are admonished not to give occasion for others' slander to be accurate. Believers must behave. They should honor the emperor and the governors. Slaves should not revolt. Even if they are mistreated, they are not to return the abuse.

> *For to this you have been called, because Christ also suffered for you, leaving you an example, so that you might follow in his steps. He committed no sin, neither was deceit found in his mouth. When he was reviled, he did not revile in return; when he suffered, he did not threaten, but continued entrusting himself to him who judges justly.*
>
> 1 Peter 2:21-23

Not just slaves, but any Christian is to repay abuse with blessing:

> *Do not repay evil for evil or reviling for reviling, but on the contrary, bless, for to this you were called, that you may obtain a blessing.*
>
> 1 Peter 3:9

Christian wives with unbelieving husbands are not to badger them, but rather to be good daughters of Sarah by displaying the beauty of a gentle and quiet spirit (3:1-6). Husbands likewise are to show proper honor to their wives lest prayers be hindered (3:7).

Christians are to remember that through baptism, like Noah through water, they have been rescued (3:20-21). As aliens, their lifestyle will be different from their environment. They should have confidence in responding to questions about the reasons for their lifestyle (3:15). Their love for each other will provide further protection (4:7-11). They must, however, be on guard against the devil who will suggest easy escapes from suffering (5:8-9).

Peter truly believed Christians were exiles. As he wrote from Rome, he described his letter as from Babylon (5:13). The city had its magnificence, attraction, and glory. But the glory of Babylon could not compare to the glory of home and the inheritance awaiting those who would faithfully endure the temporary affliction of exile.

> *And after you have suffered a little while, the God of all grace, who has called you to his eternal glory in Christ, will himself restore, confirm, strengthen, and establish you. To him be the dominion forever and ever. Amen.*
>
> 1 Peter 5:10-11

2 Peter

The second and final letter of the apostle Peter in the New Testament is poignant. As he writes, Peter has a clear sense of his own mortality. He will die very soon, martyred in the 60s AD.

The questions humans face at death's door—Peter faced. He leaves, in effect, a last will and testament.

I think it right, as long as I am in this body, to stir you up by way of reminder, since I know that the putting off of my body will be soon, as our Lord Jesus Christ made clear to me. And I will make every effort so that after my departure you may be able at any time to recall these things.

2 Peter 1:13-15

Herein Peter is concerned about final things, about the End—Jesus' coming again and God's judgment. He expresses no personal fear in the face of death, but he is anxious for others. Peter sees ominous signs in the church's future.

But false prophets also arose among the people, just as there will be false teachers among you, who will secretly bring in destructive heresies, even denying the Master who bought them, bringing upon themselves swift destruction. And many will follow their sensuality, and because of them the way of truth will be blasphemed. And in their greed they will exploit you with false words. Their condemnation from long ago is not idle, and their destruction is not asleep.

2 Peter 2:1-3

The church will hear teachers who will say that there are no rules for proper behavior: "Everyone is free in Christ to behave as he wishes. The pleasures of the body can be enjoyed to the fullest with few constraints." Such prophets may claim Paul as their authority, but they are twisting Paul's words (3:16). Such teachers are greedy men, taking money at will, enticing unsteady hearts, feeding their own undisciplined desires:

For, speaking loud boasts of folly, they entice by sensual passions of the flesh those who are barely escaping from those who live in error. They promise them freedom, but they themselves are slaves of corruption. For whatever overcomes a person, to that he is enslaved.

2 Peter 2:18-19

Why do they act this way? Peter thinks the explanation lies in part with the false prophets' denial of Jesus' return and God's judgment. With no final judgment why not live life to the fullest—fulfilling every desire of the heart? But Jesus' return was no cleverly devised myth! Peter had seen with his very own eyes a glimpse of Jesus' future coming in glory when he witnessed the Lord transfigured on the mountain (1:16-18).

God has brought judgments in human history, most noticeably in the destruction of the world by flood. God does punish the wicked. On the other hand, the Lord rescues the righteous as He did with Noah (2:4-9) and as He will do for believers at Jesus' return.

Peter anticipates scoffing prophets who will berate the idea of Jesus' return because of His having not yet come. The apostle rehearses basic theology:

> *But do not overlook this one fact, beloved, that with the Lord one day is as a thousand years, and a thousand years as one day. The Lord is not slow to fulfill his promise as some count slowness, but is patient toward you, not wishing that any should perish, but that all should reach repentance.*
>
> 2 Peter 3:8-9

Peter hopes his arguments will be remembered, bringing protection in the face of the lying prophets. Arguments, however, are never enough. Christians must be confident and continually cherish the joy of being cleansed from sins (1:9). The promises of Jesus' return help in escaping the corrupting influences of the present life through the reassurance of cleansing. One must maintain faith in the promises.

But faith is not enough. Faith is the first rung of the ladder on which one is always moving, ultimately toward love.

> *For this very reason, make every effort to supplement your faith with virtue, and virtue with knowledge, and knowledge with self-control, and self-control with steadfastness, and steadfastness with godliness, and godliness with brotherly affection, and brotherly affection with love. For if these qualities are yours and are increasing, they keep you from being ineffective or unfruitful in the knowledge of our Lord Jesus Christ.*
>
> 2 Peter 1:5-8

Peter's own life had itself been a progress from impulsive faith in Jesus to an ever-deepening love for the Lord expressed in his care for Jesus' sheep. No wonder then that Peter sees others' progress through the eyes of his own experience.

Peter had stumbled in his own life. He hoped others might learn from his own struggles in faith and be better prepared to meet Jesus in glory.

> *Therefore, brothers, be all the more diligent to confirm your calling and election, for if you practice these qualities you will never fall. For in this way there will be richly provided for you an entrance into the eternal kingdom of our Lord and Savior Jesus Christ.*
>
> 2 Peter 1:10-11

1 John

In the first century, nobody was born a Christian. No Christian parents or grandparents could make a baby a Christian. Nobody, whatever their age, could become a Christian through somebody else's decision. Each person had to make that commitment on their own.

Having become a Christian the believer was not expected, of course, to swim life's ocean alone. The church was created by God to reinforce and nurture the believer's life-changing decision.

The church available, tangible and real, was not, however, a perfect womb. Though the apostles frequently encouraged congregations to mutual sympathy and care, the church was never in an ideal state. Difficult moments came when churches split, when Christians walked away, disrupting the fellowship.

The letter of 1 John deals with just such a painful situation:

> *They went out from us, but they were not of us; for if they had been of us, they would have continued with us. But they went out, that it might become plain that they all are not of us.*
>
> 1 John 2:19

The apostle John writes a tender letter to those who have remained in order to stabilize their convictions and answer their doubts. Naturally, questions would arise about who is at fault. The insecure could blame themselves and question their own convictions. The over-confident could label the opposing brother as wrong.

In 1 John, those who have left the church are strong-willed and vocal. They claim they are not sinning but are in the right; they are the true children of God. They reiterate their own strong love of God. They boldly declare that they speak the truth and are in the true light, abiding in God.

John says just as strongly that such people are liars.

> *If we say we have fellowship with him while we walk in darkness, we lie and do not practice the truth. ... If we say we have no sin, we deceive ourselves, and the truth is not in us.*
>
> *Whoever says "I know him" but does not keep his commandments is a liar, and the truth is not in him.*
>
> *If anyone says, "I love God," and hates his brother, he is a liar; for he who does not love his brother whom he has seen cannot love God whom he has not seen.*
>
> 1 John 1:6, 8; 2:4; 4:20

By leaving the fellowship these people are "antichrists."

> *Children, it is the last hour, and as you have heard that antichrist is coming, so now many antichrists have come. Therefore we know that it is the last hour.*
>
> 1 John 2:18

They are antichrists because they are demonstrating hatred for the fellowship of Christians. Such people are in darkness (2:11). Their malice is akin to the hatred of Cain for his brother (3:12-15). What has caused the split in church is a fundamental difference in the respective confessions about Jesus.

> *Beloved, do not believe every spirit, but test the spirits to see whether they are from God, for many false prophets have gone out into the world. By this you know the Spirit of God: every spirit that confesses that Jesus Christ has come in the flesh is from God, and every spirit that does not confess Jesus is not from God. This is the spirit of the antichrist, which you heard was coming and now is in the world already.*
>
> *... and whatever we ask we receive from him, because we keep his commandments and do what pleases him.*
>
> 1 John 4:1-3; 3:22

Those who left were denying in some way that Christ was fully human. They are antichrists. By contrast, John is quick to remind the church of what he had personally seen, heard, and touched. The Word of life was very much human! (1:1-3) His own very tangible blood came from His very physical body. By such He has cleansed us from our sins.

This is he who came by water and blood—Jesus Christ; not by the water only but by the water and the blood. And the Spirit is the one who testifies, because the Spirit is the truth.

1 John 5:6

Jesus had come in the flesh, in a human body. Moreover, Jesus' coming was an act and initiative of God's love. How could one claim to know the God of love and deny His Son's humanity?

In this the love of God was made manifest among us, that God sent his only Son into the world, so that we might live through him. In this is love, not that we have loved God but that he loved us and sent his Son to be the propitiation for our sins.

1 John 4:9-10

How could one claim to love God and not love those who are His?

Beloved, let us love one another, for love is from God, and whoever loves has been born of God and knows God. Anyone who does not love does not know God, because God is love.

Beloved, if God so loved us, we also ought to love one another. No one has ever seen God; if we love one another, God abides in us and his love is perfected in us.

1 John 4:7-8, 11-12

John speaks to the church throughout the letter as dear children. John himself knew the warmth of a loving family. He had experienced the loving friendship of Jesus and Mary. He understood that the church must feel itself to be the children of God if it is to be healthy and to survive:

See what kind of love the Father has given to us, that we should be called children of God; and so we are. The reason why the world does not know us is that it did not know him. Beloved, we are God's children now, and what we will be has not yet appeared; but we know that when he appears we shall be like him, because we shall see him as he is. And everyone who thus hopes in him purifies himself as he is pure.

1 John 3:1-3

It's tough when friends you trusted with your life desert you. John reassures abandoned Christians to remember God's command:

And this is his commandment, that we believe in the name of his Son Jesus Christ and love one another, just as he has commanded us. Whoever keeps his commandments abides in God, and God in him. And by this we know that he abides in us, by the Spirit whom he has given us.

1 John 4:23-24

They will endure if they confess and believe Jesus came in the flesh—and if they love each other. Alone, such would be impossible; by God's Spirit, love is truly possible.

2-3 John

Admittedly, it is difficult to understand how God could become a man! We think of God as unlimited in power, knowledge, and presence. How could He limit himself in human flesh? We think of God as separated and untouched by evil and sin. How then could He be intertwined with the desires of the body?

Some early Christians were so troubled by such thinking that they came to believe that Jesus only appeared to be fleshly. He wasn't really a human at all—at least, the way *we* are humans. Some who heard the apostle John's recollections about Jesus wrestled with the nature of His humanity. John's Gospel recalled Jesus' own words that He was from above and from the beginning—that He and the Father were one. Some Christians understood these words to imply or at least allow the possibility that Jesus was never completely human.

In writing as an elder in the church to his children, the apostle John makes it unequivocally clear that such an idea is false. In 2 John, the shortest letter of the New Testament, John tells his sister church what to do about such missionary teachers:

For many deceivers have gone out into the world, those who do not confess the coming of Jesus Christ in the flesh. Such a one is the deceiver and the antichrist. Watch yourselves, so that you may not lose what we have worked for, but may win a full reward. Everyone who goes on ahead and does not abide in the teaching of Christ, does not have God. Whoever abides in the teaching has both the Father and the Son. If anyone comes to you and does not bring this teaching, do not receive him into your house or give him any greeting, for whoever greets him takes part in his wicked works.

2 John 7-11

For many, taking the actual step of excluding certain "believers" from the assembly could not have been easy. It must have been done with sadness and considerable trepidation. There was also the risk that the church would become suspicious of any and every unfamiliar Christian coming to town and categorically refuse to show hospitality or support. In his third letter, John is grateful that Gaius' congregation overcame any such defensiveness in its welcome to strangers.

Beloved, it is a faithful thing you do in all your efforts for these brothers, strangers as they are, who testified to your love before the church. You will do well to send them on their journey in a manner worthy of God. For they have gone out for the sake of the name, accepting nothing from the Gentiles. Therefore we ought to support people like these, that we may be fellow workers for the truth.

3 John 5-8

For a few, however, it became too easy to exclude; it turned into a selfish display of control and power. Unhappily, such permission to exclude gave some Christians an opening to completely misuse the authority. In his third letter, the apostle John warned about just such an individual who abused the use of exclusion.

I have written something to the church, but Diotrephes, who likes to put himself first, does not acknowledge our authority. So if I come, I will bring up what he is doing, talking wicked nonsense against us. And not content with that, he refuses to welcome the brothers, and also stops those who want to and puts them out of the church.

Beloved, do not imitate evil but imitate good. Whoever does good is from God; whoever does evil has not seen God.

3 John 9-11

Having to think and decide when not to be hospitable had to put considerable strain on the church and its unity. With wisdom and insight, John reminded the church that in the midst of the difficulties they should maintain their balance by remembering the primacy of love:

I rejoiced greatly to find some of your children walking in the truth, just as we were commanded by the Father. And now I ask you, dear lady—not as though I were writing you a new commandment, but the one we have had from the beginning—that we love one another. And this is love, that we walk according to his commandments; this is the commandment, just as you have heard from the beginning, so that you should walk in it.

2 John 4-6

It is sobering to be reminded that belief in Jesus' full humanity was of such critical importance to the apostles, that indeed the first "believers" who rejected the idea were not even to be welcomed in church. John understood such teaching as fertile ground for evil deeds.

The apostle John, the beloved friend of Jesus, insisted that confessing Jesus as fully man was indispensable to the Christian's life. The Word had become flesh—with all the risks and limitations involved. It was God the Father's intentional decision to do this. Ever since, Christians have had to fight the tendency to think of the body as fundamentally evil. At the same time, Christians have continued to wonder why God chose to let His Son become flesh and suffer so that the world might be saved.

Jude

Grace, real grace, is often so foreign to our experience that when we encounter it we may feel terribly awkward. Either we may try to deserve it, or we try to receive it too casually. The grace of God in Jesus is so unwarranted, unmerited, unexpected that when we finally begin to understand and receive it we risk misunderstanding and mishandling it.

In the first century, there were Christians who believed and taught that the grace of God was so big and wide and deep that it didn't really matter how one acted. Grace was the freedom and license to indulge one's appetites.

Jude, the brother of James, knew better. He remembered the teachings of his half-brother Jesus. He could recall the Jewish stories his mother Mary told, accounts he had learned growing up in the synagogues of Palestine. Now as a slave of Jesus, his Master and Lord, he writes a letter warning fellow saints of the dangers of ungodly teachers.

Beloved, although I was very eager to write to you about our common salvation, I found it necessary to write appealing to you to contend for the faith that was once for all delivered to the saints. For certain people have crept in unnoticed who long ago were designated for this condemnation, ungodly people, who pervert the grace of our God into sensuality and deny our only Master and Lord, Jesus Christ.

Jude 3-4

The ungodly teachers who have infiltrated the church seem oblivious to any punishment awaiting them. But punished they will be. Israel learned this in the wilderness. Even God's angels do not escape God's punishment. The teachers are immoral like the Sodomites, insulting angels (vss. 5-7).

The ungodly teachers arrogantly slander angels who are the very guardians of the law and moral order. Jude remembers the story of the archangel Michael who contended with the devil over the burial of Moses' body. When the devil called Moses a murderer, Michael did not condemn such falsehood but rather left the matter to God's tribunal. By contrast, the ungodly teachers revile the angels, rejecting their representations of the law (vss. 8-10).

Evidently the teachers delivered their "dreamy" oracles during the Lord's meal. Jude warns that such instruction is like a dangerous shallow reef awaiting the unsuspecting ship. These infiltrators feed off the flock rather than feed the flock. In a series of vivid comparisons to nature out of control, Jude describes the teachers:

These are hidden reefs at your love feasts, as they feast with you without fear, shepherds feeding themselves; waterless clouds, swept along by winds; fruitless trees in late autumn, twice dead, uprooted; wild waves of the sea, casting up the foam of their own shame; wandering stars, for whom the gloom of utter darkness has been reserved forever.

These are grumblers, malcontents, following their own sinful desires; they are loud-mouthed boasters, showing favoritism to gain advantage.

But you must remember, beloved, the predictions of the apostles of our Lord Jesus Christ. They said to you, "In the last time there will be scoffers, following their own ungodly passions." It is these who cause divisions, worldly people, devoid of the Spirit.

Jude 12-13, 16-19

The church, however, is not merely to become defensive. There is an active fight to be waged. "But you, beloved, building yourselves up in your most holy faith and praying in the Holy Spirit" (vs. 20). Faith, love and hope will sustain the church—and prayer in the Spirit.

And what about the ungodly teachers? Unlike John's counsel to not fellowship false teachers, Jude cautiously recommends rescuing the ungodly guides and their students.

> *And have mercy on those who doubt; save others by snatching them out of the fire; to others show mercy with fear, hating even the garment stained by the flesh.*
>
> Jude 22-23

And what does such labor bring? What is the hope which sustains the intensity? Nothing short of experiencing the glory of God. Jude captures the goal and purpose of such striving—paradoxically, in grace—at the ending of his letter:

> *Now to him who is able to keep you from stumbling and to present you blameless before the presence of his glory with great joy, to the only God, our Savior, through Jesus Christ our Lord, be glory, majesty, dominion, and authority, before all time and now and forever. Amen.*
>
> Jude 24-25

Revelation 1-5

The New Testament begins and ends with Jesus Christ. The Gospels begin with Jesus' humiliation. Revelation ends with Jesus' exaltation. The final impressions are of the exalted Christ who offers strength and endurance to believers through life's difficult times.

In Hebrews, the greatness of Jesus' priesthood as He sits at God's right hand is magnified. Christians are losing stamina and need renewal to finish the race. The great high priest, Jesus, who hears their prayers and understands their weaknesses, emboldens them to endure.

In the last book of the Bible, the magnificence of Jesus' kingship over all the powers of the earth is unveiled. In Revelation, Christians in western

Asia are facing a crisis of allegiance—whether they should worship Rome and its emperors, or honor Jesus alone as the true King. In dramatic fashion, Revelation opens the heavens to reveal Jesus in splendor, the one who knows the churches and who blesses (sevenfold!) those who conquer through patiently enduring hardship.

Revelation is a book of prophecy (so named) of "what is and what is to take place soon" (1:3, 19). It records what John saw one Sunday in the Spirit while on a tiny island named Patmos (1:9). There John was instructed to write what he saw in a book and send it to seven churches in western Asia (1:11).

Just as Paul had encountered Jesus in a frightening moment on a highway to Damascus, so John also encounters Jesus in splendor—now amidst His churches:

> *Then I turned to see the voice that was speaking to me, and on turning I saw seven golden lampstands, and in the midst of the lampstands one like a son of man, clothed with a long robe and with a golden sash around his chest. The hairs of his head were white, like white wool, like snow. His eyes were like a flame of fire, his feet were like burnished bronze, refined in a furnace, and his voice was like the roar of many waters. In his right hand he held seven stars, from his mouth came a sharp two-edged sword, and his face was like the sun shining in full strength.*
>
> *When I saw him, I fell at his feet as though dead. But he laid his right hand on me, saying, "Fear not, I am the first and the last, and the living one. I died, and behold I am alive forevermore, and I have the keys of Death and Hades. Write therefore the things that you have seen, those that are and those that are to take place after this. As for the mystery of the seven stars that you saw in my right hand, and the seven golden lampstands, the seven stars are the angels of the seven churches, and the seven lampstands are the seven churches.*
>
> Revelation 1:12-20

The Revelation of Jesus reveals the Lord knowing His churches and caring for them. The angels who represent each church are clutched in Jesus' right hand. The revelation attempts to rivet in the churches' imagination a firm memory of a watchful Lord spurring His people to perseverance and repentance.

Jesus knows the works of the churches in the seven cities as He knows today the works of every church in the world. In His words to the seven churches of Asia are captured the needs of the church universal.

Jesus knew the patient endurance of the church of Ephesus, but He also knew they had lost their first love (2:2-4). He knew the poverty of the church in Smyrna and that they were facing imprisonment (2:9-10). Jesus knew the pain in the church at Pergamum over the murder of one of their brothers, but He warned of their toleration of false teachers (2:13-15). Jesus knew the good works of the church at Thyatira but also their toleration of a false prophetess (2:19-23). Jesus knew that the church at Sardis was dead, despite its reputation for being alive (3:1-2). Jesus knew that the church in Philadelphia had little power, but it had been faithful (3:8-10). And finally Jesus knew that the church at Laodicea was ineffective even though it considered itself successful.

> *"'For you say, I am rich, I have prospered, and I need nothing, not realizing that you are wretched, pitiable, poor, blind, and naked. I counsel you to buy from me gold refined by fire, so that you may be rich, and white garments so that you may clothe yourself and the shame of your nakedness may not be seen, and salve to anoint your eyes, so that you may see. Those whom I love, I reprove and discipline, so be zealous and repent. Behold, I stand at the door and knock. If anyone hears my voice and opens the door, I will come in to him and eat with him, and he with me. The one who conquers, I will grant him to sit with me on my throne, as I also conquered and sat down with my Father on his throne. He who has an ear, let him hear what the Spirit says to the churches.'"*
>
> Revelation 3:17-22

These edicts of Jesus to endure and repent are preparatory to His churches being able to truly hear, receive, and understand what is happening in heaven. And what John sees next is an open door in heaven which he is invited to enter. In the Spirit, he sees the throne of God, with flashes of lightning emitting from it. Around it are 24 thrones with 24 elders singing,

> *"Worthy are you, our Lord and God,*
> *to receive glory and honor and power,*
> *for you created all things,*
> *and by your will they existed and were created."*
>
> Revelation 4:11

On each side of the throne, four living creatures full of eyes, sing continually,

> *"Holy, holy, holy, is the Lord God Almighty,*
> *who was and is and is to come!"*

Revelation 4:8b

At this moment, God, seated on His throne, appears ready to have announced His climactic judgments from the scroll which He holds in His right hand. But there is a surprise: No one appears worthy to open the seven seals, allowing the scroll to be unrolled and its message enacted! John weeps—until One does appear who is worthy:

> *And one of the elders said to me, "Weep no more; behold, the Lion of the tribe of Judah, the Root of David, has conquered, so that he can open the scroll and its seven seals."*

Revelation 5:5

The Lion, however, is a Lamb; and that, a Lamb slaughtered! He takes the scroll. And with this, the elders, the creatures, and the angels break forth in praise,

> *saying with a loud voice,*
>
> *"Worthy is the Lamb who was slain,*
> *to receive power and wealth and wisdom and might*
> *and honor and glory and blessing!"*
>
> *And I heard every creature in heaven and on earth and under the earth and in the sea, and all that is in them, saying,*
>
> *"To him who sits on the throne and to the Lamb*
> *be blessing and honor and glory and might forever and ever!"*
>
> *And the four living creatures said, "Amen!" and the elders fell down and worshiped.*

Revelation 5:12-14

The churches who read aloud this vision of John in their assemblies needed to see into heaven, because they were facing circumstances which had led on another occasion to a lamb being slaughtered.

They would feel powerless. They were powerless. Yet an open heaven revealed the paradox: the slaughtered Lamb was actually the Lion who conquered. On earth only blood could be seen; an open heaven revealed another story!

In their seemingly mundane acts of allegiance to Jesus, not Caesar, they were worshipping the true King, to whom belonged all power, wealth, wisdom, might, honor, glory, and blessing. Their eyes saw one thing; their imaginations were touched by the true reality.

Revelation 6-22

Much happens behind the scenes. The audience sees the play, but who or what controls the drama and its plot is unseen. What is above, below, and behind may be invisible. The audience does not meet the writer, the producer, the director. The play is experienced without knowing the playwright.

Life, however, is far different. We want to know, we need to know, who or what is in control. Our urgency to know is all the greater when tragedy strikes, when circumstances are harsh, when events seem unexplainable.

The Christians in Asia addressed by John lived in a world filled with images and reminders of Rome's power, success, and domination. The seen and perceived luxury, adornment, and wealth of Rome attracted the allegiances of many. For others, however, the solicitations to worship the emperor were resisted. Some Christians, as a result, were killed (2:13). The prospect of more persecutions (1:9), with no immediate vindication, prompted concerns about God's purposes and His control of events.

> *When he opened the fifth seal, I saw under the altar the souls of those who had been slain for the word of God and for the witness they had borne. They cried out with a loud voice, "O Sovereign Lord, holy and true, how long before you will judge and avenge our blood on those who dwell on the earth?"*
>
> Revelation 6:9-10

Revelation addresses the temptations to accommodation for some (2:20; 20:4) and the promotion of endurance for others (13:10; 14:12) by showing "what is" in heaven in order to shape expectations of "what will be" on earth (1:19).

God's opening of heaven to human view is fraught with risk. The actions, characters, and drama in heaven's reality stretch the familiar of earth's reality. The apostle Paul was ordered on one occasion not to share what he had seen in heaven (2 Cor. 12:4). In Revelation, however, John is not only shown the throne room of God and the war in heaven, he is told not to seal up his book which records what he has seen (Rev 22:10).

Many Christians have read Revelation out of context as predicting a whole series of very specific historical events. While the meaning of specific details in the book may be unclear, the message of the drama and of its poetry in song is unambiguous:

> God is in control. The Lion is a Lamb.
> The Lamb has been slaughtered.
> Christians will conquer by the blood of the Lamb.

What conveys this message is not a reasoned philosophical essay, but a barrage of word-pictures of beings and events by vision. What is seen are angels and creatures executing God's plan, and the response of a great multitude singing praises to God and to the Lamb! With the Lamb opening the seals to a scroll and judgment sweeping through creation (chap. 6), angels blow trumpets (chap. 8) and pour out bowls of God's wrath on the earth (chap. 16). God has His plans and He moves them to completion.

> *And the twenty-four elders who sit on their thrones before God fell on their faces and worshiped God, saying,*
>
> *"We give thanks to you, Lord God Almighty,*
> *who is and who was,*
> *for you have taken your great power*
> *and begun to reign.*
> *The nations raged,*
> *but your wrath came,*
> *and the time for the dead to be judged,*
> *and for rewarding your servants, the prophets and saints,*
> *and those who fear your name,*
> *both small and great,*
> *and for destroying the destroyers of the earth."*
>
> Revelation 11:16-18

Revealed in heaven is *war*. Earth is not alone in war. Far more significant than wars on earth, God's angel Michael battles and defeats the ancient serpent.

And the great dragon was thrown down, that ancient serpent, who is called the devil and Satan, the deceiver of the whole world—he was thrown down to the earth, and his angels were thrown down with him. And I heard a loud voice in heaven, saying, "Now the salvation and the power and the kingdom of our God and the authority of his Christ have come, for the accuser of our brothers has been thrown down, who accuses them day and night before our God. And they have conquered him by the blood of the Lamb and by the word of their testimony, for they loved not their lives even unto death.

Revelation 12:9-11

The defeat of the "accuser" of Christians is assured. The manner of defeat is surprising; it is by the blood of the Lamb. Retaliation and revenge have won no victory. Conquering comes by absorbing abuse, even death.

The banishment of the serpent from heaven does not mean an immediate cessation to the war on the saints. Two beasts, subservient to the dragon, continue the assault.

Also it was allowed to make war on the saints and to conquer them. And authority was given it over every tribe and people and language and nation, and all who dwell on earth will worship it, everyone whose name has not been written before the foundation of the world in the book of life of the Lamb who was slain.

Revelation 13:7-8

An angel announces the fall of Babylon (chap. 18). The Christians in Asia understand that Rome's pomp and pride will come to an end as even every human city and civilization eventually will. What is revealed, however, is a holy city, coming down out of heaven, from God.

And I saw no temple in the city, for its temple is the Lord God the Almighty and the Lamb. And the city has no need of sun or moon to shine on it, for the glory of God gives it light, and its lamp is the Lamb. By its light will the nations walk, and the kings of the earth will bring their glory into it, and its gates will never be shut by day—and there will be no night there. They will bring into it the glory and the honor of the nations. But nothing unclean will ever enter it, nor anyone who does what is detestable or false, but only those who are written in the Lamb's book of life.

Then the angel showed me the river of the water of life, bright as crystal, flowing from the throne of God and of the Lamb through the middle of the street of the city; also, on either side of the river, the tree of life with its twelve kinds of fruit, yielding its fruit each month. The leaves of the tree were for the healing of the nations. No longer will there be anything accursed, but the throne of God and of the Lamb will be in it, and his servants will worship him. They will see his face, and his name will be on their foreheads. And night will be no more. They will need no light of lamp or sun, for the Lord God will be their light, and they will reign forever and ever.

Revelation 21:22-22:5

An open heaven reveals God in control of events outside/inside time and space. It is God's way for the conqueror to become the defeated one. The seemingly unending spiral of violence and war is coming to a definitive conclusion. The end had its beginning in the blood of the Lamb. It is the conquering moment.

The moment of defeat is the moment of victory!

"Behold, I am coming soon, bringing my recompense with me, to repay each one for what he has done. I am the Alpha and the Omega, the first and the last, the beginning and the end."

Blessed are those who wash their robes, so that they may have the right to the tree of life and that they may enter the city by the gates. Outside are the dogs and sorcerers and the sexually immoral and murderers and idolaters, and everyone who loves and practices falsehood.

"I, Jesus, have sent my angel to testify to you about these things for the churches. I am the root and the descendant of David, the bright morning star."

The Spirit and the Bride say, "Come." And let the one who hears say, "Come." And let the one who is thirsty come; let the one who desires take the water of life without price.

I warn everyone who hears the words of the prophecy of this book: if anyone adds to them, God will add to him the plagues described in this book, and if anyone takes away from the words of the book of this prophecy, God will take away his share in the tree of life and in the holy city, which are described in this book.

He who testifies to these things says, "Surely I am coming soon." Amen. Come, Lord Jesus!

The grace of the Lord Jesus be with all. Amen.

Revelation 22:12-21